CAT

N
T
E
R
A
C
T
I
V
E

T
E
X
T

INTERMEDIATE
PAPER 4
ACCOUNTING FOR COSTS

BPP is the **official provider** of training materials for the ACCA's CAT qualification. This Interactive Text forms part of a suite of learning tools, which also includes CD-ROMs for tuition and computer based assessment, and the innovative, internet-based Learn Online.

This text has been specifically written to the **current syllabus** and Teaching Guide.

- Clear language and presentation

- Plenty of questions, examples and quizzes to demonstrate and practise techniques

- Syllabus and teaching guide

- A question and answer bank prepared by BPP Learning Media authors

FOR EXAMS IN DECEMBER 2007 AND JUNE 2008

LEARNING MEDIA

First edition 2003
Fifth edition June 2007

ISBN 978075 173571 0 (Previous ISBN 0 7517 2685 0)

British Library Cataloguing-in-Publication Data
A catalogue record for this book
is available from the British Library

Published by

BPP Learning Media Ltd
BPP House, Aldine Place
London W12 8AA

www.bpp.com/learningmedia

Printed in Great Britain by
Page Bros
Mile Cross Lane
Norwich
NR6 6SA

Your learning materials, published by BPP Learning
Media Ltd, are printed on paper sourced from
sustainable, managed forests.

We are grateful to the Association of Chartered Certified
Accountants for permission to reproduce past
examination questions. The suggested solutions in the
exam answer bank have been prepared by BPP Learning
Media Ltd, unless where otherwise stated.

Contents

Computer based learning products from BPP Learning Media

If you want to reinforce your studies by **interactive** learning, try BPP Learning Media's **i-Learn** product, covering major syllabus areas in an interactive format. For **self-testing**, try **i-Pass,** which offers a large number of **objective test questions**, particularly useful where objective test questions form part of the exam.

Go to www.bpp.com/cat for details of these innovative learning tools.

Learn online

Learn Online is a fully **interactive** e-learning resource **delivered via the Internet**. The site offers comprehensive **tutor support** and features areas such as **study**, **practice**, **email service**, **revision** and **useful resources**.

Visit our website www.bpp.com/cat/learnonline to sample aspects of Learn Online free of charge.

Learning to learn accountancy

BPP Learning Media's ground-breaking **Learning to Learn Accountancy** book is designed to be used both at the outset of your CAT studies and throughout the process of learning accountancy. It challenges you to consider how you study and gives you helpful hints about how to approach the various types of paper which you will encounter. It can help you **focus your studies on the subject and exam**, enabling you to **acquire knowledge, practise and revise efficiently and effectively**.

How to Use this Interactive Text

Aim of this Interactive Text

To provide the knowledge and practice to help you succeed in the examination for Paper 4 *Accounting for Costs.*

To pass the examination you need a thorough understanding in all areas covered by the syllabus and study guide.

Recommended approach

(a)   To pass you need to be able to answer questions on **everything** specified by the syllabus and study guide. Read the text very carefully and do not skip any of it.

(b)   Learning is an **active** process. Do **all** the questions as you work through the text so you can be sure you really understand what you have read.

(c)   After you have covered the material in the Interactive Text, work through the **Question Bank**, checking your answers carefully against the **Answer Bank**.

(d)   Before you take the exam, check that you still remember the material using the following quick revision plan.

   (i)   Read through the **chapter topic list** at the beginning of each chapter. Are there any gaps in your knowledge? If so, study the section again.

   (ii)   Read and learn the **key terms**.

   (iii)   Look at the **exam alerts**. These show the ways in which topics might be examined.

   (iv)   Read the **chapter roundups**, which are a summary of the **fast forwards** in each chapter.

   (v)   Do the **quick quizzes** again. If you know what you're doing, they shouldn't take long.

This approach is only a suggestion. You or your college may well adapt it to suit your needs.

Remember this is a **practical** course.

(a)   Try to relate the material to your experience in the workplace or any other work experience you may have had.

(b)   Try to make as many links as you can to other papers at the Introductory and Intermediate levels.

Introduction

This booklet contains the Study Guide for Paper 4: Accounting for Costs.

The Study Guide is designed to help you plan your studies and to provide more detailed interpretation of the syllabus for ACCA's Certified Accounting Technician examinations. It contains both the Syllabus and the Study Sessions for the paper, which you can follow when preparing for the examination.

The Syllabus outlines the content of the paper and how that content is examined. The Study Sessions take the syllabus and expand it into teaching or study sessions of similar length. These sessions indicate what the examiner expects of candidates for each part of the syllabus, and therefore gives you guidance in the skills you are expected to demonstrate in the examinations. The time to complete each session will vary according to your individual capabilities and the time you have available to study. Tuition providers offering face-to-face tuition are recommended to design courses with a minimum of two hours tuition per study session. However, repeated coverage of the material is vital to ensure your understanding and recall of the subject. Be sure to practice past examination questions to consolidate your knowledge and read your *student accountant* magazine regularly.

The study guide for December 2007 will be unchaged from this version. However, please note that the terminology used by examiners will be based on International accounting standards, rather than the UK accounting standards. An article will appear in *student accountant* to help explain this terminology clearly.

If you have any queries concerning the study guide, please direct them to:

Education Department
ACCA 29 Lincoln's Inn Fields London WC2A 3EE United Kingdom
tel: +44 (0)20 7059 5833 fax: +44 (0)20 7059 5968
e-mail: info@accaglobal.com

Additional information can be accessed on the ACCA website at:
www.accaglobal.com

© The Association of Chartered Certified Accountants
June 2006

ABOUT ACCA
ACCA is the largest and fastest-growing international accountancy body with 260,000 students and 110,000 members in 170 countries. We aim to offer first choice qualifications to people of application, ability and ambition around the world who seek a rewarding career in accountancy, finance and management. ACCA works to achieve and promote the highest professional, ethical and governance standards and advance the public interest.

PAGE 2

Accounting for Costs

AIMS

To develop knowledge and understanding of how organisations record, analyse and report current and future costs and revenue data for use within the organisation.

OBJECTIVES

On completion of this paper, candidates should be able to:

- explain the role of management accounting within an organisation and the requirement for management information
- describe costs by classification and behaviour
- identify appropriate material, labour and overhead costs
- understand and be able to apply the principles of marginal costing and absorption costing
- understand and be able to calculate product and service costs
- understand and be able to apply methods of estimating costs and revenues.

POSITION OF THE PAPER IN THE OVERALL SYLLABUS

Knowledge of Paper 2, *Information for Management Control*, is required before commencing study for Paper 4.

This paper provides the basic techniques required to enable candidates to develop the various methods for recording and evaluating costs into more complex problems at the Advanced Level.

Candidates will need a sound understanding of the methods and techniques introduced in this paper to ensure that they can take them further in subsequent papers. The methods introduced in this paper are revisited and extended in Paper 7, *Planning, Control and Performance Management*.

SYLLABUS CONTENT

1   **Management information**

    (a)   Nature and purpose of internal reporting

        (i)   financial and non-financial information for managers

        (ii)   cost centres, profit centres and investment centres and the impact of these on management information and appraisal

    (b)   Management information requirements

        (i)   definition and importance of good information

        (ii)   presentation of information

        (iii)   role of accounting technicians and accounting information

        (iv)   role of information technology

    (c)   Maintaining an appropriate cost accounting system

        (i)   cost units and responsibility centres

        (ii)   sources of relevant information

        (iii)   methods for recording, processing and storing relevant information

        (iv)   analysis and dissemination of output information

2   **Cost classification and cost behaviour**

    (a)   Cost classification

        (i)   classifications used in cost accounting according to purpose

    (b)   Cost behaviour

        (i)   cost behaviour patterns

        (ii)   identification of fixed, variable and semi-variable costs

        (iii)   use of fixed, variable and semi-variable costs in cost analysis

        (iv)   analysis of the effect of changing activity levels on unit costs

3   **Elements of cost**

    (a)   Materials

        (i)   direct and indirect material costs

        (ii)   methods of stock control and valuation including First In First Out, Last In First Out and weighted average cost

        (iii)   relationship between the materials costing system and the stock control system

    (b)   Labour

        (i)   direct and indirect labour costs

        (ii)   methods of payment for and calculation of payments for labour

        (iii)   relationship between the labour costing system and the payroll accounting system

    (c)   Overheads

        (i)   direct and indirect expenses

        (ii)   procedures and documentation relating to expenses

PAGE 3

Accounting for Costs

(iii) relationship between the accounting system and the expenses costing system

4 Marginal costing and absorption costing

(a) Marginal costing

(b) Absorption costing

    (i) bases of allocating and apportioning indirect costs (overheads) to responsibility centres

    (ii) bases of absorption

    (iii) over and under absorption of overheads

(c) Marginal versus absorption costing for costing and reporting purposes

5 Product and service costs

(a) Job and batch costing

    (i) characteristics

    (ii) direct and indirect costs

(b) Process costing

    (i) characteristics

    (ii) normal losses and abnormal losses and gains

    (iii) accounting for scrap

    (iv) closing work in progress and equivalent units

    (v) joint products and by-products

(c) Service costing

    (i) characteristics

    (ii) cost units

6 Estimating costs and revenues

(a) CVP analysis

    (i) break-even analysis

    (ii) margin of safety

    (iii) target profit

    (iv) contribution / sales ratio

    (v) simple break-even chart and profit/volume graph

(b) Decision-making

    (i) concept of relevant costs

    (ii) short-term decisions

    (iii) optimal production plan given a scarce resource

(c) Discounted cash flow techniques

    (i) simple and compound interest

    (ii) nominal and effective interest

    (iii) discounted cash flow

    (iv) annuities and perpetuities

    (v) payback period.

EXCLUDED TOPICS

The following topics are specifically excluded from Paper 4:

- activity based costing
- process costing – opening work in progress
- process costing – losses and work in progress in same process
- multi-product cost / volume / profit analysis
- linear programming.

KEY AREAS OF THE SYLLABUS

All areas of the syllabus are equally important.

APPROACH TO EXAMINING THE SYLLABUS

Paper 4 is a two-hour paper. It can be taken as a written paper or a computer based examination. The questions in the computer based examination are objective test questions – multiple choice, number entry and multiple response. The written examination consists of two sections, structured as follows:

	No. of marks
Section A – 20 compulsory multiple choice questions of two marks each	40
Section B – four compulsory written questions of between 10 and 20 marks each	60
Total	100

RELEVANT TEXTS

There are a number of sources from which you can obtain a series of materials written for the ACCA CAT examinations. These are listed below:

ACCA's approved publishers:

BPP Professional Education
Contact number: +44(0)20 8740 2222
Website: www.bpp.com

Accounting for Costs

Kaplan Publishing Foulks Lynch
Contact number: +44(0)118 989 0629
Website: www.kaplanfoulkslynch.com

Additional reading:

Accountancy Tuition Centre (ATC)
International
Contact number: +44(0)141 880 6469
Website: www.atc-global.com

Wider reading is also desirable, especially regular study of relevant articles in ACCA's *student accountant* magazine.

STUDY SESSIONS

1 Management information

(a) Discuss the purpose of management information: planning, control and decision-making

(b) Describe the features of useful management information

(c) Discuss the nature, source and importance of both financial and non-financial information for managers

(d) Describe management responsibilities (for cost, profit and investment) and their effect on management information and performance measurement

(e) Discuss the role of information technology in management information

(f) Discuss the role of the accounting technician

(g) Present management information in suitable formats according to purpose

2 Maintaining an appropriate cost accounting system

(a) Explain the relationship between the cost/management accounting system and the financial accounting/ management information systems (including interlocking and integrated bookkeeping systems)

(b) Describe the process of accounting for input costs and relating them to work done

(c) Identify the documentation required, and the flow of documentation, for different cost accounting transactions

(d) Explain the use of codes in categorising and processing transactions, and the importance of correct coding

(e) Explain and illustrate the concept of cost units

(f) Describe the different methods of costing final outputs and their appropriateness to different types of business organisation

(g) Describe methods of capturing, processing, storing and outputting cost and management accounting data by computer

3 Cost classification and cost behaviour

(a) Describe the variety of cost classifications used for different purposes in a cost accounting system, including by responsibility, function, direct/indirect, behaviour

(b) Explain and illustrate the nature of variable, fixed and mixed (semi-variable, stepped-fixed) costs

(c) Use the high-low method to separate semi-variable costs

(d) Use variable, fixed and semi-variable costs in cost analysis

(e) Analyse the effect of changing activity levels on unit costs

4 Costing of materials

(a) Describe the main types of material classification

(b) Describe the procedures and documentation required to ensure the correct authorisation, coding, analysis and recording of direct and indirect material costs

(c) Explain, illustrate and evaluate the FIFO, LIFO and weighted average methods used to price materials issued from stock

(d) Describe and illustrate the accounting for material costs

(e) Calculate material input requirements, and control measures, where wastage occurs

5 Material stock control

(a) Describe the procedures required to monitor stock and to minimise stock discrepancies and losses

(b) Explain and illustrate the costs of stockholding and stockouts

(c) Explain, illustrate and evaluate stock control levels (minimum, maximum, re-order)

(d) Calculate and interpret optimal order quantities

(e) Discuss the relationship between the materials costing system and the stock control system

Accounting for Costs

6 Costing of labour

(a) Explain, illustrate and evaluate labour remuneration methods

(b) Describe the operation of a payroll accounting system

(c) Distinguish between direct and indirect labour costs

(d) Describe the procedures and documentation required to ensure the correct coding, analysis and recording of direct and indirect labour

(e) Describe and illustrate the accounting for labour costs

(f) Discuss the relationship between the labour costing system and the payroll accounting system

(g) Explain the causes and costs of, and calculate, labour turnover

(h) Describe and illustrate measures of labour efficiency and utilisation (efficiency, capacity utilisation, production volume and idle time ratios)

7 Costing of other expenses

(a) Describe the nature of expenses by function

(b) Describe the procedures and documentation required to ensure the correct authorisation, coding, analysis and recording of direct and indirect expenses

(c) Describe capital and revenue expenditure and the relevant accounting treatment

(d) Calculate and explain depreciation charges using straight-line, reducing balance and machine hour methods

(e) Discuss the relationship between the expenses costing system and the expense accounting system

8 Overhead allocation and apportionment

(a) Explain the rationale for absorption costing

(b) Describe the nature of production and service cost centres and their significance for production overhead allocation, apportionment and absorption

(c) Describe the process of allocating, apportioning and absorbing production overheads to establish product costs

(d) Apportion overheads to cost centres using appropriate bases

(e) Re-apportion service cost centre overheads to production cost centres using direct and step down methods

9 Overhead absorption

(a) Justify, calculate and apply production cost centre overhead absorption rates using labour hour and machine hour methods

(b) Explain the relative merits of actual and pre-determined absorption rates

(c) Describe and illustrate the accounting for production overhead costs, including the analysis and interpretation of over/under absorption

(d) Describe and apply methods of attributing non-production overheads to cost units

(e) Calculate product costs using the absorption costing method

10 Absorption and marginal costing

(a) Prepare profit statements using the absorption costing method

(b) Explain and illustrate the concept of contribution

(c) Prepare profit statements using the marginal costing method

(d) Compare and contrast the use of absorption and marginal costing for period profit reporting and stock valuation

(e) Reconcile the profits reported by absorption and marginal costing

(f) Discuss the usefulness of profit and contribution information respectively

11 Job and batch costing

(a) Describe the characteristics of job and batch costing respectively

(b) Identify situations where the use of job or batch costing is appropriate

(c) Calculate unit costs using job and batch costing

(d) Discuss the control of costs in job and batch costing

(e) Apply cost plus pricing in job costing

12 Process costing - losses

(a) Describe the characteristics of process costing

(b) Identify situations where the use of process costing is appropriate

(c) Calculate unit costs and prepare process accounts where

Accounting for Costs

losses occur in process

(d) Explain and illustrate the nature of normal and abnormal losses/gains

(e) Calculate unit costs where losses are separated into normal and abnormal

(f) Prepare process accounts where losses are separated into normal and abnormal

(g) Account for scrap

13 Process costing - work-in-progress

(a) Describe and illustrate the concept of equivalent units

(b) Calculate unit costs where there is closing work-in-progress in a process

(c) Allocate process costs between finished output and work-in-progress

(d) Prepare process accounts where there is closing work-in-progress

14 Process costing - joint products and by-products

(a) Distinguish between joint products and by-products

(b) Explain the treatment of joint products and by-products at the point of separation

(c) Apportion joint process costs using net realisable values and weight/volume of output respectively

(d) Discuss the usefulness of product cost/profit data from a joint process

(e) Evaluate the benefit of further processing

15 Service costing

(a) Describe the characteristics of service costing

(b) Describe the practical problems relating to the costing of services

(c) Identify situations (cost centres and industries) where the use of service costing is appropriate

(d) Illustrate suitable cost units that may be used for a variety of services

(e) Calculate service unit costs in a variety of situations

16 Cost / volume / profit (CVP) analysis

(a) Calculate contribution per unit and the contribution/sales ratio

(b) Explain the concept of break-even and margin of safety

(c) Use contribution per unit and contribution/sales ratio to calculate break-even point and margin of safety

(d) Analyse the effect on break-even point and margin of safety of changes in selling price and costs

(e) Use contribution per unit and contribution/sales ratio to calculate the sales required to achieve a target profit

(f) Construct break-even and profit/volume charts for a single product or business

17 Decision-making

(a) Explain the importance of the limiting factor concept

(b) Identify the limiting factor in given situations

(c) Formulate and determine the optimal production solution when there is a single resource constraint

(d) Solve make/buy-in problems when there is a single resource constraint

(e) Explain the concept of relevant costs

(f) Apply the concept of relevant costs in business decisions

18 & 19 Discounted cash flow

(a) Explain and illustrate the difference between simple and compound interest, and between nominal and effective interest rates

(b) Explain and illustrate compounding and discounting

(c) Explain the distinction between cash flow and profit and the relevance of cash flow to capital investment appraisal

(d) Explain and illustrate the net present value (NPV) and internal rate of return (IRR) methods of discounted cash flow

(e) Calculate present value using annuity and perpetuity formulae

(f) Calculate payback (discounted and non-discounted)

(g) Interpret the results of NPV, IRR and payback calculations of investment viability

20 Revision

Approach to examining the syllabus

Paper 4 is a two-hour paper. It can be taken as a written paper or a computer based examination. The questions in the computer based examination are objective test questions – multiple choice, number entry and multiple response. (See page xvi for frequently asked questions about computer based examinations.)

The written examination consists of two sections, structured as follows:

		Number of marks
Section A	20 compulsory multiple choice questions of 2 marks each	40
Section B	4 compulsory written questions of between 10 and 20 marks each	60
	Total	100

December 2006

Section A

Twenty multiple choice questions covering various accounting for costs topics	40

Section B

1	Cost centres, profit centres, investment centres	10
2	Labour costing	15
3	Overhead absorption	16
4	Relevant costing; NPV	19

Examiner's comments

Overall the results were disappointing on what was considered to be a fair exam. There were many opportunities for candidates with a basic understanding of the subject to gain sufficient marks to gain a pass. In Section B, answers to the narrative Question 1 were especially disappointing. Lack of understanding of the principles of relevant costs for decision making, and of discounted cash flow, were widely demonstrated in the answers to Question 4.

Answers to the other two Section B questions demonstrated a very serious lack of understanding, and a lack of preparation on the part of many candidates. They also demonstrated a failure to read the question carefully.

June 2006

Section A

Twenty multiple choice questions covering various accounting for costs topics	40

Section B

1	Job costing	14
2	Break even; contribution/sales ratio	13
3	Coding systems; apportionment	17
4	Process costing – joint products; further processing	16

Examiner's comments

The overall performance was an improvement on recent sittings with a significant number of scripts gaining very high marks. Many candidates however were poorly prepared for the exam.

Poor time management was a problem for quite a few candidates.

Failure to show workings was a particular problem in Questions 1 and 3.

December 2005

Section A

Twenty multiple choice questions covering various accounting for costs topics   40

Section B

1	Compound interest formula; NPV	16
2	Overhead apportionment and absorption	14
3	Cost function formula and calculation	12
4	Profit/volume chart; contribution	18

Examiner's comments

Overall, the results were somewhat disappointing. While a significant number of scripts gained very high marks, demonstrating what is achievable by the well-prepared candidate, many other candidates were insufficiently prepared and had simply not mastered the basics. Many very low marks were seen as a result.

Most candidates attempted all questions and there was little evidence of time pressure being a factor. Questions 2 and 3 were on average reasonably well-answered with questions 1 and 4 less so. In question 2 performance was boosted by consistent high marks in part (a) but candidates often scored much less well in part (b), especially (ii) and (iii).

A few candidates still fail to show workings to calculation questions, making it very difficult to award appropriate marks for 'own figure' work in incorrect answers. At times, however, candidates' time is wasted on unnecessarily detailed workings. This is especially the case where formulae are used, as in questions 1(a) and 3(b). Candidates should refer to the published answers as a guide to the number of stages, and detail, required in an answer.

June 2005

Section A

Twenty multiple choice questions covering various cost accounting systems topics   40

Section B

1	Absorption and marginal costing	14
2	Process costing	14
3	Stock control	15
4	Cost-volume-profit (CVP) analysis	17

Examiner's comments

Several candidates achieved very high marks, and overall there was an improvement in performance compared with the two previous examination sessions. Candidates obtained higher than average marks on the Section A multiple-choice questions which, along with relatively high marks on Question 2 in Section B, were the main factors contributing to the improved result. Most candidates made a reasonable attempt at all questions although too many candidates, as always, were not well-prepared and failed to complete the paper.

It is also important for candidates to manage their time effectively in the examination. The first few marks in a question are often the easiest to gain. A further factor here is that candidates all too often failed to read question requirements carefully, resulting in a lot of unnecessary work and few, if any, marks gained. This was especially the case in Question 1(b), where detailed marginal costing profit statements were commonplace, and in Question 4(b), where full break-even charts were, at times, prepared. Failure to read questions carefully was also evident in the answers to Questions 1(a), 3(d) and 4(a).

A number of candidates still fail to provide adequate workings, despite this being regularly highlighted in past examiners' reports, and as a consequence may well miss gaining marks for 'own figure' work.

December 2004

Section A

Twenty multiple choice questions covering various cost accounting systems topics   40

Section B

1	Labour costs	16
2	Process costing-joint products	14
3	Service costing	16
4	Decision making and limiting factor analysis	14

Examiner's comments

Some excellent answers were presented with well-prepared candidates ably demonstrating what could be achieved. However, the overall performance was disappointing. A large number of candidates seemed unprepared for the examination. Average marks achieved in Section A were disappointing and, once again, a number of candidates did not attempt all twenty multiple-choice questions.

In Section B, Question 2 and part (a) of Question 1 were consistently well-answered. The remainder of Section B was considerably less well-answered, especially Question 4. At times there is was a lack of workings being shown making it very difficult to award appropriate marks for incorrect answers. Presentation and labelling of answers were also often poor.

June 2004

Section A

Twenty multiple choice questions covering various cost accounting systems topics   40

Section B

1	Stock control	12
2	Overheads and absorption costing	14
3	Job costing and service costing	19
4	Capital investment appraisal	15

Examiner's comments

Some excellent answers were presented but the performance overall was disappointing, with a large number of candidates appearing to be unprepared for the first sitting of this new paper. Average marks achieved in Section A were disappointing and although Questions 1 and 2 in Section B were generally fairly well-answered, Questions 3 and 4 were considerably less well-completed, especially Question 4. Lack of thought, or lack of understanding, was demonstrated in various ways in the answers presented (note particularly the comments below on answers presented to Question 1(b), Question 2(c) and Question 4(b) in Section B).

A reasonable number of candidates did not attempt all four questions in Section B. Question 4 in particular was not attempted. This is likely to have been a combination of the fact that it was the last question on the exam paper and that it covered subject matter not within the previous CAT Scheme Paper B2 syllabus. It is a concern that so many candidates were apparently unprepared for this new topic at this level, seemingly concentrating their studies on the previous syllabus coverage. It is also a concern that a significant number of candidates did not attempt all 20 multiple-choice questions in Section A.

There were too many instances of failure to show workings, especially in the answers to Question 2(a) and Question 3(b), making it difficult to award appropriate marks. Candidates must also try to present their answers clearly, including clear labelling. It would be preferable if each question was started on a new page of the answer booklet.

Pilot paper

Section A

Twenty multiple choice questions covering various cost accounting systems topics   40

Section B

1	Marginal costing and absorption costing	17
2	Job costing	13
3	Process costing: joint products	12
4	Discounted cash flow	18

The Computer Based Examination

The ACCA has introduced a computer based examination (CBE) for CAT Papers 1–4 (in addition to the conventional paper based examination).

Computer based examinations must be taken at an ACCA CBE Licensed Centre.

How does CBE work?

- Questions are displayed on a monitor

- Candidates enter their answer directly onto the computer

- Candidates have two hours to complete the examination

- When the candidate has completed their examination, the computer automatically marks the file containing the candidate's answers

- Candidates are provided with a certificate showing their results before leaving the examination room

- The CBE Licensed Centre uploads the results to the ACCA (as proof of the candidate's performance) within 48 hours

Benefits

- **Flexibility** as a CBE can be sat at any time.

- **Resits** can also be taken at any time and there is no restriction on the number of times a candidate can sit a CBE.

- **Instant feedback** as the computer displays the results at the end of the CBE.

- Results are notified to ACCA **within 48 hours**.

- **Extended closing date periods** (see ACCA website for further information)

CBE question types

- Multiple choice – choose one answer from four options

- Multiple response 1 – select more than one response by clicking the appropriate tick boxes

- Multiple response 2 – select a response to a number of related part questions by choosing one option from a number of drop down menus

- Number entry – key in a numerical response to a question

CAT CBE

You will have two hours in which to answer a number of questions, which are worth a total of 100 marks. See the ACCA website for a demonstration and up to date information (www.acca.org.uk/colleges/cbe_demo).

Tackling Multiple Choice Questions

Of the total marks available for the paper based exam, multiple choice questions (MCQs) comprise 50 per cent. MCQs also feature in the computer based exam.

The MCQs in your exam contain four possible answers. You have to **choose the option that best answers the question**. The three incorrect options are called distracters. There is a skill in answering MCQs quickly and correctly. By practising MCQs you can develop this skill, giving you a better chance of passing the exam.

You may wish to follow the approach outlined below, or you may prefer to adapt it.

Step 1   Skim read all the MCQs and identify what appear to be the easier questions.

Step 2   Attempt each question – **starting with the easier questions** identified in Step 1. Read the question **thoroughly**. You may prefer to work out the answer before looking at the options, or you may prefer to look at the options at the beginning. Adopt the method that works best for you.

Step 3   Read the four options and see if one matches your own answer. Be careful with numerical questions as the distracters are designed to match answers that incorporate common errors. Check that your calculation is correct. Have you followed the requirement exactly? Have you included every stage of the calculation?

Step 4   You may find that none of the options matches your answer.

- Re-read the question to ensure that you understand it and are answering the requirement
- Eliminate any obviously wrong answers
- Consider which of the remaining answers is the most likely to be correct and select the option

Step 5   If you are still unsure make a note and continue to the next question

Step 6   Revisit unanswered questions. When you come back to a question after a break you often find you are able to answer it correctly straight away. If you are still unsure have a guess. You are not penalised for incorrect answers, so **never leave a question unanswered!**

After extensive practice and revision of MCQs, you may find that you recognise a question when you sit the exam. Be aware that the detail and/or requirement may be different. If the question seems familiar read the requirement and options carefully – do not assume that it is identical.

Part A
Introduction to accounting for costs

BPP
LEARNING MEDIA

1

Management information

Chapter topic list

Study guide reference

			Syllabus reference
1	(a)	Discuss the purpose of management information: planning, control and decision making	1b(i)
	(b)	Describe the features of useful management information	1(b)(i)/1(c)(ii)
	(c)	Discuss the nature, source and importance of both financial and non-financial information for managers	1(a)(i)
	(f)	Discuss the role of the accounting technician	1(b)(iii)
	(g)	Present management information in suitable formats according to purpose	1(b)(ii)
2	(a)	Explain the relationship between the cost/management accounting system and the financial accounting/management information systems	1(c)
	(b)	Describe the process of accounting for input costs and relating them to work done	1(c)
	(c)	Identify the documentation required, and the flow of documentation, for different cost accounting transactions	1(c)
	(d)	Explain the use of codes in categorising and processing transactions, and the importance of correct coding	1(c)
	(e)	Explain and illustrate the concept of cost units	1(c)
	(f)	Describe the different methods of costing final outputs and their appropriateness to different types of business organisation	1(c)

1 Management information

FAST FORWARD

Information is data that has been processed to make it **meaningful**. **Useful** management information should be:

- Relevant
- Complete
- Accurate
- Clear
- Manageable volume
- Timely
- Cost effective

1.1 Information

Key terms

- **Data** is the raw material for data processing. Data relates to facts, events and transactions.

- **Information** is data that has been processed in such a way as to be **meaningful** to the person who receives it. It is anything that is communicated.

Information is sometimes referred to as **processed data**. The terms 'information' and 'data' are often used interchangeably. It is important to understand the difference between these two terms.

Researchers who conduct market research surveys might ask members of the public to complete questionnaires about a product or a service. These completed questionnaires are **data**; they are processed and analysed in order to prepare a report on the survey. This resulting report is **information**.

As you probably know, managers (including your own manager!) are always asking for reports, analyses, schedules of costs and so on. Well, broadly speaking, these reports, analyses and schedules are part of what is known as **management information**. Management information, as we shall see, is most likely to be used for the following

- Planning
- Control
- Decision making

1.2 Features of useful management information

The main features of useful management information are as follows.

- It should be **relevant** for its purpose
- It should be **complete** for its purpose
- It should be sufficiently **accurate** for its purpose
- It should be **clear** to the user
- The user should have **confidence** in it
- It should be **communicated** to the right person
- Its **volume** should be manageable
- It should be **timely** – in other words communicated at the most appropriate time
- It should be communicated by an appropriate **channel** of communication
- It should be provided at a **cost** which is less than the value of its benefits

Let us look at those qualities in more detail.

(a) **Relevance**. Management information must be relevant to the purpose for which a manager wants to use it. In practice, far too many reports fail to 'keep to the point' and contain irrelevant paragraphs which only annoy the managers reading them.

(b) **Completeness**. An information user should have all the information he needs to do his job properly. If he does not have a complete picture of the situation, he might well make bad decisions.

(c) **Accuracy**. Management information should obviously be accurate because using incorrect information could have serious and damaging consequences. However, management information should only be accurate enough for its purpose and there is no need to go into unnecessary detail for pointless accuracy.

(d) **Clarity**. Management information must be clear to the user. If the user does not understand it properly he cannot use it properly. Lack of clarity is one of the causes of a breakdown in communication. It is therefore important to choose the most appropriate presentation medium or channel of communication.

(e) **Confidence**. Management information must be trusted by the managers who are expected to use it. However not all management information is certain. Some information has to be certain, especially operating information, for example, related to a production process. Strategic information, especially relating to the environment, is uncertain. However, if the assumptions underlying it are clearly stated, this might enhance the confidence with which the management information is perceived.

(f) **Communication**. Within any organisation, individuals are given the authority to do certain tasks, and they must be given the information they need to do them. An office manager might be made responsible for controlling expenditures in his office, and given a budget expenditure limit for the year. As the year progresses, he might try to keep expenditure in check but unless he is told throughout the year what is his current total expenditure to date, he will find it difficult to judge whether he is keeping within budget or not.

(g)   **Volume**. There are physical and mental limitations to what a person can read, absorb and understand properly before taking action. An enormous mountain of management information, even if it is all relevant, cannot be handled. Reports to management must therefore be **clear** and **concise** and in many systems, control action works basically on the 'exception' principle.

(h)   **Timing**. Management information which is not available until after a decision is made will be useful only for comparisons and longer-term control, and may serve no purpose even then. Management information prepared too frequently can be a serious disadvantage. If, for example, a decision is taken at a monthly meeting about a certain aspect of a company's operations, management information to make the decision is only required once a month, and weekly reports would be a time-consuming waste of effort.

(i)   **Channel of communication**. There are occasions when using one particular method of communication will be better than others. For example, job vacancies should be announced in a medium where they will be brought to the attention of the people most likely to be interested. The channel of communication might be the company's in-house journal, a national or local newspaper, a professional magazine, a job centre or school careers office. Some internal memoranda may be better sent by 'electronic mail'. Some information is best communicated informally by telephone or word-of-mouth, whereas other information ought to be formally communicated in writing or figures.

(j)   **Cost**. Management information should have some value, otherwise it would not be worth the cost of collecting and filing it. The benefits obtainable from the management information must also exceed the costs of acquiring it, and whenever management is trying to decide whether or not to produce management information for a particular purpose (for example whether to computerise an operation or to build a financial planning model) a cost/benefit study ought to be made.

1.3 Purpose of management information

The successful management of any organisation depends on information. For example, consider the following problems and what management information would be useful in solving these problems.

1.4 Example: purpose of management information

Problem 1

A company wishes to launch a new product. The company's pricing policy is to set the price at total cost + 20%. What should the price of the product be?

⇩

MANAGEMENT NEED INFORMATION ABOUT THE TOTAL COST OF THE PRODUCT

Problem 2

A company's bottle making machine has a fault and the company has to decide whether to repair the machine, to buy a new machine or to hire a machine. If the company aims to minimise costs, which decision should management take?

⇩

MANAGEMENT NEED COST INFORMATION RELATING TO THE FOLLOWING DECISIONS.   • REPAIRING THE CURRENT MACHINE   • BUYING A NEW MACHINE   • HIRING A SIMILAR MACHINE

The examples above show that information is a vital part of the following processes.

- Planning
- Control
- Decision making

AST FORWARD

- **Planning** involves establishing **objectives** for the company and developing **strategies** in order to achieve those objectives.

- **Control** is the action of monitoring something in order to keep it on course.

1.5 Planning

Planning involves the following.

- Establishing **objectives** for the company
- Developing **strategies** in order to achieve the company's objectives

An **objective** is the aim or goal of an organisation.

A **strategy** is a possible course of action that might enable an organisation to achieve its objectives.

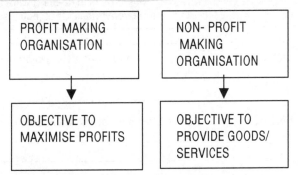

The objectives of an organisation might include one or more of the following.

- Maximise profits
- Maximise shareholder value
- Minimise costs
- Maximise revenue
- Increase market share

Remember that the type of activity undertaken by an organisation will have an impact on its objectives.

1.6 Control

Control is the action of monitoring something in order to keep it on course. Most companies will set out a plan for a future period (for example, a **budget**) and then compare the actual results during the period with the budget. Any deviations from the budget can then be identified and corrected as necessary. Such deviations are known as **variances** (you studied variances at Introductory level in Paper 2).

You will go on to study variances and variance analysis in detail at Final level in Paper 7, *Planning, Control and Performance Management.*

1.7 Decision making

Managers at all levels within an organisation take decisions. Decision making always involves a **choice between alternatives** and it is the role of the accounting technician to provide information so that management can reach an informed decision. It is therefore useful if accounting technicians understand the decision-making process so that they can supply the appropriate type of management information.

Decision-making process

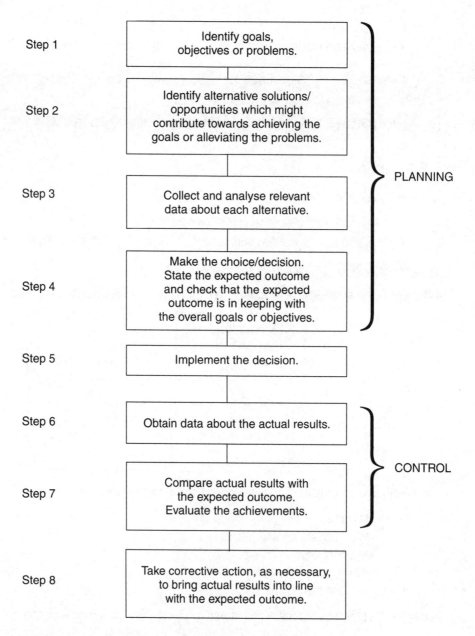

1.8 Internal sources of management information

The main **internal sources of management information** within an organisation include the following.

- Financial accounting records
- Personnel records
- Production department records
- Detailed time records (especially in service organisations)

There is no need for us to give a detailed description of the constituents of the **financial accounting records**. You are probably familiar with the idea of a system of sales ledgers and purchase ledgers, general ledgers, cash books and so on. These records provide a history of an organisation's monetary transactions. Some of this information is of great value outside the accounts department, for example sales information for the marketing function.

You will also be aware that to maintain the integrity of its financial accounting records, an organisation of any size will have systems for and controls over transactions. These also give rise to valuable information.

An inventory control system is the classic example. Besides actually recording the monetary value of purchases and inventory in hand for external financial reporting purposes, the system will include purchase orders, goods received notes, goods returned notes and so on, and these can be analysed to provide management information about speed of delivery, say, or the quality of supplies.

Much of the information that is not strictly part of the financial accounting records is in fact closely tied in to the accounting system.

(a) Information relating to **personnel** will be linked to the **payroll system**. Additional information may be obtained from this source if, say, a project is being costed and it is necessary to ascertain the availability and rate of pay of different levels of staff, or the need for and cost of recruiting staff from outside the organisation.

(b) Much information will be produced by a **production department** about machine capacity, fuel consumption, movement of people, materials, and work in progress, set up times, maintenance requirements and so on. A large part of the traditional work of cost accounting involves ascribing costs to the physical information produced by this source.

(c) Many service businesses – notably accountants and solicitors - need to keep **detailed records of the time** spent on various activities, both to justify fees to clients and to assess the efficiency of operations.

1.9 External sources of management information

We hardly need say that an organisation's files are also full of invoices, letters, advertisements and so on received from customers and suppliers. These documents provide information from an **external source**. There are many occasions when an active search outside the organisation is necessary.

(a) A **primary source** of information is, as the term implies, as close as you can get to the origin of an item of information: the eyewitness to an event, the place in question, the document under scrutiny.

(b) A **secondary source**, again logically enough, provides 'second-hand' information: books, articles, verbal or written reports by someone else.

1.10 Financial and non-financial information for management

Most organisations require the following types of information for management.

- Financial
- Non-financial
- A combination of financial and non-financial information

Suppose that the management of ABC Co have decided to provide a canteen for their employees.

(a) The **financial information** required by management might include the following

- Canteen staff costs
- Costs of subsidising meals
- Capital costs
- Costs of heat and light

(b) The **non-financial information** might include the following.

- Management comment on the effect on employee morale of the provision of canteen facilities

- Details of the number of meals served each day

- Meter readings for gas and electricity

- Attendance records for canteen employees

ABC Co could now **combine financial and non-financial information** to calculate the **average cost** to the company of each meal served, thereby enabling them to predict total costs depending on the number of employees in the work force.

Most people probably consider that management accounting is only concerned with financial information and that people do not matter. This is, nowadays, a long way from the truth. For example, managers of business organisations need to know whether employee morale has increased due to introducing a canteen, whether the bread from particular suppliers is fresh and the reason why the canteen staff are demanding a new dishwasher. This type of non-financial information will play its part in **planning, controlling** and **decision making** and is therefore just as important to management as financial information is.

Non-financial information must therefore be **monitored** as carefully, **recorded** as accurately and **taken into account** as fully as financial information. There is little point in a careful and accurate recording of total canteen costs if the recording of the information on the number of meals eaten in the canteen is uncontrolled and therefore produces inaccurate information.

While management accounting is mainly concerned with the provision of **financial information** to aid planning, control and decision making, the accounting technician cannot ignore any **non-financial influences** which might be present.

2 Recording management information

Financial accounts are prepared for individuals **external** to an organisation whereas **management accounts** are prepared for **internal** managers of an organisation. There are a number of differences between financial accounts and management accounts – make sure that you know what they are.

2.1 Financial accounts and management accounts

Management information provides a common source from which is drawn information for two groups of people.

(a) **Financial accounts** are prepared for individuals **external** to an organisation.

- Shareholders
- Customers
- Suppliers
- The Inland Revenue, employees

(b) **Management accounts** are prepared for **internal** managers of an organisation.

Financial accounts	Management accounts
Financial accounts detail the performance of an organisation over a defined period and the state of affairs at the end of that period.	Management accounts are used to aid management record, plan and control the organisation's activities and to help the decision-making process.
Limited companies must, by law, prepare financial accounts.	There is no legal requirement to prepare management accounts.
The format of published financial accounts is determined by law (mainly the Companies Acts) and by Financial Reporting Standards. In principle the accounts of different organisations can therefore be easily compared.	The format of management accounts is entirely at management discretion: no strict rules govern the way they are prepared or presented. Each organisation can devise its own management accounting system and format of reports.

Financial accounts	Management accounts
Financial accounts concentrate on the business as a whole, aggregating revenues and costs from different operations, and are an end in themselves.	Management accounts can focus on specific areas of an organisation's activities. Information may be produced to aid a decision rather than to be an end product of a decision.
Most financial accounting information is of a monetary nature.	Management accounts incorporate non-monetary measures. Management may need to know, for example, tons of aluminium produced, monthly machine hours, or miles travelled by salesmen.
Financial accounts present an essentially historic picture of past operations.	Management accounts are both an historical record and a future planning tool.

2.2 Cost accounts

Cost accounting and management accounting are terms which are often used interchangeably. It is *not* correct to do so.

Cost accounting is concerned with the following.

- Preparing statements (eg budgets, costing)
- Cost data collection
- Applying costs to inventory, products and services

Management accounting is concerned with the following.

- Using financial data and communicating it as information to users

Cost accounting is part of management accounting. Cost accounting provides a bank of data for the management accountant to use. Cost accounts aim to establish the following.

(a) The **cost** of goods produced or services provided.

(b) The **cost** of a department or work section.

(c) What **revenues** have been.

(d) The **profitability** of a product, a service, a department, or the organisation in total.

(e) **Selling prices** with some regard for the costs of sale.

(f) The **value of inventories of goods** (raw materials, work in progress, finished goods) that are still held in store at the end of a period, thereby aiding the preparation of a balance sheet of the company's assets and liabilities.

(g) **Future costs** of goods and services (costing is an integral part of budgeting (planning) for the future).

(h) **How actual costs compare with budgeted costs** (If an organisation plans for its revenues and costs to be a certain amount, but they actually turn out differently, the differences can be measured and reported. Management can use these reports as a guide to whether corrective action (or 'control' action) is needed to sort out a problem revealed by these differences between budgeted and actual results. This system of control is often referred to as budgetary control).

(i) **What information management needs** in order to make sensible decisions about profits and costs.

It would be wrong to suppose that cost accounting systems are restricted to manufacturing operations, although they are probably more fully developed in this area of work. **Service industries**, **government departments** and **welfare activities** can all make use of cost accounting information. Within a manufacturing organisation, the cost accounting system should be applied not only to **manufacturing** but also to **administration**, **selling and distribution**, **research and development** and all other departments.

3 The role of the accounting technician

You have now had a brief introduction to management information and cost accounting. Let us now consider the role of the accounting technician in a cost accounting system.

Remember that the accounting technician will have access to a large amount of information which is all recorded in the cost accounting records. With so much information at his fingertips, it is inevitable that many people are going to want to ask him lots of questions!

So, what sort of questions is the accounting technician going to provide answers for? Well, here are a few examples.

(a)   What has the cost of goods produced or services provided been?
(b)   What has the cost of operating a department been?
(c)   What have revenues been?

All of these questions may relate to different periods. For example, if someone wants to know what revenues have been for the past ten years, the accounting technician will need to extract this information from the cost accounting records. It is important therefore that the cost accounting system is capable of analysing such information.

If the accounting technician knows all about the costs incurred or revenues earned, he may also be asked to do the following types of task.

(a)   To assess how profitable certain products or departments are.

(b)   To review the costs of products, and to use this information to enable him to set suitable selling prices.

(c)   To put a value to inventories of goods (such as raw materials) which are unsold at the end of a period. As you will learn later on in your studies, the valuation of inventory is a very important part of cost accounting.

In order for the accounting technician to provide all of this information, the organisation must have a cost accounting system which is capable of analysing cost information quickly and easily.

The accounting technician may also need to provide information on future costs of goods and services. This is an integral part of the planning or budgeting process.

By comparing current costs with budgeted costs, the accounting technician should be able to highlight areas which show significant variances. These variances should then be investigated.

Most cost accounting systems should be capable of producing regular performance statements, though the accounting technician himself is likely to be the person producing them, and distributing them to the relevant personnel.

The role of an accounting technician in a cost accounting system is therefore fairly varied. The role is likely to include spending much time providing answers to the many questions which may be directed at the accounting technician (such as those that we have considered here).

Exam focus point

When answering paper-based examinations, always make sure that your answers are neat and well-presented. Marks are usually awarded for presentation – don't throw them away!

4 Costs in outline

Let us suppose that in your hand you have a red biro which you bought in the newsagent's down the road for 50c. Why does the newsagent charge 50c for it? In other words what does that 50c represent?

From the newsagent's point of view the cost can be split into two.

Price paid by newsagent to wholesaler	Z
Newsagent's 'mark-up'	Y
	50 c

If the newsagent did not charge more for the biro than he paid for it (Y) there would be no point in him selling it. The mark-up itself can be split into further categories.

Pure profit	X
Amount paid to shop assistants	X
Expenses of owning and operating a shop (rent, electricity, cleaning and so on)	X
	Y

The newsagent's **profit** is the amount he personally needs to live: it is like your salary. Different newsagents have different ideas about this: this is why you might pay 60c for an identical biro if you went into another newsagent's. The shop expenses are amounts that have to be paid, whether or not the newsagent sells you a biro, simply to keep the shop going. Again, if other newsagents have to pay higher rent than our newsagent, this might be reflected in the price of biros.

The amount paid to the wholesaler can be split in a similar way: there will be a profit element and amounts to cover the costs of running a wholesaling business. There might also be a cost for getting the biro from the wholesaler's premises to the shop and, of course, there will be the amount paid to the manufacturer.

The majority of the remainder of this Interactive Text takes the point of view of the manufacturer of products since his costs are the most diverse. If you understand the costing that a manufacturer has to do, you will understand the costing performed by any other sort of business. Let us go on to have a look at costs in detail.

5 Costs in detail

FAST FORWARD

- **Direct costs** can be traced directly to specific units of production.

- A **cost unit** is a unit of product which has costs attached to it. The cost unit is the basic control unit for costing purposes.

- **Cost centres** are the essential building blocks of a costing system. They act as a collecting place for certain costs before they are analysed further.

- **Overheads (indirect costs)** cannot be identified with any one product because they are incurred for the benefit of all products rather than for any one specific product.

5.1 Production costs

Look at your biro and consider what it consists of. There is probably a red plastic cap and a little red thing that fits into the end, and perhaps a yellow plastic sheath. There is an opaque plastic ink holder with red ink inside it. At the tip there is a gold plastic part holding a metal nib with a roller ball.

Let us suppose that the manufacturer sells biros to wholesalers for 20c each. How much does the little ball cost? What share of the 20c is taken up by the little red thing in the end of the biro? How much did somebody earn for putting it there?

To elaborate still further, the manufacturer probably has machines to mould the plastic and do some of the assembly. How much does it cost, per biro, to run the machines: to set them up so that they produce the right shape of moulded plastic? How much are the production line workers' wages per biro?

Any of these separate production costs, known as **direct costs** because they can be traced directly to specific units of production, could be calculated and recorded on a unit cost card which records how the total cost of a unit (in this instance, a biro) is arrived at.

BIRO - UNIT COST CARD	$	$
Direct materials		
Yellow plastic	X	
Red plastic	X	
Opaque plastic	X	
Gold plastic	X	
Ink	X	
Metal	X̲	
		X
Direct labour		
Machine operators' wages	X	
Manual assembly staff wages	X	
		X̲
		X
Direct expenses		
Moulding machinery – operating costs	X	
Assembly machinery – operating costs	X	
		X̲
Total direct cost (or prime cost)		X
Overheads (production)		X̲
Manufacturing cost (or factory cost)		X
Overheads (administration, distribution and selling)		X̲
Total cost		X̲

Don't worry if you are a bit unsure of the meaning of some of the terms in the unit cost card above as we will be looking at them in detail as we work through the text.

5.2 Cost units

Key term

> A **cost unit** is a unit of product or service which has costs attached to it. The cost unit is the basic control unit for costing purposes.

The only difficult thing about this is that a cost unit is not always a single item. It might be a **batch** of 1,000 if that is how the individual items are made. In fact, a cost per 1,000 (or whatever) is often more meaningful information, especially if calculating a cost for a single item gives an amount that you cannot hold in your hand, like 0.003c. Examples of cost units are a construction contract, a batch of 1,000 pairs of shoes, a passenger mile (in other words, the transportation of a passenger for a mile) and a patient night (the stay of a patient in hospital for a night).

5.3 Cost centres

Key term

> **Cost centres** are the essential 'building blocks' of a costing system. They are a production or service location function, activity or item of equipment. They act as a collecting place for certain costs before they are analysed further.

A cost centre might be a place, and this is probably what you think of first because the word 'centre' is often used to mean a place. On the other hand it might be a person, or it might be an item of equipment such as a machine which incurs costs because it needs to be oiled and maintained.

Cost centres may vary in nature, but what they have in common is that they **incur costs**. It is therefore logical to **collect costs** initially under the headings of the various different cost centres that there may be in an organisation. Then, when we want to know how much our products cost, we simply find out how many cost units have been produced and share out the costs incurred by that cost centre amongst the cost units.

5.4 Overheads

Overheads (or indirect costs) include costs that go into the making of the biro that you do not see when you dismantle it. You can touch the materials and you can appreciate that a combination of man and machine put them together. It is not so obvious that the manufacturer has had to lubricate machines and employ foremen to supervise the assembly staff. He also has to pay rent for his factory and for somewhere to house his stock of materials, and he has to pay someone to buy materials, recruit labour and run the payroll. Other people are paid to deliver the finished biros to the wholesalers; still others are out and about persuading wholesalers to buy biros, and they are supported at head office by staff taking orders and collecting payments.

In addition certain costs that could be identified with a specific product are classified as overheads and not direct costs. Nails used in the production of a cupboard can be identified specifically with the cupboard. However, because the cost is likely to be relatively insignificant, the expense of tracing such costs does not justify the possible benefits from calculating more accurate direct costs. Instead of keeping complex and time consuming records which might enable us to trace such costs directly to specific units of production, we try to apportion them and other overheads (indirect costs) to each cost unit in as fair a way as possible.

Overheads are the biggest problem for cost accountants because it is not easy to tell by either looking at or measuring the product, what overheads went into getting it into the hands of the buyer. Overheads, or indirect costs, unlike direct costs, will not be identified with any one product because they are incurred for the benefit of all products rather than for any one specific product.

Make sure that you understand the distinction between direct and indirect costs, as it is a very important part of your studies.

5.5 Direct and indirect costs

To summarise so far, the cost of an item can be divided into the following cost elements.

    (a)   Materials
    (b)   Labour
    (c)   Expenses

Each element can be split into two, as follows.

Materials	=	Direct materials	+	Indirect materials
+		+		+
Labour	=	Direct labour	+	Indirect labour
+		+		+
Expenses	=	Direct expenses	+	Indirect expenses
Total cost	=	Direct cost		Overhead

Question
Costs

List all of the different types of cost that a large supermarket might incur. Arrange them under headings of labour, materials used and other expenses.

Answer

Labour	Materials	Expenses
Petrol station staff	Saleable stocks	Heating
Car park attendant	Carrier bags	Lighting
Check-out staff	Other packaging	Telephone
Supervisors	Cleaning materials	Post
Delicatessen staff	Bakery ingredients	Stationery
Bakery staff		Rent
Shelf fillers		Business rates
Warehouse staff		Water rates
Cleaners		Vehicle running costs
Security staff		Advertising
Administrative staff		Discounts
Managers		Bank charges
Delivery staff		Waste disposal
Maintenance staff		

5.6 Fixed costs and variable costs

FAST FORWARD

Costs are either **variable** or **fixed**, depending upon whether they change when the volume of production changes.

We must mention one other important distinction and that is between fixed costs and variable costs.

(a)   If you produce two identical biros you will use twice as many direct materials as you would if you only produced one biro. Direct materials are in this case a **variable cost**. They vary according to the volume of production.

(b)   If you oil your machines after every 1,000 biros have been produced, the cost of oil is also a variable cost. It is an indirect material cost that varies according to the volume of production.

(c)   If you rent the factory that houses your biro-making machines you will pay the same amount of rent per annum whether you produce one biro or 10,000 biros. Factory rental is an indirect expense and it is **fixed** no matter what the volume of activity is.

The examples in (b) and (c) are both indirect costs, or overheads, but (b) is a variable overhead and (c) is a fixed overhead. The example in (a) is a variable direct cost. Direct costs usually are variable although they do not have to be.

We are elaborating this point because it can be a source of great confusion. Variable cost is **not** just another name for a direct cost. The distinctions that can be made are as follows.

(a)   **Costs are either variable or fixed, depending upon whether they change when the volume of production changes.**

(b)   **Costs are either direct or indirect, depending upon how easily they can be traced to a specific unit of production.**

Question

Are the following likely to be fixed or variable costs?

(a)   Charges for telephone calls made
(b)   Charges for rental of telephone
(c)   Annual salary of the chief accountant
(d)   Managing director's subscription to the Institute of Directors
(e)   Cost of materials used to pack 20 units of product X into a box

Answer

(a)   Variable
(b)   Fixed
(c)   Fixed
(d)   Fixed
(e)   Variable

6 Product costing

AST FORWARD **Job**, **batch** and **process costing** are methods used to cost end products.

6.1 Job costing

There are several different ways of arriving at a value for the different cost elements (material, labour and expenses) which make up a unit cost of production. The most straightforward case is where the thing to be costed is a **one-off item**. For example, a furniture maker may make a table, say, to a customer's specific requirements. From start to finish the costs incurred to make that table are identifiable. It will cost so much for the table top, so much for the legs, and so on. This form of costing is known as **job costing**.

6.2 Batch costing

An item like a biro, however, will be produced as one of a **batch** of identical items, because it would clearly be uneconomical to set up the machinery, employ labour and incur overheads to produce each biro individually. There might be a production run of, say, 5,000 biros. The cost of producing 5,000 biros would be calculated and if we wanted to know the cost of one biro we would divide this total by 5,000. The answer would however be a fraction of a penny and this is not very meaningful information.

This method of costing is called **batch costing** and it applies to many everyday items. So far as costing techniques are concerned, job and batch costing are much the same. We will be looking at job and batch costing in detail in Chapter 11.

6.3 Process costing

Another approach can be used when the product results from a series of **continuous** or **repetitive** operations or processes, and is not distinguishable as a separate unit of product until the final stage. For example oil refining, paper production, food and drink production or chemical processing.

The **output** of one process becomes the **input** to the next until the finished product is made in the final process. It is not possible to build up cost records of the cost per unit of output because production in progress is an **indistinguishable homogenous mass**.

There is often a **loss in process** due to spoilage , wastage, evaporation and so on.

We will be looking at process costing in detail in Chapter 12.

6.4 Service costing

Service organisations do not make or sell **tangible** goods. **Service costing** is used by organisations operating in a service industry (for example electricians, hotels, rail companies) or by organisations wishing to establish the cost of services carried out by some of their departments (for example the staff canteen, computer department or distribution).

We will be looking at service costing in detail in Chapter 11.

6.5 Accounting for overheads

Whether job costing, batch costing or process costing is used, there is still a problem in attributing to units of product overhead costs like factory rental, canteen costs and head office lighting. The pros and cons of trying to work out an amount per unit for such costs are open to debate. Most businesses actually do try to do this in practice, and one very good reason for doing so is to make sure that all costs are covered when prices are set.

This practice of working out an amount per unit for overheads is known as **absorption costing**. Absorption costing is a technique that is used in conjunction with the product costing methods described above. We will look at absorption costing in detail in Chapter 8.

| Question | | | Costing methods |

For each of the items listed below decide which type of costing method would be used. Mark an X in the appropriate column.

	Job	Batch	Process
Suit (off the peg)			
Suit (tailored)			
Soap			
Yoghurt			
House decoration			
Car alarm			
Paper			
Poster			
Audit			

| Answer | | | |

	Job	Batch	Process
Suit (off the peg)		X	
Suit (tailored)	X		
Soap			X
Yoghurt			X
House decoration	X		
Car alarm		X	
Paper			X
Poster		X	
Audit	X		

7 Cost codes

AST FORWARD

> A **code** is a system of symbols designed to be applied to a classified set of items to give a brief, accurate reference, facilitating entry, collection and analysis.

Once costs have been classified, a coding system can be applied to make it easier to manage the cost data, both in manual systems and in computerised systems.

A **code** is 'a system of symbols designed to be applied to a classified set of items to give a brief, accurate reference, facilitating entry, collection and analysis'. (CIMA *Official Terminology*)

Coding systems can take many forms, but an efficient and effective coding system should incorporate the following features.

(a) The code must be **easy to use and communicate**.

(b) Each item should have a **unique code**.

(c) The coding system must **allow for expansion**.

(d) The code should be **flexible** so that small changes in a cost's classification can be incorporated without major changes to the coding system itself.

(e) The coding system should provide a **comprehensive** system, whereby every recorded item can be suitably coded.

(f) The coding system should be **brief**, to save clerical time in writing out codes and to save storage space in computer memory and on computer files. At the same time codes must be **long enough** to allow for the suitable coding of all items.

(g) The likelihood of **errors** going undetected should be minimised.

(h) Code numbers should be **issued from a single central point**. Different people should not be allowed to add new codes to the existing list independently.

(i) Codes should be **uniform** (that is, have the same length and the same structure) to assist in the detection of missing characters and to facilitate processing.

(j) The coding system should avoid problems such as confusion between I and 1, O and 0 (zero), S and 5 and so on.

(k) The coding system should, if possible, be **significant** (in other words, the actual code should signify something about the item being coded).

(l) If the code consists of alphabetic characters, it should be derived from the item's description or name (that is, **mnemonics** should be used).

7.1 Example

An illustration of the use of a four digit code to apply code numbers to consumable stores might be as follows.

Department 2

Cost centre	1	2	3	4
Consumable stores	2109	2209	2309	2409

The four-digit codes above indicate the following.

- The first digit, 2, refers to department 2
- The second digit, 1, 2, 3 or 4, refers to the cost centre which incurred the cost
- The last two digits, 09, refer to 'materials costs, consumable stores'

Question Codes

Using the above code, describe the expenditure that is represented by the code number 6209.

Answer

- The first digit, 6, refers to department 6
- The second digit, 2, refers to cost centre 2
- The last two digits, 09, refer to 'material costs, consumable stores'

Therefore the code number 6209 depicts the use of consumable stores which are to be charged to cost centre 2 within department 6.

7.2 The advantages of a coding system

(a) A code is usually **briefer** than a description, thereby saving clerical time in a manual system and storage space in a computerised system.

(b) A code is **more precise** than a description and therefore **reduces ambiguity**.

(c) Coding **facilitates data processing.**

8 Presentation of management information

Most information is likely to be presented to managers in the form of a **report**. In small organisations it is possible, however, that management information will be communicated less formally (orally or using informal reports/memos).

Throughout this Interactive Text, you will come across a number of techniques which allow management information to be collected. Once it has been collected it is usually analysed and reported back to management in the form of a **report**.

Main features of a report are as follows.

- **TITLE**

  Most reports are usually given a heading to show that it is a report.

- **WHO IS THE REPORT INTENDED FOR?**

  It is vital that the intended recipients of a report are clearly identified. For example, if you are writing a report for Joe Bloggs, it should be clearly stated at the head of the report.

- **WHO IS THE REPORT FROM?**

  If the recipients of the report have any comments or queries, it is important that they know who to contact.

- **DATE**

  We have already mentioned that management information should be communicated at the most appropriate **time**. It is also important to show this timeliness by giving your report a date.

- **SUBJECT**

  What is the report about? Managers are likely to receive a great number of reports that they need to review. It is useful to know what a report is about before you read it!

- **APPENDIX**

    In general, management information is summarised in a report and the more detailed calculations and data are included in an appendix at the end of the report.

We recommend that you should use the following format when writing a report in an examination.

REPORT

To: Board of Directors
From: Cost Accountant   Date:
Subject: Report Format
Body of report
Signed: Cost Accountant

Exam focus point

When producing reports in the paper-based examination, remember that they must include the following.

- **Title** – REPORT
- **To** – Who is the report to?
- **From** – Who is the report from?
- **Date** – What is the date of report?
- **Subject** – What is the subject of the report?

Chapter Roundup

- **Information** is data that has been processed to make it **meaningful. Useful management information** should be:

    - Relevant
    - Complete
    - Accurate
    - Clear
    - Manageable volume
    - Timely
    - Cost effective

- **Planning** involves establishing **objectives** for the company and developing **strategies** in order to achieve those objectives.

- **Control** is the action of monitoring something in order to keep it on course.

- **Financial accounts** are prepared for individuals **external** to an organisation whereas **management accounts** are prepared for **internal** managers of an organisation. There are a number of differences between financial accounts and management accounts – make sure that you know what they are.

- **Direct costs** can be traced directly to specific units of production.

- A **cost unit** is a unit of product which has costs attached to it. The cost unit is the basic control unit for costing purposes.

- **Cost centres** are the essential building blocks of a costing system. They act as a collecting place for certain costs before they are analysed further.

- **Overheads (indirect costs)** cannot be identified with any one product because they are incurred for the benefit of all products rather than for any one specific product.

- Costs are either **variable** or **fixed**, depending upon whether they change when the volume of production changes.

- **Job**, **batch** and **process costing** are methods used to cost end products.

- A **code** is a system of symbols designed to be applied to a classified set of items to give a brief, accurate reference, facilitating entry, collection and analysis.

Quick quiz

1   Define the terms **data** and **information**.

2   The four main qualities of good information are:

*   ....

*   ....

*   ....

*   ....

3   Secondary sources of information include documents or reports written for a specific purpose.

☐   True

☐   False

4   In terms of cost accounting, information is most likely to be used for (1) ...., (2) .... or (3) ....

5   A strategy is the aim or goal of an organisation.

☐   True

☐   False

6   What is a cost unit?

7   Which cost elements make up overheads?

8   When preparing reports, what are the five key points to remember.

(1)   ....

(2)   ....

(3)   ....

(4)   ....

(5)   ....

Answers to quick quiz

1   **Data** is the raw material for data processing. **Information** is data that has been processed in such a way as to be meaningful to the person who receives it. **Information** is anything that is communicated.

2   • Relevance
    • Completeness
    • Accuracy
    • Clarity

3   False. Secondary information sources would include items that have not been prepared for a specific purpose (these would be primary information sources).

4   (1) Planning
    (2) Control
    (3) Decision making

5   False. This is the definition of an **objective**. A strategy is a possible course of action that might enable an organisation to **achieve** its objectives.

6   A unit of product which as costs attached to it. The cost unit is the basic control unit for costing purposes.

7   • Indirect materials
    • Indirect labour
    • Indirect expenses

8   (1) Title
    (2) Who is the report to
    (3) Who is the report from
    (4) Date
    (5) Subject

Now try the question below from the Exam Question Bank

Number	Level	Marks	Time
Q1	MCQ	N/A	N/A

The role of information technology

2

Chapter topic list

1   Role of information technology
2   Capturing and processing cost and management accounting data
3   Storing cost and management accounting data
4   Outputting cost and management accounting data
5   Management information systems

Study guide reference

			Syllabus reference
1	(e)	Discuss the role of information technology in management information	1(b)(iv)
2	(a)	Explain the relationship between the cost/management accounting system and the financial accounting/management information systems	1(c)
	(g)	Describe methods of capturing, processing, storing and outputting cost and management accounting data by computer	1(c)(iii), (iv)

1 Role of information technology

FAST FORWARD

Computers are widely used for data processing because they have certain advantages over humans.

- Speed
- Accuracy
- Volume and complexity
- Access to information

Here is a very simple example of a **data processing model.**

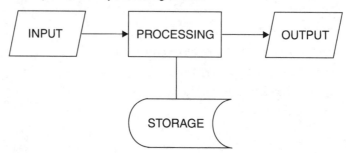

The processing of business data can be illustrated by a person working at their desk dealing with matters from their in-tray.

(a)   A person receives **input from the in-tray**, which must be dealt with.

(b)   The person may have a procedures manual or have learned a set of rules which are applied to do the work. Tools such as a calculator or a PC may also be used.

(c)   To process data from the in-tray, it may be necessary to refer to other information held on file (either paper or computer-based files).

(d)   As a result of doing the work, the person may:

(i)   Produce **output**, perhaps a report or a completed routine task.
(ii)   Add to the information held on file, or change the information to bring it up to date.

Data processing is essentially the same, no matter whether it is done manually or by computer. The **input, process, output,** storage steps apply to manual and computerised processing.

1.1 Advantages of computers

Computers are widely used for data processing because they have certain advantages over humans.

(a)   **Speed**. Computers can process data much more quickly than a human. This means that using a computer to process large volumes of data should be cheaper than doing the work manually. As computer costs have fallen, this cost advantage of the computer has increased.

The ability to process data more quickly means that a computer can produce more timely information, when information is needed as soon as possible.

(b) **Accuracy**. If set-up and programmed correctly, computers are generally accurate, whereas humans are prone to error. Errors in computer processing occur if the people involved inputting data or programming software have made errors, or if faults are present in the computer hardware.

(c) **Volume and complexity**. As businesses grow and become more complex, their data processing requirements increase in volume and complexity too. More managers need better quality information. More transactions have to be processed. The volume of processing required is beyond the capability of even the largest clerical workforce to do manually. Clearing banks, for example, would be unable to function without electronic data processing to ease the demands on their workforce.

(d) **Access to information**. The use of databases and the ability to link a number of users via some form of network improves the distribution of information within and beyond the organisation.

However, the 'manual' or 'human' method of data processing is more suitable when human judgement is involved in the work. For example, the human brain stores a lifetime of experiences and emotions that influence decisions and it is capable of drawing on them and making connections between them when making decisions.

2 Capturing and processing cost and management accounting data

FAST FORWARD

> Stages of **data input**
> – Origination of data
> – Transcription of data
> – Data input

The collection of data and its subsequent input to the computer can be a time-consuming and costly task. The computer will only accept data which is in machine-sensible form, data held on a source document must be manually input to produce a computer file.

The stages of data input are as follows.

(a) **Origination** of data (transactions giving rise to data which needs to be recorded and processed).

(b) **Transcription** of data onto a paper document suitable for operators to refer to while keying in data.

(c) Data **input**.

The ideal methods of data collection and input are those which minimise the following.

- The time needed to record the original data, and transmit, prepare and input the data to the computer

- Costs

- Errors

2.1 Direct data entry with a keyboard

The principal method of direct data entry is by means of a keyboard.

2.1.1 Keyboard layout and functions

A basic keyboard includes the following.

- **Ordinary typing keys** used to enter data or text
- A **numeric key pad** for use with the built-in calculator
- **Cursor control keys** (basically up/down/left/right keys to move the cursor)
- A number of **function keys** for use by the system and application software

In addition to the function keys, there are special keys that are used to communicate with the operating programs, to let the computer know that you have finished entering a command, that you wish to correct a command and so on. Nothing appears at the cursor point when these keys are used, but they affect operations on screen.

2.2 The VDU

A **VDU** (or monitor) **displays text** and **graphics** and serves a number of purposes.

- It allows the operator to carry out a visual check on what he or she has keyed in
- It helps the operator to input data by providing 'forms' on the screen for filling in
- It displays output such as answers to file enquiries
- It gives messages to the operator

Graphical user interfaces have become the principal means by which humans communicate with machines. Features include the following.

(a)   **Windows**. This basically means that the screen can be divided into sections or 'windows' of flexible size which can be opened and closed. This enables two or more documents to be viewed and edited together, and sections of one to be inserted into another. This is particularly useful for word processed documents and spreadsheets, which are too large for the VDU screen.

(b)   **Icons**. An icon is an image of an object used to represent an abstract idea or process. In software design, icons may be used instead of numbers, letters or words to identify and describe the various functions available for selection, or files to access. A common icon is a waste paper bin to indicate the deletion of a document.

(c)   **Mouse**. This is a device used with on-screen graphics and sometimes as an alternative to using the keyboard to input instructions. It can be used to pick out the appropriate icon (or other option), to mark out the area of a new window, mark the beginning and end of a block for deletion/insertion and so on. It also has a button to execute the current command.

(d)   **Pull-down menu**. An initial menu (or 'menu-bar') will be shown across the top of the VDU screen. Using the mouse to move the pointer to the required item in the menu, the pointer 'pulls down' a subsidiary menu, somewhat similar to pulling down a window blind in a room of a house. The pointer and mouse can then be used to select the required item on the pulled-down menu.

(e)   Many GUIs (such as Microsoft Windows) also display dialogue boxes, buttons, sliders, check boxes, and a plethora of other graphical widgets that let you tell the computer what to do and how to do it.

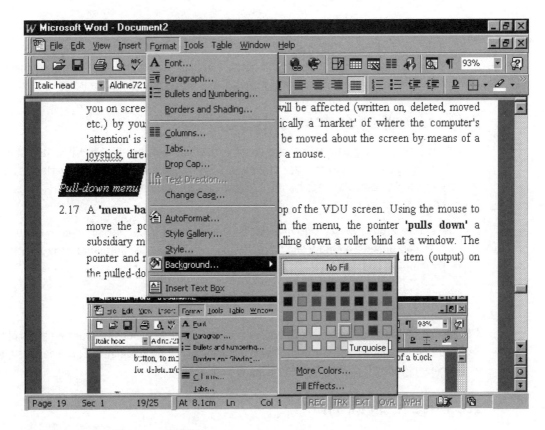

2.3 Automatic input devices

In the following paragraphs we explain some of the most common document reading methods. Document reading methods reduce the manual work involved in data input. This **saves time and money** and also **reduces errors.**

(a)   **Magnetic ink character recognition (MICR)** involves the recognition by a machine of special formatted characters printed in magnetic ink. The characters are read using a specialised reading device. The main advantage of MICR is its speed and accuracy, but MICR documents are expensive to produce. The main commercial application of MICR is in the banking industry – on cheques and deposit slips.

(b)   **Optical mark reading** involves the marking of a pre-printed form with a ballpoint pen or typed line or cross in an appropriate box. The card is then read by an OMR device which senses the mark in each box using an electric current and translates it into machine code. Applications in which OMR is used include **Lotto** entry forms, and answer sheets for multiple choice questions.

(c)   A **scanner** is device that can **read text or illustrations printed on paper** and translate the information into a **form the computer can use**. A scanner works by digitising an image, the resulting matrix of bits is called a **bit map.**

To edit text read by an optical scanner, you need **optical character recognition (OCR)** software to translate the image into text. Most optical scanners sold today come with OCR packages. Businesses may use a scanner and OCR to obtain 'digital' versions of documents they have only paper copies of. For good results the copy must be of good quality.

(d)   **Bar codes** are groups of marks which, by their spacing and thickness, indicate specific codes or values.

Large retail stores have Electronic Point of Sale (EPOS) devices, which include bar code readers. This enables the provision of immediate sales and stock level information.

(e)   Many retailers have now introduced **EFTPOS systems (Electronic Funds Transfer at the Point of Sale)**. An EFTPOS terminal is used with a customers credit card or debit card to pay for goods or services. The customer's credit card account or bank account will be debited automatically. EFTPOS systems combine point of sale systems with electronic funds transfer.

2.4 Card reading devices

(a)   The standard **magnetic stripe card** contains machine-sensible data on a thin strip of magnetic recording tape stuck to the back of the card. The magnetic card reader converts this information into directly computer-sensible form. The widest application of magnetic stripe cards is as bank credit or service cards.

(b)   A **smart card** is a plastic card in which is embedded **a microprocessor chip**. A smart card would typically contain a **memory** and a **processing capability**. The information held on smart cards can therefore be updated (eg using a PC and a special device).

2.5 Touch screens

A **touch screen** is a display screen that enables users to make selections by touching areas of the screen. Sensors, built into the screen surround, detect which area has been touched. These devices are widely used in vending situations, such as the selling of train tickets.

2.6 Voice recognition

Computer software has been developed that can convert speech into computer-sensible form via a microphone. Users are required to speak clearly and reasonably slowly.

3 Storing cost and management accounting data

FAST FORWARD   Data can be **stored** on disks, tapes or memory sticks.

3.1 Hard disks

Disks offer **direct access** to data. Almost all PCs have an **internal hard disk** to store software and data. At the time of writing the average new **PC** has a hard disk size of around **40 Gigabytes**, a massive increase from just a couple of years ago.

3.2 Floppy disks

The floppy disk provides a **cost-effective** means of on-line storage for **small** amounts of information. A 3½' disk can hold up to **1.44 Mb** of data.

3.3 Zip disks

A **Zip disk** is a different type of **removable** disk, with much larger capacity (up to 750 Mb – the equivalent of 521 floppy disks). Zip disks require a special Zip drive. They are suitable for back-up, general storage or for moving files between computers.

3.4 Tape storage

Tape cartridges have a **much larger capacity** than floppy disks and they are still widely used as a **backing storage** medium. Fast tapes which can be used to create a back-up file very quickly are known as **tape streamers**.

Like an audio or video cassette, data has to be recorded **along the length** of a computer tape and so it is **more difficult to access** than data on disk (ie direct access is not possible with tape). Reading and writing are separate operations.

3.5 CD-ROM (Compact Disc – Read Only Memory)

A CD-ROM can store 650 megabytes of data.

The **speed** of a CD-ROM drive is relevant to how fast data can be retrieved: an **eight speed** drive is quicker than a **four speed** drive.

CD recorders are now available for general business use with blank CDs (CD-R) and **rewritable disks** (CD-RW) are now available.

3.6 DVD (Digital Versatile Disc)

DVD development was encouraged by the advent of multimedia files with video graphics and sound requiring greater disk capacity.

Digital Versatile Disc (DVD) technology can store up to 6 gigabytes of data on one disk. Access speeds are improved as is sound and video quality.

3.7 Memory stick or 'Pen drive'

A pen drive or memory stick is a physically small external storage device usually connected via a USB port. Capacity ranges from 16Mb to 512Mb.

4 Outputting cost and management accounting data

AST FORWARD Data can be output via printers or a VDU.

4.1 Printers

Laser printers print a whole page at a time, rather than line by line. The **quality** of output is very **high**. Laser printers are relatively expensive to purchase, but compared with inkjet printers, running costs are relatively low.

Inkjet printers are small and reasonably cheap. They work by sending a jet of ink on to the paper to produce the required characters.

Older style printers, that use tractor-fed rolls of paper are still used in some organisations for printing high volumes. An example is a **dot matrix printer**, which is a character printer which prints a single character at a time. Their main drawback is their **low-resolution.** They are also relatively **slow** and **noisy**.

4.2 The VDU or monitor

Screens were described earlier in this chapter, as they are used together with computer keyboards for **input**. It should also be clear that they can be used as an **output** medium, primarily where the output **volume is low** (for example a single enquiry) and **no permanent output** is required (for example the current balance on an account).

4.3 The choice of output medium

As with choosing an input medium, choosing a suitable output medium depends on a number of factors, which you should bear in mind when we go on to consider each type of output in turn. These factors are as follows.

(a) **Is a 'hard' copy of the output required**; in other words, is a printed version of the output needed? If so, what quality must the output be?

    (i) If the output includes documents that are going to be used as OCR turnround documents, the quality of printing must be good.

    (ii) If the information will be used as a working document with a short life or limited use (eg a copy of text for type-checking) then a low quality output on a dot matrix printer might be sufficient.

(b) **The volume of information produced**. For example, a VDU screen can hold a certain amount of data, but it becomes more difficult to read when information goes 'off-screen' and can only be read a bit at a time.

(c) **The speed at which output is required**. For example, to print a large volume of data, a high speed printer might be most suitable to finish the work more quickly (and release the CPU for other jobs).

(d) **The suitability of the output medium to the application** – ie the purpose for which the output is needed.

    (i) A VDU is well-suited to interactive processing with a computer.

    (ii) A graph plotter would be well-suited to output in the form of graphs.

    (iii) Output on to a magnetic disk or tape would be well-suited if the data is for further processing.

    (iv) Large volumes of reference data for human users to hold in a library might be held on microfilm or microfiche, and so output in these forms would be appropriate.

(e) **Cost**: some output devices would not be worth having because their advantages would not justify their cost, and so another output medium should be chosen as 'second best'.

5 Management information systems

FAST FORWARD

A **management information system** is the hardware and software used to drive a database system which provides useful information for management.

5.1 Introduction

Key term

A **management information system** (MIS) is defined as a collective term for the hardware and software used to drive a database system with the outputs, both to screen and print, being designed to provide easily assimilated information for management.

Management information is by no means confined to accounting information, but until relatively recently accounting information systems have been the most formally-constructed and well-developed part of the overall information system of a business enterprise.

An alternative definition of a management information system is 'an information system making use of available resources to provide managers at all levels in all functions with the information from all relevant sources to enable them to make timely and effective decisions for planning, directing and controlling the activities for which they are responsible.'

A management information system is therefore **a system of disseminating information which will enable managers to do their job**. Since managers must have information, there will always be a management information system in any organisation.

Most management information systems are not designed, but grow up **informally**, with each manager making sure that he or she gets all the information considered necessary to do the job. It is virtually taken for granted that the necessary information flows to the job, and to a certain extent this is so. Much accounting information, for example, is easily obtained, and managers can often get along with frequent face-to-face contact and co-operation with each other. Such an informal system works best in **small organisations**.

However, some information systems are **specially designed**, often because the introduction of computers has forced management to consider its information needs in detail. This is especially the case in **large** companies.

5.2 The need for formal planning

Management should try to develop/implement a management information system for their enterprise with care. If they allow the MIS to develop without any formal planning, it will almost certainly be **inefficient** because data will be obtained and processed in a random and disorganised way and the communication of information will also be random and hit-and-miss.

(a) Some managers will prefer to keep **data in their heads** and will not commit information to paper. When the manager is absent from work, or is moved to another job, his stand-in or successor will not know as much as he could and should about the work because no information has been recorded to help him.

(b) The organisation will not collect and process all the information that it should, and so valuable information that ought to be available to management will be missing from **neglect**.

(c) Information may be available but not **disseminated** to the managers who are in a position of authority and so ought to be given it. The information would go to waste because it would not be used. In other words, the wrong people would have the information.

(d) Information is **communicated late** because the need to communicate it earlier is not understood and appreciated by the data processors.

The consequences of a poor MIS might be **dissatisfaction** amongst employees who believe they should be told more, a **lack of understanding** about what the targets for achievement are and a **lack of information** about how well the work is being done.

5.3 Essential characteristics

Whether a management information system is formally or informally constructed, it should therefore have certain essential characteristics.

(a) The functions of individuals and their areas of responsibility in achieving company objectives should be defined.

(b) Areas of control within the company (eg cost centres, investment centres) should also be clearly defined.

(c)   Information required for an area of control should flow to the manager who is responsible for it.

An organisation's cost accounting system will be part of the overall management information system. It will both provide information to assist management with planning, control and decision making as well as accumulating historical costs to establish inventory valuations, profits and balance sheet items.

Chapter Roundup

- Computers are widely used for data processing because they have certain advantages over humans.

    - Speed
    - Accuracy
    - Volume and complexity
    - Access to information

- Stages of **data input**

    - Origination of data
    - Transcription of data
    - Data input

- Data can be **stored** on disks, tapes or memory sticks.

- Data can be output via printers or a VDU.

- A **management information system** is the hardware and software used to drive a database system which provides useful information for management.

Quick quiz

1   List four advantages that computers have over humans.

2   List four things that a basic keyboard includes.

3   What is the main function of a graphical user interface?

4   What sort of automatic input device is issued on Lotto entry forms?

5   Which gives better quality output?

    ☐ Dot matrix printer
    ☐ Laser printer

6   What is ROM and what does it stand for?

Answers to quick quiz

1.
   - Speed
   - Accuracy
   - Volume and complexity
   - Access to information

2.
   - Ordinary typing keys
   - Numeric key pad
   - Cursor control keys
   - A number of function keys

3. To enable humans to communicate with machines

4. OMR (Optimal Mark Reading) which involves the marking of a pre-printed form with a ball point pen or typed line or cross in an appropriate box. The card is then read by an OMR device which senses the mark in each box using an electronic current and translates it into machine code.

5. ☑ Laser printer

6. ROM (Read-Only Memory) means that all data is implanted onto a disk when it is made and subsequent users can only retrieve information (they cannot overwrite or delete what is already on the disk).

Now try the question below from the Exam Question Bank

Number	Level	Marks	Time
Q2	MCQ	N/A	N/A

Cost classification

Chapter topic list

Study guide reference

			Syllabus reference
1	(d)	Describe management responsibilities (for cost, profit and investment) and their effect on management information and performance measurement	1(a)(ii) 1(c)(i)
2	(e)	Explain and illustrate the concept of cost units	1(c)(i)
3	(a)	Describe the variety of cost classifications used for different purposes in a cost accounting system, including by responsibility, function, direct/indirect, behaviour.	2(a)
6	(a)	Distinguish between direct and indirect labour costs	3(b)(i)
7	(a)	Describe the nature of expenses by function	3(c)(i)

1 Cost classifications in a cost accounting system

The total cost of making a product or providing a service consists of the following.

    (a)   Cost of **materials**

    (b)   Cost of the **wages** and **salaries** (labour costs)

    (c)   Cost of **other expenses**

        • Rent and rates
        • Electricity and gas bills
        • Depreciation

2 Direct costs and indirect costs

FAST FORWARD

A **direct cost** is a cost that can be traced in full to the product or service being costed. An **indirect cost** (or overhead) is a cost that is incurred in the course of making a product or providing a service, but which cannot be traced directly and in full to the product or service.

We saw in Chapter 1 how materials, labour costs and other expenses can be classified as either **direct costs** or **indirect costs**.

Key term

• A **direct cost** is a cost that can be traced in full to saleable cost units (products or services) that are being costed.

• An **indirect cost** or **overhead** is a cost that is incurred in the course of making a product or providing a service, but which cannot be traced directly and in full to the product or service.

    (a)   **Direct material costs** are the costs of materials that are known to have been used in making and selling a product (or even providing a service).

    (b)   **Direct labour costs** are the specific costs of the workforce used to make a product or provide a service to an external customer. Direct labour costs are established by measuring the time taken for a job, or the time taken in 'direct production work'.

    (c)   **Direct expenses** are those expenses that have been incurred in full as a direct consequence of making a product or providing a service.

Examples of **indirect costs** include supervisors' wages, cleaning materials and buildings insurance.

As we saw in Chapter 1, **total expenditure** may therefore be analysed as follows.

Materials	=	Direct materials	+	Indirect materials
+		+		+
Labour	=	Direct labour	+	Indirect labour
+		+		+
Expenses	=	Direct expenses	+	Indirect expenses
Total cost	=	Total direct cost	+	Overhead

Total direct cost is also known as **prime cost**.

2.1 Direct material

y term

> **Direct material** is all material becoming part of the product (unless used in negligible amounts and/or having negligible cost).

Direct material costs are charged to the product as part of the **prime cost**. Examples of direct material are as follows.

(a) **Component parts**, specially purchased for a particular job, order or process.

(b) **Part-finished work** which is transferred from department 1 to department 2 becomes finished work of department 1 and a direct material cost in department 2.

(c) **Primary packing materials** like cartons and boxes.

2.2 Direct labour

ey term

> **Direct wages** are all wages paid for labour (either as basic hours or as overtime) expended on work on the product itself.

Direct wages costs are charged to the product as part of the **prime cost**.

Examples of groups of labour receiving payment as direct wages are as follows.

(a) Workers engaged in **altering** the condition or composition of the product.
(b) Inspectors, analysts and testers **specifically required** for such production.
(c) Foremen, shop clerks and anyone else whose wages are **specifically identified.**

Two **trends** may be identified in **direct labour costs.**

(a) The ratio of direct labour costs to total product cost is falling as the use of machinery increases, and hence depreciation charges increase.

(b) Skilled labour costs and sub-contractors' costs are increasing as direct labour costs decrease.

2.3 Direct expenses

ey term

> **Direct expenses** are any expenses which are incurred on a specific product other than direct material cost and direct wages.

Direct expenses are charged to the product as part of the **prime** cost. Examples of direct expenses are as follows.

- The cost of special designs, drawings or layouts
- The **hire of tools** or equipment for a particular job

Direct expenses are also referred to as **chargeable expenses.**

3 Classification by function

Classification by function involves classifying costs as production/manufacturing costs, administration costs or marketing/selling and distribution costs.

In a 'traditional' costing system for a manufacturing organisation, costs are classified as follows.

(a)   **Production** or **manufacturing costs.** These are costs associated with the factory.

(b)   **Administration costs.** These are costs associated with general office departments.

(c)   **Marketing**, or **selling** and **distribution costs.** These are costs associated with sales, marketing, warehousing and transport departments.

Classification in this way is known as **classification by function.** Expenses that do not fall fully into one of these classifications might be categorised as **general overheads** or even listed as a classification on their own (for example research and development costs).

In costing a small product made by a manufacturing organisation, direct costs are usually restricted to some of the production costs. A commonly found build-up of costs is therefore as follows.

	$
Production costs	
Direct materials	A
Direct wages	B
Direct expenses	C
Prime cost	A+B+C
Production overheads	D
Full production cost	A+B+C+D
Administration costs	E
Selling and distribution costs	F
Full cost of sales	A+B+C+D+E+F

Functional costs include the following.

(a)   **Production costs** are the costs which are incurred by the sequence of operations beginning with the supply of raw materials, and ending with the completion of the product ready for warehousing as a finished goods item. Packaging costs are production costs where they relate to 'primary' packing (boxes, wrappers and so on).

(b)   **Administration costs** are the costs of managing an organisation, that is, planning and controlling its operations, but only insofar as such administration costs are not related to the production, sales, distribution or research and development functions.

(c)   **Selling costs** sometimes known as marketing costs, are the costs of creating demand for products and securing firm orders from customers.

(d)   **Distribution costs** are the costs of the sequence of operations with the receipt of finished goods from the production department and making them ready for despatch and ending with the reconditioning for reuse of empty containers.

(e)   **Research costs** are the costs of searching for new or improved products, whereas **development costs** are the costs incurred between the decision to produce a new or improved product and the commencement of full manufacture of the product.

(f)   **Financing costs** are costs incurred to finance the business such as loan interest.

Question

Within the costing system of a manufacturing company the following types of expense are incurred.

Reference number

1	Cost of oils used to lubricate production machinery
2	Motor vehicle licences for lorries
3	Depreciation of factory plant and equipment
4	Cost of chemicals used in the laboratory
5	Commission paid to sales representatives
6	Salary of the secretary to the finance director
7	Trade discount given to customers
8	Holiday pay of machine operatives
9	Salary of security guard in raw material warehouse
10	Fees to advertising agency
11	Rent of finished goods warehouse
12	Salary of scientist in laboratory
13	Insurance of the company's premises
14	Salary of supervisor working in the factory
15	Cost of typewriter ribbons in the general office
16	Protective clothing for machine operatives

Required

Complete the following table by placing each expense in the correct cost classification.

Cost classification	Reference number					
Production costs						
Selling and distribution costs						
Administration costs						
Research and development costs						

Each type of expense should appear only once in your answer. You may use the reference numbers in your answer.

Answer

Cost classification	Reference number					
Production costs	1	3	8	9	14	16
Selling and distribution costs	2	5	7	10	11	
Administration costs	6	13	15			
Research and development costs	4	12				

4 Fixed costs and variable costs

FAST FORWARD

A different way of analysing and classifying costs is into **fixed costs** and **variable costs**. Many items of expenditure are part-fixed and part-variable and hence are termed **semi-fixed** or **semi-variable**. This is also known as **classification by behaviour**.

We also saw in Chapter 1 that a different way of analysing and classifying costs is into **fixed costs** and **variable costs.** Some items of expenditure are part-fixed and part-variable. In cost accounting, **semi-fixed** or **semi-variable costs** may be divided into their fixed and variable elements.

Key terms

> A **fixed cost** is a cost which is incurred for a particular period of time and which, within certain activity levels, is unaffected by changes in the level of activity.
>
> A **variable cost** is a cost which tends to vary with the level of activity.

Examples of fixed and variable costs are as follows.

(a) Direct material costs are **variable costs** because they rise as more units of a product are manufactured.

(b) Sales commission is often a fixed percentage of sales turnover, and so is a **variable cost** that varies with the level of sales.

(c) Telephone call charges are likely to increase if the volume of business expands, and so they are a **variable overhead cost.**

(d) The rental cost of business premises is a constant amount, at least within a stated time period, and so it is a **fixed cost.**

5 Classification by responsibility

FAST FORWARD

- **Cost centres** are collecting places for costs before they are further analysed. Costs are further analysed into cost units once they have been traced to cost centres.

- A **cost unit** is a unit of product or service to which costs can be related.

- A **cost object** is any activity for which a separate measure of costs is desired.

- **Profit centres** are similar to cost centres but are accountable for both costs and revenues.

- **Revenue centres** are similar to cost centres and profit centres but are accountable for revenues only.

- An **investment centre** is a profit centre with additional responsibilities for capital investment and possibly financing.

- A **responsibility centre** is a department or organisational function whose performance is the direct responsibility of a specific manager.

5.1 Allocation of costs to cost centres

As we have seen, costs consist of the costs of the following.

- Direct materials
- Direct labour
- Direct expenses
- Production overheads
- Administration overheads
- Selling and distribution overheads

When costs are incurred, they are generally allocated to a **cost centre** (the **collecting place** for certain costs before they are analysed further).

- A department
- A machine, or group of machines
- A project (eg the installation of a new computer system)

Cost centres are an essential 'building block' of a costing system. They are the starting point for the following.

(a) The classification of actual costs incurred.
(b) The preparation of budgets of planned costs.
(c) The comparison of actual costs and budgeted costs (management control).

5.2 Cost units

Once costs have been traced to cost centres, they can be further analysed in order to establish a **cost per cost unit**.

Question   Cost units

Suggest suitable cost units which could be used to aid control within the following organisations.

(a) A hotel with 50 double rooms and 10 single rooms
(b) A hospital
(c) A road haulage business

Answer

(a) • Guest/night
     • Bed occupied/night
     • Meal supplied

(b) • Patient/night
     • Operation
     • Outpatient visit

(c) • Tonne/mile
     • Mile

5.3 Cost objects

A **cost object (or objective)** is any activity for which a separate measurement of costs is desired.

If the users of management information wish to know the cost of something, this something is called a **cost object**. Examples include the following.

• The cost of a product
• The cost of a service
• The cost of operating a department

5.4 Profit centres

A **profit centre** is similar to a cost centre but is accountable for **costs** *and* **revenues**. Profit centre managers should normally have control over how revenue is raised and how costs are incurred. Often, several cost centres will comprise one profit centre.

5.5 Revenue centres

A **revenue centre** is similar to a cost centre and a profit centre but is accountable for **revenues only**. Revenue centre managers should normally have control over how revenues are raised.

5.6 Investment centres

An **investment centre** is a profit centre with additional responsibilities for capital investment and possibly for financing, and whose performance is measured by its return on investment.

5.7 Responsibility centres

Cost centres, revenue centres, profit centres and investment centres are also known as **responsibility centres**.

A **responsibility centre** is a department or organisational function whose performance is the direct responsibility of a specific manager.

6 Responsibility accounting and performance measurement

FAST FORWARD

In responsibility accounting, three commonly used **performance measures** are as follows.

  –   Cost per unit
  –   Profitability ratios
  –   Resource utilisation ratios

Responsibility accounting is a system of accounting that segregates revenues and costs into areas of personal responsibility in order to monitor and assess the performance of each part of an organisation.

The performance of each manager or each part of an organisation is monitored by a number of commonly used **performance measures**.

- Cost per unit
- Profitability ratios
- Resource utilisation ratios

6.1 Cost per unit

The **cost per unit** of a product is a performance measure which is used to monitor the total costs which are collected in cost centres.

Key term

The **cost per unit** of a product or service may be calculated as follows.

$$\text{Cost per unit} = \frac{\text{Cost of input}}{\text{Units of ouput}}$$

6.2 Example: cost per unit

Tandridge Co makes two products, the 'Oxted' and the 'Edenbridge'. Management believe that the company is performing more efficiently since the introduction of a bonus scheme for its factory workers one year ago. The following information relates to the costs and production of Tandridge Co for 20X7 and 20X8.

	20X7		20X8	
	Oxted	Edenbridge	Oxted	Edenbridge
	$	$	$	$
Direct material	20,000	16,000	18,000	14,000
Direct labour	15,000	20,000	14,000	18,000
Direct expenses	12,000	12,000	10,000	10,000
Total direct costs	47,000	48,000	42,000	42,000
Output (units)	10,000	16,000	12,000	18,000

Using cost per unit as a performance indicator, comment on the performance of the company in the years 20X7 and 20X8.

Solution

Firstly, we need to calculate the cost per unit for each product for each of the years 20X7 and 20X8.

		Cost per unit $	
		20X7	20X8
Oxted			
20X7 $= \dfrac{47,000}{10,000}$		4.70	
20X8 $= \dfrac{42,000}{12,000}$			3.50
Edenbridge			
20X7 $= \dfrac{48,000}{16,000}$		3.00	
20X8 $= \dfrac{42,000}{18,000}$			2.33

The results show that the cost per unit for both the Oxted and the Edenbridge has fallen quite significantly between 20X7 and 20X8. This is an example of a situation in which the cost per unit may be used as a performance indicator.

6.3 Profitability

AST FORWARD

Profitability ratios are an important performance measure of profit centres. The **profit margin** determines the profitability of an operation.

Profitability is a measure of how profitable something is. Profit has two components, cost and income. All parts of an organisation and all activities within it incur costs, and so their success needs to be judged in relation to costs. Only some parts of an organisation receive income, for example **profit centres,** and their success should be judged in terms of both cost and income, ie **profit.**

The main indicator of profitability in profit centres and in individual organisations is the **profit margin.**

6.4 Profit margin

ey term

The **profit margin (profit to sales ratio)** is calculated as (profit ÷ sales) × 100%.

The profit margin is a particularly useful way of analysing information.

(a)   It provides a measure of performance for management.

(b)   Investigation of unsatisfactory profit margins enables control action to be taken, either by reducing excessive costs or, possibly, by raising selling prices.

Profit margin is usually calculated using the **net profit**.

6.5 Example: the profit to sales ratio

A company compares its 20X1 results with 20X0 results as follows.

	20X1	20X0
	$	$
Sales	160,000	120,000
Cost of sales		
Direct materials	40,000	20,000
Direct labour	40,000	30,000
Production overhead	22,000	20,000
Marketing overhead	42,000	35,000
	144,000	105,000
Profit	16,000	15,000
Profit to sales ratio	10%	12½%

Ratio analysis on the above information shows that there is a decline in profitability in spite of the $1,000 increase in profit, because the profit margin is less in 20X1 than 20X0.

6.6 Gross profit margin

The **gross profit margin** is a measure of a company's manufacturing and distribution efficiency during the production process. It is calculated as follows.

Gross profit margin = $\dfrac{\text{Gross profit}}{\text{Turnover}}$ × 100%.

Remember that gross profit excludes non-production overheads.

For the company in Paragraph 6.6 the gross profit margins would be as follows.

20X1 $\dfrac{16,000 + 42,000}{160,000}$ × 100% = 36.25%

20X0 $\dfrac{15,000 + 35,000}{120,000}$ × 100% = 41.67%

Question	Profit margin

The following results are for Macbeth Co a company which has just two profit centres, A and B. Calculate the profit margin for each profit centre in each of the years 20X4, 20X5 and 20X6, and comment on your results.

	20X4		20X5		20X6	
	A	B	A	B	A	B
	$'000	$'000	$'000	$'000	$'000	$'000
Sales	25	44	60	47	62	49
Net profit	10	11	24	14	27	16

Answer

Net profit margin is calculated as $\dfrac{\text{Net profit}}{\text{Sales}} \times 100\%$

	20X4		20X5		20X6	
	A	*B*	*A*	*B*	*A*	*B*
Net profit margin	40%	25%	40%	30%	44%	33%

The profit margin is used as an indicator of profitability. In this example it is used to compare the profitability of profit centres A and B from 20X4 to 20X6, and also to compare the profitability of profit centre A with profit centre B.

The results show that profit centre A is as profitable in 20X4 as it is in 20X5, and that in 20X6 it appears to become more profitable.

Profit centre B, on the other hand, shows a net profit margin which is increasing steadily between 20X4 and 20X6.

In each of the years 20X4 to 20X6, profit centre A is found to be more profitable than profit centre B, as indicated by A having a higher net profit margin than B.

6.7 Resource utilisation ratios

There are two main resource utilisation ratios.

- Return on capital employed
- Asset turnover

y term

> **Return on capital employed (ROCE)** (also called **return on investment (ROI)**) is calculated as (profit/capital employed) × 100% and shows how much profit has been made in relation to the amount of resources invested.

Profits alone do not show whether the return achieved by an organisation is sufficient, because the profit measure takes no account of the volume of assets committed. Thus if Company A and Company B have the following results, Company B would have the better performance.

	A	B
	$	$
Profit	5,000	5,000
Sales	100,000	100,000
Capital employed	50,000	25,000
ROCE	10%	20%

The profit of each company is the same but Company B only invests $25,000 to achieve these results whereas Company A needs $50,000.

ROCE may be calculated in a number of ways, but management accountants usually prefer to exclude from profits all revenues and expenditures which are not related to the operation of the business itself (such as interest payable and income from trade investments). **Profit before interest and tax** is therefore often used.

Similarly **all assets of a non-operational nature** (for example trade investments and intangible assets such as goodwill) **should be excluded** from capital employed.

Profits should be related to average capital employed but, in practice, the **ratio is usually computed using the year-end assets**. Using year-end figures can, however, distort trends and comparisons. If a new investment is undertaken near to a year end and financed, for example, by an issue of shares, the capital employed will rise by the finance raised but profits will only have a month or two of the new investment's contribution.

What does the ROCE tell us? What should we be looking for? There are **two principal comparisons** that can be made.

- The change in ROCE from one year to the next
- The ROCE being earned by other entities

Question   Profitability

Figaro is a travelling opera company. During 20X6 the company produced three different operas, each running for fifteen weeks. The sales revenue and costs of each production were collected in individual profit centres which are shown as follows.

Production	Profit centre	Sales $	Variable costs $	Fixed costs $
Carmen	W	143,000	41,000	39,000
Don Giovanni	A	127,500	23,000	42,000
Tosca	M	152,000	26,000	45,000

Required

Calculate the profitability of the three opera productions, Carmen, Don Giovanni and Tosca.

Answer

In order to calculate the profitability of each of the different opera productions, we need to calculate the profit margin of each of the different profit centres.

Profit margin is calculated as $\frac{\text{Net profit}}{\text{Sales}} \times 100\%$

Remember that Net profit = Sales revenue − variable costs − fixed costs.

The net profit and profit margin for each of the different profit centres are therefore as follows.

Production	Profit centre	Net profit $	Profit margin
Carmen	W	63,000 (W1)	44%
Don Giovanni	A	62,500 (W2)	49%
Tosca	M	81,000 (W3)	53%

Workings

(1)   Net profit = $143,000 − $(41,000 + 39,000) = $63,000
(2)   Net profit = $127,500 − $(23,000 + 42,000) = $62,500
(3)   Net profit = $152,000 − $(26,000 + 45,000) = $81,000

If the profit margin is used to indicate the profitability of each of the different productions, the results show that Tosca was the most profitable production, with a profit margin of 53%.

6.8 Asset turnover

term

> **Asset turnover** is a measure of how well the assets of a business are being used to generate sales. It is calculated as (sales ÷ capital employed).

For example, suppose two companies each have capital of $100,000 and Company A makes sales of $400,000 per annum whereas Company B makes sales of only $200,000 per annum. Company A is making a higher turnover from the same amount of assets, in other words twice as much asset turnover as Company B, and this will help A to make a higher return on capital employed than B. Asset turnover is **expressed as 'x times' so that assets generate x times their value in annual turnover.** Here, Company A's asset turnover is 4 times and B's 2 times.

6.9 Interrelationships between ratios

Profit margin and asset turnover together explain the ROCE. The relationship between the three ratios is as follows.

Profit margin × asset turnover = ROCE

$$\frac{\text{Profit}}{\text{Sales}} \times \frac{\text{Sales}}{\text{Capital employed}} = \frac{\text{Profit}}{\text{Capital employed}}$$

7 Classification by behaviour

So far in this Interactive Text we have introduced you to the subject of management information and explained in general terms what it is and what it does. In this chapter, we have looked at the principal methods of classifying costs and management responsibilities (for cost, profit and investments) and their effect on management information and performance measurement.

One of the cost classifications that we have looked at is variable and fixed costs. You will remember that **variable costs vary directly with changes in activity levels** and **fixed costs do not**. This particular classification is also known as **classification by behaviour** and the next chapter will explain further this two-way split of cost behaviour and explain an important method of splitting **total costs** into **fixed costs and variable costs.**

am focus
int

> This chapter has introduced a number of new terms and definitions. The topics covered in this chapter are very important and are likely to be tested in the **Accounting for Costs** examination that you will be facing.

Chapter Roundup

- A **direct cost** is a cost that can be traced in full to the product or service being costed. An **indirect cost** (or overhead) is a cost that is incurred in the course of making a product or providing a service, but which cannot be traced directly and in full to the product or service.

- **Classification by function** involves classifying costs as production/manufacturing costs, administration costs or marketing/selling and distribution costs.

- A different way of analysing and classifying costs is into **fixed costs** and **variable costs**. Many items of expenditure are part-fixed and part-variable and hence are termed **semi-fixed** or **semi-variable**. This is also known as **classification by behaviour**.

- **Cost centres** are collecting places for costs before they are further analysed. Costs are further analysed into cost units once they have been traced to cost centres.

- A **cost unit** is a unit of product or service to which costs can be related.

- A **cost object** is any activity for which a separate measure of costs is desired.

- **Profit centres** are similar to cost centres but are accountable for both costs and revenues.

- **Revenue centres** are similar to cost centres and profit centres but are accountable for revenues only.

- An **investment centre** is a profit centre with additional responsibilities for capital investment and possibly financing.

- A **responsibility centre** is a department or organisational function whose performance is the direct responsibility of a specific manager.

- In responsibility accounting, three commonly used **performance measures** are as follows.

  - Cost per unit
  - Profitability ratios
  - Resource utilisation ratios

- Profitability ratios are an important performance measure of profit centres. The **profit margin** determines the profitability of an operation.

Quick quiz

1 Give two examples of direct expenses.

2 Give an example of an administration overhead, a selling overhead and a distribution overhead.

3 What are functional costs?

4 What is the distinction between fixed and variable costs?

5 What is a cost centre?

6 What is a cost unit?

7 What is a profit centre?

8 What is an investment centre?

9 What is the formula for return on capital employed?

10 What is the most suitable measure of profitability?

11 What is the formula for gross profit margin?

Answers to quick quiz

1 • The hire of tools or equipment for a particular job
   • Maintenance costs of tools, fixtures and so on

2 • **Administration overhead** = Depreciation of office administration overhead, buildings and machinery
   • **Selling overhead** = Printing and stationery (catalogues, price lists)
   • **Distribution overhead** = Wages of packers, drivers and despatch clerks

3 Functional costs are classified as follows.

   • **Production** or **manufacturing costs**
   • **Administration costs**
   • **Marketing** or **selling and distribution costs**

4 A **fixed cost** is a cost which is incurred for a particular period of time and which, within certain activity levels, is unaffected by changes in the level of activity.

   A **variable cost** is a cost which tends to vary with the level of activity.

5 A **cost centre** acts as a collecting place for certain costs before they are analysed further.

6 A **cost unit** is a unit of product or service to which costs can be related. The cost unit is the basic control unit for costing purposes.

7 A **profit centre** is similar to a cost centre but is accountable for **costs** and **revenues**.

8 An **investment centre** is a profit centre with additional responsibilities for capital investment and possibly financing.

9 $\dfrac{\text{Profit}}{\text{Capital employed}} \times 100\%$

10 Profit margin

11 $\dfrac{\text{Gross profit}}{\text{Sales}} \times 100\%$

Now try the question below from the Exam Question Bank

Number	Level	Marks	Time
Q3	Examination	N/A	20 mins

Cost behaviour

4

Chapter topic list

Study guide reference

			Syllabus reference
3	(b)	Explain and illustrate the nature of variable, fixed and mixed (semi-variable, stepped-fixed) costs	2(b)(i)
3	(c)	Use the high-low method to separate semi-variable costs	2(b)(ii)
3	(d)	Use variable, fixed and semi-variable costs in cost analysis	2(b)(iii)
3	(e)	Analyse the effect of changing activity levels on unit costs	2(b)(iv)

1 Cost behaviour

Cost behaviour is the way in which costs are affected by changes in the **volume of output** and is important for planning, control and decision-making.

Key term

> **Cost behaviour** is the way in which costs are affected by changes in the volume of output.

Management decisions will often be based on how costs and revenues vary at different activity levels. Examples of such decisions are as follows.

- What should the **planned activity level** be for the next period?
- Should the **selling price** be reduced in order to sell more units?
- Should a particular component be **manufactured internally** or **bought in**?
- Should a **contract** be undertaken?

If the accountant does not know the level of costs which should have been incurred as a result of an organisation's activities, how can he or she hope to control costs?

Knowledge of cost behaviour is obviously essential for the tasks of **budgeting**, **decision making** and **control accounting**.

Exam focus point

> Remember that the behavioural analysis of costs is important for planning, control and decision-making.

1.1 Cost behaviour and levels of activity

There are many factors which may influence costs. The major influence is **volume of output**, or the **level of activity**. The level of activity may refer to one of the following.

- Value of items sold
- Number of items sold
- Number of invoices issued
- Number of units of electricity consumed

1.2 Basic principles of cost behaviour

The basic principle of cost behaviour is that **as the level of activity rises, costs will usually rise**. It will cost more to produce 2,000 units of output than it will cost to produce 1,000 units.

This principle is common sense. The problem for the accountant, however, is to determine, for each item of cost, the way in which costs rise and by how much as the level of activity increases. For our purposes here, the level of activity for measuring cost will generally be taken to be the **volume of production**.

1.3 Example: Cost behaviour and activity level

Hans Bratch Co has a fleet of company cars for sales representatives. Running costs have been estimated as follows.

(a)   Cars cost $12,000 when new, and have a guaranteed trade-in value of $6,000 at the end of two years. Depreciation is charged on a straight-line basis.

(b)   Petrol and oil cost 15 cents per mile.

(c)   Tyres cost $300 per set to replace; replacement occurs after 30,000 miles.

(d)   Routine maintenance costs $200 per car (on average) in the first year and $450 in the second year.

(e)   Repairs average $400 per car over two years and are thought to vary with mileage. The average car travels 25,000 miles per annum.

(f)   Tax, insurance, membership of motoring organisations and so on cost $400 per annum per car.

Required

Calculate the average cost per annum of cars which travel 20,000 miles per annum and 30,000 miles per annum.

Solution

Costs may be analysed into fixed, variable and stepped cost items, a stepped cost being a cost which is fixed in nature but only within certain levels of activity.

(a)   **Fixed costs**

	$ per annum
Depreciation $(12,000 − 6,000) ÷ 2	3,000
Routine maintenance $(200 + 450) ÷ 2	325
Tax, insurance etc	400
	3,725

(b)   **Variable costs**

	Cents per mile
Petrol and oil	15.0
Repairs ($400 ÷ 50,000 miles)	0.8
	15.8

(c)   Step costs are tyre replacement costs, which are $300 at the end of every 30,000 miles.

  (i)   If the car travels less than or exactly 30,000 miles in two years, the tyres will not be changed. Average cost of tyres per annum = $0.

  (ii)   If a car travels more than 30,000 miles and up to (and including) 60,000 miles in two years, there will be one change of tyres in the period. Average cost of tyres per annum = $150 ($300 ÷ 2).

  (iii)   If a car exceeds 60,000 miles in two years (up to 90,000 miles) there will be two tyre changes. Average cost of tyres per annum = $300. ($600 ÷ 2).

The estimated costs per annum of cars travelling 20,000 miles per annum and 30,000 miles per annum would therefore be as follows.

	20,000 miles per annum $	30,000 miles per annum $
Fixed costs	3,725	3,725
Variable costs (15.8c per mile)	3,160	4,740
Tyres	−	150
Cost per annum	6,885	8,615

2 Cost behaviour patterns

FAST FORWARD

- Costs which are not affected by the level of activity are **fixed** costs or **period** costs.

- **Step costs** are fixed within a certain range of activity.

- **Variable costs** increase or decrease with the level of activity and it is usually assumed that there is a linear relationship between cost and activity.

- **Semi-variable, semi-fixed** or **mixed costs** are costs which are part fixed and part variable.

2.1 Fixed costs

Key term

> A **fixed cost** is a cost which tends to be unaffected by increases or decreases in the volume of output.

Fixed costs are a **period charge**, in that they relate to a span of time; as the time span increases, so too will the fixed costs (which are sometimes referred to as period costs for this reason).

A sketch graph of a fixed cost would look like this.

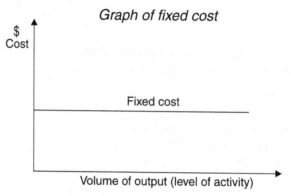

Examples of a fixed cost would be as follows.

- The salary of the managing director (per month or per annum)
- The rent of a single factory building (per month or per annum)
- Straight line depreciation of a single machine (per month or per annum)

2.2 Step costs

Key term

> A **step cost** is a cost which is fixed in nature but only within certain levels of activity.

Consider the depreciation of a machine which may be fixed if production remains below 1,000 units per month. If production exceeds 1,000 units, a second machine may be required, and the cost of depreciation (on two machines) would go up a step. A sketch graph of a step cost could look like this.

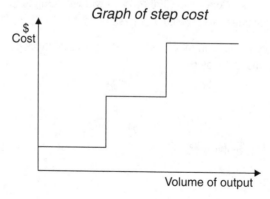

BPP LEARNING MEDIA

Other examples of step costs are as follows.

(a) **Rent** is a step cost in situations where accommodation requirements increase as output levels get higher.

(b) **Basic pay** of individual employees is nowadays usually fixed, but as output rises, more employees (supervisors, managers and so on) are required.

2.3 Variable costs

term

A **variable cost** is a cost which tends to vary directly with the volume of output. The variable cost per unit is the same amount for each unit produced.

Total variable costs will increase or decrease in **proportion** to any change in activity. This can be shown in a sketch graph like this.

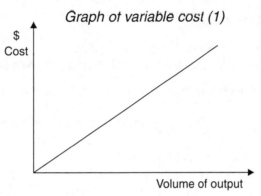

Graph of variable cost (1)

A constant variable cost per unit implies that the price per unit of say, material purchased is constant, and that the rate of material usage is also constant.

(a) The most important variable cost is the **cost of raw materials** (where there is no discount for bulk purchasing since bulk purchase discounts reduce the cost of purchases).

(b) **Sales commission** is variable in relation to the volume or value of sales.

(c) **Bonus payments** for productivity to employees might be variable once a certain level of output is achieved, as the following diagram illustrates.

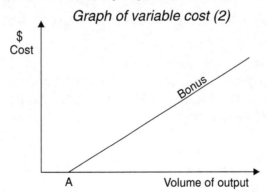

Graph of variable cost (2)

Up to output A, no bonus is earned.

2.4 Semi-variable costs

Key term

> A **semi-variable/semi-fixed/mixed cost** is a cost which contains both fixed and variable components and so is partly affected by changes in the level of activity.

Examples of these costs include the following.

(a) **Electricity and gas bills**

- Fixed cost = standing charge
- Variable cost = charge per unit of electricity used

(b) **Salesman's salary**

- Fixed cost = basic salary
- Variable cost = commission on sales made

(c) **Costs of running a car**

- Fixed cost = road tax, insurance
- Variable costs = petrol, oil, repairs (which vary with miles travelled)

A sketch graph of a semi-variable cost would look like this.

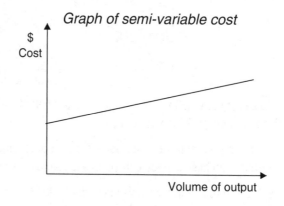

Graph of semi-variable cost

$ Cost

Volume of output

 Question

Cost behaviour

Are the following likely to be fixed, variable or semi-variable costs?

(a) Telephone bill
(b) Annual salary of the chief accountant
(c) The management accountant's annual membership fee to CIMA (paid by the company)
(d) Cost of materials used to pack 20 units of product X into a box
(e) Wages of warehousemen

Answer

(a) Semi-variable
(b) Fixed
(c) Fixed
(d) Variable
(e) Variable

2.5 Other cost behaviour patterns

Other cost behaviour patterns may be appropriate to certain cost items. Examples of two other cost behaviour patterns are shown below.

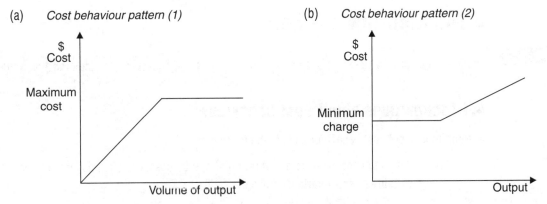

(a) *Cost behaviour pattern (1)*

(b) *Cost behaviour pattern (2)*

- Graph (a) represents an item of cost which is variable with output up to a certain maximum level of cost.

- Graph (b) represents a cost which is variable with output, subject to a minimum (fixed) charge.

3 The effect of changing activity levels on unit costs

The effect of changing activity levels on units costs is best explained by means of an example.

3.1 Example: The effect of changing activity levels on unit costs

The following table relates to different levels of production of the zed. The variable cost of producing a zed is $5. Fixed costs are $5,000.

	1 zed	10 zeds	50 zeds
	$	$	$
Total variable cost	5	50	250
Variable cost per unit	5	5	5
Total fixed cost	5,000	5,000	5,000
Fixed cost per unit	5,000	500	100
Total cost (fixed and variable)	5,005	5,050	5,250
Total cost per unit	5,005	505	105

What happens when activity levels rise can be summarised as follows.

- The variable cost per unit remains constant
- The fixed cost per unit falls
- The total cost per unit falls

The above example may be illustrated graphically as follows.

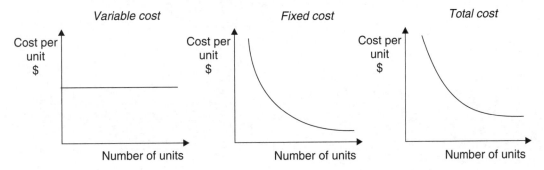

Exam focus point

> Remember that you can pick up easy marks in the paper-based examination for drawing graphs neatly. Always use a ruler, label your axes and use an appropriate scale.

4 The high-low method

FAST FORWARD

> The fixed and variable elements of semi-variable costs can be determined by the **high-low method**.

4.1 Assumptions about cost behaviour

Assumptions about cost behaviour include the following.

(a) Within the normal or **relevant range** of output, costs are often assumed to be either **fixed**, **variable** or **semi-variable** (mixed).

(b) Within the normal or relevant range of output, costs often rise in a straight line as the volume of activity increases. Such costs are said to be **linear**.

The **high-low method** of determining fixed and variable elements of mixed costs relies on the assumption that mixed costs are linear. We shall now go on to look at this method of cost determination.

4.2 High-low method

Follow the steps below to estimate the fixed and variable elements of semi-variable costs.

Step 1   Review records of activity and costs in previous periods.
- Select the period with the **highest** activity level
- Select the period with the **lowest** activity level

Step 2   Determine the following.

- Total cost at highest activity level
- Total costs at lowest activity level
- Total units at highest activity level
- Total units at lowest activity level

Step 3   Calculate the following.

$$\frac{\text{Total cost at highest activity level} - \text{total cost at lowest activity level}}{\text{Total units at highest activity level} - \text{total units at lowest activity level}}$$

= variable cost per unit (v)

Step 4   The fixed costs can be determined as follows. (Total cost at highest activity level) – (total units at highest activity level × variable cost per unit)

The following graph demonstrates the high-low method.

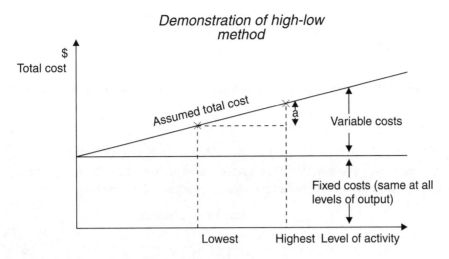

Demonstration of high-low method

4.2.1 Example: The high-low method

DG Co has recorded the following total costs during the last five years.

Year	Output volume Units	Total cost $
20X0	65,000	145,000
20X1	80,000	165,000
20X2	90,000	170,000
20X3	60,000	140,000
20X4	75,000	155,000

Required

Calculate the total cost that should be expected in 20X5 if output is 85,000 units.

Solution

Step 1
- Period with highest activity = 20X2
- Period with lowest activity = 20X3

Step 2
- Total cost at highest activity level = 170,000
- Total cost at lowest activity level = 140,000
- Total units at highest activity level = 90,000
- Total units at lowest activity level = 60,000

Step 3 Variable cost per unit

$$= \frac{\text{Total cost at highest activity level} - \text{total cost at lowest activity level}}{\text{Total units at highest activity level} - \text{total units at lowest activity level}}$$

$$= \frac{170,000 - 140,000}{90,000 - 60,000} = \frac{30,000}{30,000} = \$1 \text{ per unit}$$

Step 4 Fixed costs = (total cost at highest activity level) − (total units at highest activity level × variable cost per unit)

= 170,000 − (90,000 × 1) = 170,000 − 90,000 = $80,000

Therefore the costs in 20X5 for output of 85,000 units are as follows.

		$
Variable costs	(85,000 × $1)	85,000
Fixed costs		80,000
		165,000

The step-by-step guide has been covered in order that you fully understand the process involved.

Question

The Valuation Department of a large firm of surveyors wishes to develop a method of predicting its total costs in a period. The following past costs have been recorded at two activity levels.

	Number of valuations (V)	Total cost (TC)
Period 1	420	82,200
Period 2	515	90,275

The total cost model for a period could be represented as follows.

A   TC = $46,500 + 85V
B   TC = $42,000 + 95V
C   TC = $46,500 – 85V
D   TC = $51,500 – 95V

Chapter Roundup

- **Cost behaviour** is the way in which costs are affected by changes in the volume of output and is important for planning, control and decision-making.

- Costs which are not affected by the level of activity are **fixed** costs or **period** costs.

- **Step costs** are fixed within a certain range of activity.

- **Variable costs** increase or decrease with the level of activity and it is usually assumed that there is a linear relationship between cost and activity.

- **Semi-variable, semi-fixed** or **mixed costs** are costs which are part fixed and part variable.

- The fixed and variable elements of semi-variable costs can be determined by the **high-low method**.

Quick Quiz

1   Cost behaviour is ....

2   The basic principle of cost behaviour is that as the level of activity rises, costs will usually rise/fall.

3   Fill in the gaps for each of the graph titles below.

(a)

Graph of a ....cost

Example:

(b)

Graph of a ....cost

Example:

(c)

Graph of a ....cost

Example:

(d)

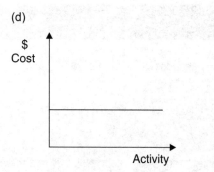

Graph of a ....cost

Example:

4 Costs are assumed to be either fixed, variable or semi-variable within the normal or relevant range of output.

☐ True

☐ False

5 The costs of operating the canteen at 'Eat a lot Company' for the past three months is as follows.

Month	Cost $	Employees
1	72,500	1,250
2	75,000	1,300
3	68,750	1,175

Variable cost (per employee per month) =

Fixed cost per month =

Answers to Quick Quiz

1   The variability of input costs with activity undertaken.

2   Rise

3   (a)   Step cost. Example: rent, supervisors' salaries
    (b)   Variable cost. Example: raw materials, direct labour
    (c)   Semi-variable cost. Example: electricity and telephone
    (d)   Fixed. Example: rent, depreciation (straight-line)

4   True

5   Variable cost = $50 per employee per month

    Fixed costs = $10,000 per month

	Activity	Cost $
High	1,300	75,000
Low	1,175	68,750
	125	6,250

    Variable cost per employee = $6,250/125 = $50

    For 1,175 employees, total cost = $68,750

    Total cost   = variable cost + fixed cost

    $68,750   = (1,175 × $50) + fixed cost

    ∴ Fixed cost   = $68,750 − $58,750

              = $10,000

Now try the questions below from the Exam Question Bank

Number	Level	Marks	Time
Q4	Examination	N/A	20 mins

Part B
Elements of cost

5

Materials

Chapter topic list

Study guide reference

			Syllabus reference
2	(b)	Describe the process of accounting for input costs and relating them to work done	1(c)
2	(c)	Identify the documentation required, and the flow of documentation, for different cost accounting transactions	1(c)
4	(a)	Describe the main types of material classification	3(a)(i)
4	(b)	Describe the procedures and documentation required to ensure the correct authorisation, coding, analysis and recording of direct and indirect material costs	3(a)(i)
4	(c)	Explain, illustrate and evaluate the FIFO, LIFO and weighted average methods used to price materials issued from inventory	3(a)(ii)
4	(d)	Describe and illustrate the accounting for material costs	3(a)
4	(e)	Calculate material input requirements, and control measures, where wastage occurs	3(a)
5	(a)	Describe the procedures required to monitor inventory and to minimise inventory discrepancies and losses	3(a)(iii)
5	(b)	Explain and illustrate the costs of inventory holding and stock outs	3(a)(iii)
5	(c)	Explain, illustrate and evaluate inventory control levels (minimum, maximum, reorder)	3(a)(iii)
5	(d)	Calculate and interpret optimal reorder quantities	3(a)(iii)
5	(e)	Discuss the relationship between the materials costing system and the inventory control system	3(a)(iii)

1 Types of material

FAST FORWARD

Materials can be **classified** according to the substances that make them up, how they are measured, or their physical properties.

1.1 Classifying materials

There are a number of different ways in which materials can be classified. The three main ways of classifying materials are as follows.

- They can be classified according to the **substances that make them up**
- They can be classified according to **how they are measured**
- They can be classified according to their **physical properties**

Materials may be made of one or more substances. For example, when classifying materials according to the substances that make them up, they may be classified as either **wood, plastic, metal, wool** and so on. Many items may be made up of a **combination of substances.**

You may also classify materials according to how they are measured. Accounting text books could make it easy for you to believe that all materials come by the **litre, metre** or **kilogram.** In practice however, you will find that materials really come in **bags, packets** or **by the thousand.**

Finally, materials may also be classified by one or more of their physical properties. The same basic piece of material may be distinguished by one or more of the following features.

- Colour
- Shape
- Fire resistance
- Water resistance
- Abrasiveness
- Flexibility
- Quality

1.2 Raw materials

y term

> **Raw materials** are goods purchased for incorporation into products for sale.

Raw materials is a term which you are likely to come across often, both in your studies and your workplace. But what are raw materials?

Examples of raw materials are as follows.

- Clay for making terracotta garden pots
- Timber for making dining room tables
- Paper for making books

Question

Raw materials

Without getting too technical, what are the main raw materials used in the manufacture of the following items?

(a)   A car
(b)   A box of breakfast cereal
(c)   A house (just the basic structure)
(d)   Your own organisation's products

Answer

(a)   Metal, rubber, plastic, glass, fabric, oil, paint, glue

(b)   Cereals, plastic, cardboard, glue. You might have included sugar and preservatives and so on, depending upon what you eat for breakfast

(c)   Sand, gravel, cement, bricks, plaster, wood, metal, plastic, glass, slate

(d)   You will have to mark your own answer. If you work for a service organisation like a firm of accountants, you could view the paper (and binding) of sets of accounts sent out to clients as raw materials, although in practice such materials are likely to be regarded as indirect costs

1.3 Work in progress

ey term

> **Work in progress** is a term used to represent an intermediate stage between the manufacturer purchasing the materials that go to make up the finished product and the finished product.

Work in progress is another term which you are likely to come across often, and valuing work in progress is one of the most difficult tasks in costing.

Work in progress means that some work has been done on the materials purchased as part of the process of producing the finished product, but **the production process is not complete.** Examples of work in progress are as follows.

(a) Terracotta pots which have been shaped, but which have not been fired, and are therefore unfinished.

(b) Dining room tables which have been assembled, but have not been polished, and are therefore not ready for sale.

(c) Paper which has been used to print books, but which has not yet been bound. The books are therefore not yet assembled, and not yet ready for sale.

1.4 Finished goods

Key term

> A **finished good** is a product ready for sale or despatch.

Did you notice how all of the examples of work in progress were items which were not ready for sale? It therefore follows that examples of finished goods are as follows.

- Terracotta pots ready for sale or despatch
- Dining room tables ready for sale or despatch
- Books ready for sale or despatch

The examples in the previous paragraph show terracotta pots which have now been fired, dining room tables which have now been polished, and books which have now been bound. These final processes have transformed our **work in progress** into **finished goods.**

Question
Materials

(a) Distinguish between raw materials, work in progress and finished goods.

(b) Give three examples of indirect materials costs.

Answer

(a) Raw materials are goods purchased for incorporation into products for sale, but not yet issued to production. Work in progress is the name given to the materials while they are in the course of being converted to the final product. Finished goods are the end products when they are ready to be sold.

(b) Some examples of indirect materials costs are as follows.

(i) Oil for machine maintenance

(ii) Cleaning fluids and substances

(iii) Rags, dusters and the like

(iv) Glue if used in small quantities

(v) Secondary packaging, for example the sort of boxes you can pick up at the check-out in supermarkets

2 Buying materials

ST FORWARD Procedures and documentation are required for material purchases.

2.1 Purchasing procedures

All businesses have to buy materials of some sort, and this means that decisions have to be made and somebody has to be responsible for doing the **buying**.

Large businesses have specialist buying departments managed by people who are very skilled at the job. One of the reasons for the success of companies like Tesco's is that they are expert at buying good quality goods at the best prices.

In spite of this, the essence of a buying transaction is simple and, in fact, familiar because you buy things every day and (mainly subconsciously) go through the following process.

- You need something
- You find out where you can buy it
- Identify the most suitable item (take into account cost, quality, and so on)
- You order the item, or perhaps several if you will need more in the future
- You receive the item
- You pay for the item

In a business this process will be more involved, but only because those spending the money are likely to be different from those looking after the goods and those using them, and because none of those people will actually own the money spent. The following diagram illustrates who will be involved.

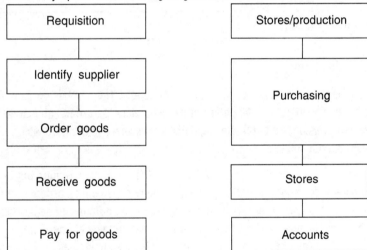

2.2 Purchasing documentation

Clearly there needs to be some means by which different departments can let each other know what they want and what is being done about it, and even the smallest business will need to keep records of some sort. We shall describe a manual system that might be used in a fairly large organisation. In reality it is likely that much of the procedure would be computerised, but this does not alter the basic principles or information flows.

2.2.1 Purchase requisition form

The first stage will be that the department requiring the goods will complete a **purchase requisition form** asking the **purchasing department** to carry out the necessary transaction. An example is shown below. Note that the purchase requisition will usually need some form of **authorisation**, probably that of a senior person in the department requiring the goods and possibly also that of a senior person in the finance department if substantial expense is involved.

PURCHASE REQUISITION		Req. No.
Department Suggested supplier:		Date Requested by: Latest date required:

Quantity	Description	Estimated Cost	
		Unit	$
Authorised signature:			

2.2.2 Order form

Often the business will use a regular source of supply. The purchasing department may, however, be aware of special offers or have details of new suppliers: part of its job is to keep up to date with what is on the market. Thus once a **purchase requisition** is received in the purchasing department, the first task is to identify the most suitable **supplier**.

Often the requisitioning department will specify the goods they require but the buying department may have a choice (for example in deciding what quality paper will be ordered for stationery). Whatever the decision made, an **order form** is then completed by the purchasing department (again, it may have to be authorised by the finance department to ensure that budgets are not being over-stepped) and this is sent to the supplier. The order form, an example of which is shown below, will contain the following details.

(a) The **name** and **address** of the ordering organisation.
(b) The **date** of order, and reference numbers for both ordering department and supplier.
(c) The **address** and **date**(s) for delivery (by road, rail, air and so on) or collection.
(d) **Details of goods/services**: quantity, code (if any), specification, unit costs and so on.

An order form should be sent even if goods are initially ordered by telephone, to confirm that the order is a legitimate one and to make sure that the supplier does not overlook it.

Purchase Order/Confirmation		Fenchurch Garden Centre Pickle Lane Westbridge Kent			

Our Order Ref: Date

To

⌐(Address)   ⌐   Please deliver to the above address

Ordered by:

Passed and checked by:

∟   ⌐   Total Order Value £

Quantity	Code	Description/Specification		£	p
			Subtotal		
			VAT (@ 17.5%)		
			Total		

The **purchase order** is important because it provides a means by which the business can later check that the goods received are the same as those ordered. Copies can be sent to the person who requisitioned the goods so that he knows they are on their way and also to the stores so that they can arrange to accommodate the goods. Either now or later a copy can be sent to the accounts department so that they can see that goods invoiced were genuinely required and that the purchase was properly authorised.

2.2.3 Despatch note

Certain other documents may arise before the goods are actually received. The supplier may acknowledge the order and perhaps indicate how long it is likely to take to be fulfilled. A **despatch note** may be sent to warn that the goods are on their way.

2.2.4 Delivery note

We now move to the stores department. When the goods are delivered, goods inwards will be presented with a **delivery note** or **advice note** (although bear in mind that smaller suppliers may not go to these lengths). This is the supplier's document (a copy is signed by the person receiving the goods and returned to the supplier) and, as such, there is no guarantee that its details are correct. If the actual goods cannot be inspected immediately, the delivery note should be signed 'subject to inspection'.

2.2.5 Goods received note

Once the goods have been delivered they should be inspected as soon as possible. A **goods received note (GRN)** will be completed by goods inwards on the basis of a physical check, which involves counting the items received and seeing that they are not damaged.

```
                                                    ACCOUNTS COPY

        GOODS RECEIVED NOTE  WAREHOUSE COPY
   DATE: __7 March 20X5__  TIME: __2.00 pm_____    NO  5565
   ORDER NO: _____.
   SUPPLIER'S ADVICE NOTE NO: _____ WAREHOUSE A

   | QUANTITY | CAT NO  | DESCRIPTION            |
   |    20    | TP 400  | Terracotta pots, medium |

   RECEIVED IN GOOD CONDITION:   L. W.           (INITIALS)
```

A copy of the GRN can be sent to the purchasing department so that it can be matched with the purchase order. This is to make sure that the correct number and specification of items have been received. Any discrepancies would be taken up with the supplier.

A copy of the GRN would also be sent to the accounts department so that it can be matched with the **purchase invoice** when it is received. The payment of the invoice is the end of the transaction (unless there is a mistake on the invoice or there was some problem with the delivery, in which case a **credit note** may later be received from the supplier).

2.3 Buying and costing

Clearly the buying department needs to retain cost information for the purpose of identifying suitable suppliers. This is likely to be in the form of catalogues and price lists.

The costing department is chiefly interested in the actual cost of materials as shown on the **invoice** and included in the accounting records as cash and credit transactions.

2.3.1 Example: Buying and costing

It is Amy Alexander's first day in the costing department and she has been told to calculate the materials cost of job 1234 which has just been completed. No invoice has yet been received for the main material used, which is known as LW32. Amy uses her initiative and pops down to the purchasing department to see if they can help. They are rather busy but someone hands her a very well-thumbed catalogue and a thick file of purchase orders, all relating to the supplier of LW32. There are many orders for LW32, one of which has today's date. How should Amy go about costing the LW32 used for job 1234?

Solution

The quickest thing to do would be to phone up the supplier and ask what price will be charged for the order in question, but there might be good reasons for not doing this (for example not wishing to prompt an earlier invoice than usual!) It seems likely that, in the absence of the actual information, the best way of ascertaining a price for LW32 is to consult the catalogue (assuming it is up to date) and to find the most recent purchase order that *has* been invoiced. If there is a discrepancy, previous invoices could be looked at to see if they show a price rise since the date of the catalogue. If the price fluctuates widely it might be better to calculate an average.

As Amy gets to know her way around the system she will learn which are the most reliable sources of information. Possibly some suppliers make frequent errors on invoices but quote correct unit prices on delivery notes. The moral is to always be on your guard for errors.

Question	Materials purchase

Draw a flow diagram illustrating the main documents involved in a materials purchase, from its initiation up until the time of delivery.

Answer

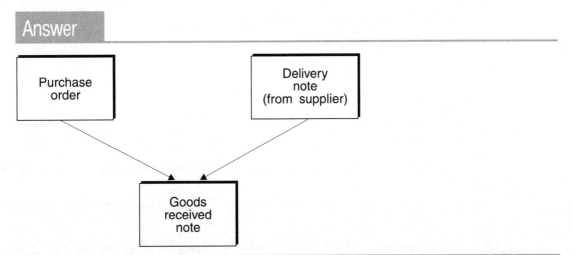

2.4 Material input requirements

Some organisations might need to buy 'extra' materials because wastage may occur as a matter of course in some production processes.

2.4.1 Example: Material input requirements

1 kg of product A is manufactured from 1 kg of Material X in a process where wastage is equivalent to 3% of material input.

How many kgs of Material X are needed in order to produce 100 kg of Product A?

100 kgs of material X will only produce 97 kgs of Product A (and there will be 3 kg of material X wasted).

$$100 \text{ kg of material X} = (100 - 0.03) \times 100 \text{ kgs Product A}$$
$$= 0.97 \times 100 \text{ kg of Product A}$$
$$= 97 \text{ kg Product A}$$

Therefore, in order to produce 100 kg of Product A, the company needs to buy 103.09 kg of Material X.

$$\frac{100\,\text{kg Material X}}{0.97} = 103.09\text{ kg Material X}$$

	Kg
Material X input	103.09
Wastage (3% × 103.09 kg)	(3.09)
Product A output	100.00

Question   Wastage

If JH Co produces 1 unit of product L from 2 kg of Material W, and wastage equates to 5% of material input, how many kgs of Material W should JH Co buy in order to produce 4,000 units of Product L? State your answer to the nearest kg.

Answer

4,000 units of product L are produced from $\dfrac{8{,}000\text{ kg}^{*}}{0.95^{**}} = 8{,}421$ kg Material W

* Each unit of product L is made from 2 kg of Material W.

**(100% − 5% wastage)

Summary

	Kg
Material W input	8,421
5% wastage (5% × 8,421 kg)	(421)
Material W processed	8,000

If 8,000 kg of Material W are processed, they will produce 4,000 units of Product L (8,000 kg ÷ 2 kg = 4,000 units).

It is important, therefore, that any wastage is taken into account when calculating material input requirements and hence quantities of materials to be purchased.

3 Valuing materials issues and inventories

FAST FORWARD

Materials issued from inventory can be valued using FIFO, LIFO and weighted average methods.

3.1 Just-in-time inventory policy

The implicit assumption in the Amy Alexander example above was that materials were bought specifically for individual jobs and therefore that each order could be identified with a particular job. This is possible in practice. Certainly, keeping large quantities of inventory is something to be avoided in the business environment of the new millennium. Holding inventory means that you have to have somewhere to put it and so it takes up space that could be used for other purposes. Often it means employing somebody to look after it, perhaps 24 hours a day if it is very valuable.

Ideally, you should receive an order for so many items of the product in question, buy exactly the right quantity of materials to make that many items and be left with no inventories of finished goods, work in progress or raw materials. This is known as the **just-in-time (JIT) approach,** that is, the just-in-time purchasing of inventories to meet just-in-time production of goods ordered. From the point of view of costing, there is very little difficulty with the JIT approach. The materials costs of each production run are known because the materials used were bought specially for that run. There was no inventory to start with and there is none left over.

3.2 Buffer inventory

However the approach more common in practice is to keep a certain amount of inventory in reserve to cope with fluctuations in demand and with suppliers who cannot be relied upon to deliver the right quality and quantity of materials at the right time. This reserve of inventory is known as **buffer inventory** (or safety inventory). Buffer inventory may also be held when it is more economical to purchase inventory in greater quantities than required (in order to obtain bulk purchase discounts). The valuation of buffer inventory is one of the most important elements of your studies at this level.

3.2.1 Example: Inventory valuation

(a)   Suppose, for example, that you have 50 litres of a chemical in inventory. You buy 2,000 litres to allow for the next batch of production. Both the opening inventory and the newly-purchased inventory cost $2 per litre.

	Litres	$
Opening inventory	50	100
Purchases	2,000	4,000
	2,050	4,100

(b)   You actually use 1,600 litres, leaving you with 450 litres. You know that each of the 1,600 litres used cost $2, as did each of the 450 litres remaining. There is no costing problem here.

(c)   Now suppose that in the following month you decide to buy 1,300 litres, but have to pay $2.10 per litre because you lose a 10c discount if buying under 1,500 litres.

	Litres	Cost per litre $	Total cost $
Opening inventory	450	2.00	900
Purchases	1,300	2.10	2,730
	1,750		3,630

For the next batch of production you use 1,600 litres, as before. What did the 1,600 litres used cost, and what value should you give to the 150 litres remaining in inventory?

Solution

If we could identify which litres were used there would be no problem. Some would cost $2 per litre but most would cost $2.10. It may not, however, be possible to identify litres used. For instance, the chemical may not be perishable, and new purchases may be simply mixed in with older inventory in a central tank. There would thus be no way of knowing which delivery the 1,600 litres used belonged to. Even if the chemical were stored in tins with date stamps it would be a tedious chore to keep track of precisely which tins were used when (and since they are all the same, the exercise has no virtue from the point of view of the quality of the final product.)

It may not therefore be possible or desirable to track the progress of each individual litre. However we need to know the cost of the litres that we have used so that we know how much to charge for the final product and so that we can compare this cost with the equivalent cost in earlier or future periods. We also need to know the cost of closing inventory both because it will form part of the usage figure in the next period and for financial accounting purposes. Closing inventory is often a significant figure in the financial statements and it appears in both the income statement and the balance sheet.

We therefore have to use a consistent method of pricing the litres which provides a reasonable approximation of the costs of the inventory.

3.3 Inventory valuation methods

There are a number of different methods of valuing inventory.

(a)   **FIFO – First in, first out**

This method values issues at the prices of the oldest items in inventory at the time the issues were made. The remaining inventory will thus be valued at the price of the most recent purchases. Say, for example, ABC Co's inventory consisted of four deliveries of raw material in the last month:

	Units		
1 September	1,000	at	$2.00
8 September	500	at	$2.50
15 September	500	at	$3.00
22 September	1,000	at	$3.50

If on 23 September 1,500 units were issued to production, 1,000 of these units would be priced at $2 (the cost of the 1,000 oldest units in inventory), and 500 at $2.50 (the cost of the next oldest 500). 1,000 units of closing inventory would be valued at $3.50 (the cost of the 1,000 most recent units received) and 500 units at $3.00 (the cost of the next most recent 500).

(b)   **LIFO – Last in, first out**

This method is the opposite of FIFO. Issues will be valued at the prices of the most recent purchases; hence inventory remaining will be valued at the cost of the oldest items. In the example above it will be 1,000 units of issues which will be valued at $3.50, and the other 500 units issued will be valued at $3.00. 1,000 units of closing inventory will be valued at $2.00, and 500 at $2.50.

(c)   **Weighted average pricing methods**

There are two main weighted average pricing methods: **cumulative** and **periodic**.

(i)   **Cumulative weighted average pricing**

With this method we calculate an **average cost** of all the litres in inventory whenever a new delivery is received.

(ii)   **Periodic weighted average pricing**

The periodic weighted average pricing method involves calculating a new inventory value at the end of a given period (rather than whenever new inventory is purchased, as with the cumulative weighted average pricing method). The periodic weighted average pricing method is easier to calculate than the cumulative weighted average method, and therefore requires less effort, but it must be applied retrospectively since the costs of materials used cannot be calculated until the end of the period.

(d)   **Standard cost**

Under the standard costing method, all issues are at a predetermined standard price. You will study standard costing in more detail in **Paper 7, Planning, Control and Performance Management**.

3.3.1 Example: FIFO, LIFO and weighted average pricing methods

The following transactions should be considered in order to demonstrate FIFO, LIFO and weighted average pricing methods.

TRANSACTIONS DURING MAY 20X3

	Quantity	Unit cost	Total cost	Market value per unit on date of transaction
	Units	$	$	$
Opening balance, 1 May	100	2.00	200	
Receipts, 3 May	400	2.10	840	2.11
Issues, 4 May	200			2.11
Receipts, 9 May	300	2.12	636	2.15
Issues, 11 May	400			2.20
Receipts, 18 May	100	2.40	240	2.35
Issues, 20 May	100			2.35
Closing balance, 31 May	200			2.38
			1,916	

(a) **FIFO**

FIFO assumes that materials are issued out of inventory in the order in which they were delivered into inventory: issues are priced at the cost of the earliest delivery remaining in inventory.

Using FIFO, the cost of issues and the closing inventory value in the example would be as follows.

Date of issue	Quantity issued	Value		
	Units		$	$
4 May	200	100 o/s at $2	200	
		100 at $2.10	210	
				410
11 May	400	300 at $2.10	630	
		100 at $2.12	212	
				842
20 May	100	100 at $2.12		212
Cost of issues				1,464
Closing inventory value	200	100 at $2.12	212	
		100 at $2.40	240	
				452
				1,916

* The cost of materials issued plus the value of closing inventory equals the cost of purchases plus the value of opening inventory ($1,916).

The market price of purchased materials is rising dramatically. In a period of inflation, there is a tendency with FIFO for materials to be issued at a cost lower than the current market value, although closing inventories tend to be valued at a cost approximating to current market value.

(b) **LIFO**

LIFO assumes that materials are issued out of inventory in the reverse order to which they were delivered: the most recent deliveries are issued before earlier ones, and are priced accordingly.

Using LIFO, the cost of issues and the closing inventory value in the example above would be as follows.

Date of issue	Quantity issued	Valuation		
	Units		$	$
4 May	200	200 at $2.10		420
11 May	400	300 at $2.12	636	
		100 at $2.10	210	
				846
20 May	100	100 at $2.40		240
Cost of issues				1,506
Closing inventory value	200	100 at $2.10	210	
		100 at $2.00	200	
				410
				1,916

Notes

(a)   The cost of materials issued plus the value of closing inventory equals the cost of purchases plus the value of opening inventory ($1,916).

(b)   In a period of inflation there is a tendency with LIFO for the following to occur.

   (i)   Materials are issued at a price which approximates to current market value.
   (ii)   Closing inventories become undervalued when compared to market value.

(c)   **Cumulative weighted average pricing**

The cumulative weighted average pricing method calculates a **weighted average price** for all units in inventory. Issues are priced at this average cost, and the balance of inventory remaining would have the same unit valuation. The average price is determined by dividing the total cost by the total number of units.

A new weighted average price is calculated whenever a new delivery of materials into store is received. This is the key feature of cumulative weighted average pricing.

In our example, issue costs and closing inventory values would be as follows.

Date	Received	Issued	Balance	Total inventory value	Unit cost	
	Units	Units	Units	$	$	$
Opening inventory			100	200	2.00	
3 May	400			840	2.10	
			* 500	1,040	2.08	
4 May		200		(416)	2.08	416
			300	624	2.08	
9 May	300			636	2.12	
			* 600	1,260	2.10	
11 May		400		(840)	2.10	840
			200	420	2.10	
18 May	100			240	2.40	
			* 300	660	2.20	
20 May		100		(220)	2.20	220
						1,476
Closing inventory value			200	440	2.20	440
						1,916

* A new inventory value per unit is calculated whenever a new receipt of materials occurs.

Notes

(a) The cost of materials issued plus the value of closing inventory equals the cost of purchases plus the value of opening inventory ($1,916).

(b) In a period of inflation, using the cumulative weighted average pricing system, the value of material issues will rise gradually, but will tend to lag a little behind the current market value at the date of issue. Closing inventory values will also be a little below current market value.

(d) **Periodic weighted average pricing**

Under the periodic weighted average pricing method, a retrospective average price is calculated for *all* materials issued during the period. The average issue price is calculated for our example as follows.

$$\frac{\text{Cost of all receipts in the period} + \text{Cost of opening inventory}}{\text{Number of units received in the period} + \text{Number of units of opening inventory}}$$

$$= \frac{\$1,716 + \$200}{800 + 100}$$

Issue price = $2.129 per unit

Closing inventory values are a balancing figure.

The issue costs and closing inventory values are calculated as follows.

Date of issue	Quantity issued Units	Valuation $
4 May	200 × $2.129	426
11 May	400 × $2.129	852
20 May	100 × $2.129	213
Cost of issues		1,491
Value of opening inventory plus purchases		1,916
Value of 200 units of closing inventory (at $2.129)		425

3.3.2 Which method is correct?

This is a trick question, because there is no one correct method. Each method has **advantages** and **disadvantages.**

The advantages and disadvantages of the **FIFO** method are as follows.

(a) **Advantages**

(i) It is a logical pricing method which probably represents what is physically happening: in practice the oldest inventory is likely to be used first.

(ii) It is easy to understand and explain to managers.

(iii) The closing inventory value can be near to a valuation based on the cost of replacing the inventory.

(b)   **Disadvantages**

    (i)   FIFO can be cumbersome to operate because of the need to identify each batch of material separately.

    (ii)   Managers may find it difficult to compare costs and make decisions when they are charged with varying prices for the same materials.

The advantages and disadvantages of the **LIFO** method are as follows.

(a)   **Advantages**

    (i)   Inventories are issued at a price which is close to current market value. This is not the case with FIFO when there is a high rate of inflation.

    (ii)   Managers are continually aware of recent costs when making decisions, because the costs being charged to their department or products will be current costs.

(b)   **Disadvantages**

    (i)   The method can be cumbersome to operate because it sometimes results in several batches being only part-used in the inventory records before another batch is received.

    (ii)   LIFO is often the opposite to what is physically happening and can therefore be difficult to explain to managers.

    (iii) As with FIFO, decision making can be difficult because of the variations in prices.

The advantages and disadvantages of weighted **average pricing** are as follows.

(a)   **Advantages**

    (i)   Fluctuations in prices are smoothed out, making it easier to use the data for decision making.

    (ii)   It is easier to administer than FIFO and LIFO, because there is no need to identify each batch separately.

(b)   **Disadvantages**

    (i)   The resulting issue price is rarely an actual price that has been paid, and can run to several decimal places.

    (ii)   Prices tend to lag a little behind current market values when there is gradual inflation.

4 Inventory control

FAST FORWARD

> **Inventory control** is the regulation of inventory levels, which includes putting a value to the amounts of inventory issued and remaining. Inventory control also includes ordering, purchasing, receiving and storing goods.

This section deals with the costs of inventory holding and the location of inventory.

4.1 Why hold inventory?

The costs of purchasing inventory are usually one of the largest costs faced by an organisation and, once obtained, inventory has to be carefully controlled and checked.

The main reasons for holding inventories can be summarised as follows.

(a) To ensure sufficient goods are available to meet expected demand.
(b) To provide a buffer between processes.
(c) To meet any future shortages.
(d) To take advantage of bulk purchasing discounts.
(e) To absorb seasonal fluctuations and any variations in usage and demand.
(f) To allow production processes to flow smoothly and efficiently.
(g) As a necessary part of the production process (such as when maturing cheese).
(h) As a deliberate investment policy, especially in times of inflation or possible shortages.

4.2 Holding costs

Holding costs are associated with high inventory levels. The reasons they occur are as follows.

(a) **Costs of storage and stores operations**. Larger inventories require more storage space and possibly extra staff and equipment to control and handle them.

(b) **Interest charges**. Holding inventories involves the tying up of capital (cash) on which interest must be paid.

(c) **Insurance costs**. The larger the value of inventories held, the greater insurance premiums are likely to be.

(d) **Risk of obsolescence**. When materials or components become out-of-date and are no longer required, existing inventories must be thrown away and their cost must be written off to the income statement.

(e) **Deterioration**. When materials in store deteriorate to the extent that they are unusable, they must be thrown away (with the likelihood that disposal costs would be incurred) and again, the value written off inventory plus the disposal costs will be a charge to the income statement.

(f) **Theft**.

4.3 Costs of obtaining inventory

Ordering costs are associated with low inventory levels, because if low inventories are maintained it will be necessary to place more frequent orders. The following costs are included in ordering costs.

(a) **Clerical and administrative costs** associated with purchasing, accounting for and receiving goods.

(b) **Transport costs**.

(c) **Production run costs**, if an organisation manufactures its own components.

4.4 Stockout costs

An additional type of cost which may arise if inventories are kept too low is the type associated with running out of inventory. There are a number of causes of **stockout costs**.

- Lost contribution from lost sales
- Loss of future sales due to disgruntled customers
- Loss of customer goodwill
- Cost of production stoppages
- Labour frustration over stoppages
- Extra costs of urgent, small quantity, replenishment orders

4.5 Locating inventory

You can probably picture a warehouse - a large room with rows and rows of high shelving, perhaps moveable ladders and maybe barrows or fork-lift trucks. Very modern 'highbay' warehouses have automatic guided vehicles (AGVs), stacker cranes and conveyors, all controlled by computer. All of this implies organisation: when they are brought into the warehouse inventories are not simply dumped in the nearest available space. There is a place for everything and everything is in its place. There is no point in keeping inventory at all if you don't know where to find it when it is needed.

Suppose, for example, that a warehouse were arranged as shown below, A to F representing rows of shelving and 1 to 7 the access bays between them. Suppose the shelves were 4m high, 10m long and 1m wide and you needed to locate five 10 mm washers in stainless steel. (To put it another way, suppose you had a haystack and you were looking for a needle!) How would you go about organising the warehouse so that you could always find what you were looking for?

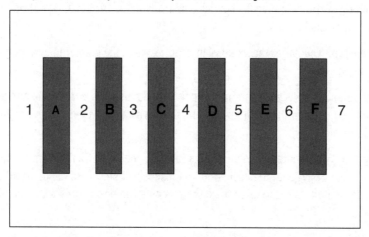

The solution is fairly obvious. You need to divide up the shelf-racks and give each section a code. A typical warehouse might organise its shelving as shown below.

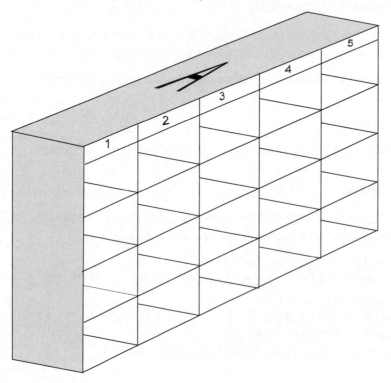

If you are reminded of a library, this is intentional: it is helpful to think of a warehouse as a library of materials.

You also need to keep a record which shows the whereabouts in the warehouse of all the different types of inventory, including the 10mm washers in stainless steel. Suppose that the washers are listed as being kept in location A234.

The reference A234 would take you to Row A, bay 2, bin 3, shelf 4. Shelf 4 might contain a series of drawers containing washers of various sizes, each drawer being labelled with a precise part number (A234/1279, say) and a description of the item. (Coding is discussed in more detail later on in this chapter.)

The term **bin** as it is used above may be new to you, but you need to get used to it meaning something other than the receptacle by your desk full of screwed up paper and apple cores! **Bin** simply means a receptacle. In warehouse terms it normally means a division of shelving (or simply one shelf) or some other container which can be located by a code letter or number. The term is in general usage but it does not have a precise meaning.

In the light of this you should understand what a **bin card** is. **In a manual inventory control system the bin card is kept with the actual inventory and is updated whenever items are removed or added** to provide an accurate record of the quantity in inventory for each stores item.

BIN CARD

Description .... Bin No: ....

Reorder Quantity .... Code No: ....
Maximum: ....
Minimum: ....
Re-order Level: ....

Receipts			Issues			Balance	Remarks
Date	G.R.N. No.	Quantity	Date	Req. No.	Quantity	Quantity	

Note that the bin card does not need to show any information about the cost of materials.

Organisations will also maintain what are known as **stores ledger accounts**, an example of an account being shown below.

STORES LEDGER ACCOUNT

Material: ....   Maximum Quantity: ....

Code: ....   Minimum Quantity: ....

Date	Receipts				Issues				Stock		
	G.R.N. No.	Quantity	Unit Price $	Amount $	Materials Req. No.	Quantity	Unit Price $	Amount $	Quantity	Unit Price $	Amount $

Details from GRNs and materials requisition notes (see later) are used to update stores ledger accounts, which then provide a record of the quantity and value of each line of inventory in the stores. The stores ledger accounts are normally kept in the cost department or in the stores office whereas the bin cards are written up and actually kept in the stores. There are two advantages to this procedure.

(a) The accounting records can be maintained more accurately and in a better condition by a cost clerk or an experienced stores clerk than by a stores assistant.

(b) A control check is provided. The balances on the bin cards in the stores can be compared with the balances on the stores ledger accounts.

The use of bin cards and stores ledger accounts ensures that every issue and receipt of inventory is recorded as it occurs so that there is a continuous clerical record of the balance of each item of inventory. This is known as a **perpetual inventory system.**

You may be thinking that the system we have described is rather over-complicated. Why not, for example, start at one end of the room and end at the other numbering each separate location in sequence and numbering each inventory item accordingly? The reasons are for practicality and flexibility. If item 1 is a 10mm washer and item 2 is an exhaust pipe they are hardly going to fit into the same size drawer. If item 1 is a 10mm washer and item 2 is a 15mm washer, what happens when a new product needs 12mm washers? If item 1 is used twice a year and item 10,001 is used every day the storekeeper will be collapsing with exhaustion by the end of the day if item 1 is the one nearest the issue point. If item 1 is a large heavy item and item 10,001 is also a large heavy item the storeman will be driving the fork-lift from one end of the warehouse to the other all day. It is therefore far better to have large heavy items in close proximity and to have frequently used items near to the issue point.

The last point is worth developing a little. Storekeeping involves a good deal of commonsense and a considerable knowledge of the types of inventory held, and an effective storekeeping system should take the following points into account.

(a) Heavy items should not be stored on high shelves (in case the shelves collapse and to make handling as safe and unstrenuous as possible).

(b) Dangerous items (for example items with sharp edges) should not be stored above eye level.

(c) Items liable to be damaged by flood (for example paper inventory) should not be stored on low shelves.

(d)   Special arrangements should be made for the storage and handling of chemicals and flammable materials.

(e)   Some inventories are sensitive to temperature or light and should be stored accordingly.

(f)   Other inventories may have special hygiene or 'clean air' requirements.

4.6 Coding of materials

Each item held in stores must be unambiguously identified and this can best be done by numbering them with inventory codes. The advantages of this are as follows.

(a)   **Ambiguity is avoided**. Different people may use different descriptions for materials. This is avoided if numbers are used.

(b)   **Time is saved**. Descriptions can be lengthy and time-consuming, particularly when completing written forms.

(c)   **Production efficiency is improved**. If the correct material can be accurately identified from a code number, production hold-ups caused by the issue of incorrect material can be avoided.

(d)   **Computerised processing** is made easier.

(e)   Numbered code systems can be designed to be **flexible**, and can be **expanded** to include more inventory items as necessary.

The digits in a code can stand for the type of inventory, supplier, location and so forth. For example inventory item A234/1279 might refer to the item of inventory kept in row A, bay 2, bin 3, shelf 4. The item might be identified by the digits 12 and its supplier might be identified by the digits 79.

4.7 Issuing materials

The sole point of holding inventories is so that they can be used to make products. This means that they have to be issued from stores to production. This transaction will be initiated by production who will complete a **materials requisition note** and pass it to the warehouse.

MATERIALS REQUISITION						
Material Required for: (Job or Overhead Account) Department:				No. Date:		
Quantity	Description	Code No.	Weight	Rate	$	Notes
Foreman:						

The stores department will locate the inventory, withdraw the amount required and update the bin card as appropriate. The stores ledger account will also be updated.

If the amount of materials required is overestimated the excess should be put back into store accompanied by a **materials returned note**. The form in our illustration is almost identical to a requisition note. In practice it would be wise to colour code the two documents (one white, one yellow, say) to prevent confusion.

MATERIALS RETURNED NOTE						
Material not needed for: (Job or Overhead Account) Department:					No. Date:	
Quantity	Description	Code No.	Weight	Rate	$	Notes
Foreman:						

There may be occasions when materials already issued but not required for one job can be used for another job in progress. In this case there is no point in returning the materials to the warehouse. Instead a **materials transfer note** can be raised. This prevents one job being charged with too many materials and another with too little.

You will note that all of the forms shown above have spaces for cost information (that is, monetary values). This will be inserted either by the stores department or in costing, depending upon how the system is organised. We have already described the various bases which may be used to put a value on inventory - FIFO, LIFO or an average figure.

4.8 Stocktaking

Stocktaking involves counting the physical inventory on hand at a certain date and then checking this against the balance shown in the clerical records. There are two methods of carrying out this process.

Key term

- **Periodic stocktaking**. This is usually carried out annually and the objective is to count all items of inventory on a specific date.

- **Continuous stocktaking**. This involves counting and checking a number of inventory items on a regular basis so that each item is checked at least once a year, and valuable items can be checked more frequently. This has a number of advantages over periodic stocktaking. It is less disruptive, less prone to error, and achieves greater control.

4.9 Inventory discrepancies

There will be occasions when inventory checks disclose **discrepancies between the physical amount of an item in inventory and the amount shown in the inventory records**. When this occurs, the cause of the discrepancy should be investigated, and appropriate action taken to ensure that it does not happen again. Possible causes of discrepancies are as follows.

(a)   Suppliers deliver a different quantity of goods than is shown on the goods received note. Since this note is used to update inventory records, a discrepancy will arise. This can be avoided by ensuring that all inventory is counted as it is received, and a responsible person should sign the document to verify the quantity.

(b)   The quantity of inventory issued to production is different from that shown on the materials requisition note. Careful counting of all issues will prevent this.

(c)   Excess inventory is returned from production without documentation. This can be avoided by ensuring that all movements of inventory are accurately documented - in this case, a materials returned note should be raised.

(d)   Clerical errors may occur in the inventory records. Regular checks by independent staff should detect and correct mistakes.

(e)   Inventory items may be wasted because, for example, they get broken. All wastage should be noted on the inventory records immediately so that physical inventory equals the inventory balance on records. (The cost of the wastage is then written off to the profit and loss account.)

(f)   Employees may steal inventory. Regular checks or continuous stocktaking will help to prevent this, and only authorised personnel should be allowed into the stores.

If the inventory discrepancy is found to be caused by clerical error, then the records should be rectified immediately. If the discrepancy occurs because units of inventory appear to be missing, the lost inventory must be written off. If actual inventory is greater than recorded inventory, extra units of inventory are added to the inventory records. The accounting transaction will be recorded by a stores credit note, where items of inventory have been lost, or a **stores debit note**, when there is more actual inventory than recorded.

A stores **credit note** may have the following format.

STORES CREDIT NOTE			
Quantity	Item code	Description	$

Continuous stocktaking report number...
Credit note authorised by..
Date...

5 Reordering inventory

FAST FORWARD

Inventory control levels can be calculated in order to maintain inventories at the optimum level. The four critical control levels are **reorder level, reorder quantity, minimum inventory control level and maximum inventory control level.**

As noted earlier, the ideal is for businesses not to have any inventories on the premises unless they are about to be used in production which can be sold immediately. In practice many businesses would regard this approach as too risky or impractical because they are unable to predict either their own levels of demand or the reliability of their suppliers or both. They therefore set various **control levels**, the purpose of which is to ensure the following.

(a)   The business **does not run out of inventory** and **suffer disruption to production** as a result.

(b)   The business **does not carry an excessive amount of inventories** which take up space, incur storage costs and possibly deteriorate with age.

The problems of when to reorder inventory and how much to reorder are the most significant practical problems in inventory management. To illustrate the problems in detail and the way in which they may be solved, we shall consider an example.

5.1 Example: Inventory control levels

(a)   A new manufacturing business is being set up to make a single product. The product is to be made by moulding plastic. Owen, the manager, expects to make 10 units per day and has found that each unit will require 5kg of plastic. He decides to obtain enough materials to last a week (5 days). How much should he order?

(b)   This is not difficult. Owen should order 5 days × 10 units × 5kg = 250kg.

The materials are placed in the stores ready for the commencement of production on the following Monday.

(c)   The following week everything goes as planned, causing great celebration over the weekend. The following Monday however, Owen realises that he has no materials left. (You will remember that this is called a **stockout**). He rings up a number of suppliers but to his dismay none can deliver in less than 2 days. There is therefore no production for the whole of Monday and Tuesday.

(d)   Owen doesn't want this to happen again so he orders four weeks worth of materials, even though this means increasing his overdraft at the bank by $4,000. The materials duly arrive on Wednesday morning but of the 1,000kg delivered (20 × 10 × 5 = 1,000) Owen finds he only has room to store 500kg. To accommodate the remainder he has to rent space in the factory next door at a cost of $20.

(e)   Twenty days go by and production goes as planned. Owen doesn't want to get caught out again, so two days before he is due to run out of materials he places a fresh order, this time for only 500kg.

(f)   Unfortunately, this time the suppliers are unable to deliver in 2 days as promised, but take 4 days. Another 2 days production is lost.

(g)   As Owen's product establishes itself in the market, demand starts to increase. He starts to produce 15 units a day but again he is caught out because, obviously, this means that the materials are used up more quickly. He often runs out before the next delivery has arrived.

(h)   So it goes on for the whole of Owen's first year in business. By the end of this time he works out that he has lost nearly three weeks production due to materials shortages. In despair he contacts a management consultant for advice.

Solution

(a)   Owen is told to calculate a number of figures from his records.

    (i)   The **maximum daily usage**

    (ii)   The **maximum lead time** (**Lead time** is the time it takes between ordering inventories and having them delivered)

(iii)   The **average daily usage**

(iv)   The **average lead time**

(v)   The **minimum daily usage** and **minimum lead time**

(vi)   The cost of holding one unit of inventory for one year (**holding cost**)

(vii)   The **cost of ordering** a consignment of inventory

(viii)   The **annual demand** for materials

(b)   Owen has kept careful records and some of these figures cause him little bother.

Maximum usage	100kg per day
Average usage	75kg per day
Minimum usage	50kg per day
Annual demand	19,500kg ($52 \times 5 \times 75$kg)
Maximum lead time	4 days
Average lead time	3 days
Minimum lead time	2 days

(c)   The calculation of the **holding cost** is quite complicated. Owen has to work out a number of figures.

     (i)   Materials can only be bought in 5kg boxes and therefore 'one unit' of inventory is 5kg, not 1kg.

     (ii)   The total cost of having one box in inventory is made up of a number of separate costs.

          (1)   Interest paid on the money borrowed to buy one box

          (2)   Rental of the floor space taken up by one box

          (3)   The warehouse keeper's wages

          (4)   Administrative costs of taking deliveries, issuing materials, and keeping track of them

          (5)   The cost of insuring the inventory

     Eventually Owen works out that the figure is $0.62 per 'unit' of 5kg. He is shocked by this and wonders whether he should order smaller quantities more frequently. (Fortunately for Owen, there is little risk of obsolescence or deterioration of boxes. Many organisations have to include the cost of obsolescence or deterioration in holding costs, however.)

(d)   **Ordering costs** are also quite difficult to calculate. Owen has to take into account:

     (i)   The cost of stationery and postage
     (ii)   The cost of phoning round to suppliers
     (iii)   The time taken up by doing this

     He is surprised to find that the figure works out to $19.87 per order and now wonders whether he should make fewer larger orders to keep these costs down.

(e)   Now that Owen has these figures the consultant tells him how to calculate four inventory control levels that will help him to avoid running out of inventory and to keep down the costs of holding and ordering inventory.

     (i)   **Reorder level**. Owen already realises that inventories have to be reordered before they run out completely. This number tells him how low inventories can be allowed to fall before an order should be placed. It assumes that maximum usage and maximum lead time, the two worst events from the point of view of inventory control, coincide.

Key term

> **Reorder level** = maximum usage × maximum lead time

Reorder level = 100kg × 4 days = 400kg

Using the maximum usage and lead time figures allows for some safety inventory. However the formula for the reorder level needs to be amended slightly if the organisation in question holds a level of safety inventory. This is because some organisations aim to keep a reserve of inventory in order to cope with fluctuations in demand and with unreliable suppliers.

The adjusted reorder level formula is as follows.

Reorder level (with safety inventory) = safety inventory + (average usage × average lead time)

(ii)   **Reorder quantity**

Key term

> The **reorder quantity** is the quantity of inventory which is to be re-ordered when inventory reaches the reorder level.

Owen has never known what the best amount to order would be. He is beginning to understand that there must be some way of juggling the costs of holding inventory, the costs of ordering inventory and the amount of inventory needed but he does not know how to work it out. His consultant fortunately does and she gives him the following formula.

Formula to learn

> $$Q = \sqrt{\frac{2cd}{h}}$$ **Economic order quantity**, or **EOQ**
>
> where   h   is the cost of holding one unit of inventory for one year
>   c   is the cost of ordering a consignment
>   d   is the annual demand
>   Q   is the 'economic order quantity' (EOQ), that is, the best amount to order

Remembering that a 'unit' of inventory is 5kg and therefore annual demand is 19,500kg/5kg = 3,900 units, we can calculate the reorder quantity as follows.

$$Q = \sqrt{\frac{2 \times 19.87 \times 3,900}{0.62}}$$

= 500 units (approximately) = 2,500kg

(f)   Owen is not entirely convinced by the EOQ calculation but promises to try it out since it seems like a reasonable amount to order. He then asks what the other two control levels are, since he seems to have all the information he needs already. The consultant points out that the calculations done so far don't allow for other uncertain factors like a severe shortage of supply or unexpected rises or falls in demand. As a precaution Owen needs a **minimum inventory control level** below which inventories ideally should never fall, and a **maximum inventory control level** above which inventory should not be able to rise. There is a risk of stockouts if inventory falls below the minimum level and a risk of inventory being at a wasteful level if above the maximum level.

Key term

> **Minimum inventory control level** = reorder level − (average usage × average lead time)

Minimum **inventory** control level = 400kg − (75kg × 3 days) = 175kg

Key term

> **Maximum inventory control level** = reorder level + reorder quantity − (minimum usage × minimum lead time)

Maximum inventory control level = 400kg + 2,500kg − (50kg × 2 days) = 2,800kg

Note that the minimum and maximum inventory control levels are **extreme control levels**. Inventory may fall below the minimum control level and if it does so, then it will alert staff to check whether the system is still in control or whether there is a longer term change in the situation concerned. Such control levels are adjustable, especially in an organisation where **stockouts** are acceptable (ie where the minimum inventory control level = 0).

The story has a happy ending. Owen finds that the EOQ works very well in practice. His costs are reduced and he suffers no stockouts in the following year. The derivation of the EOQ formula is quite complicated and we suggest that you, too, simply accept it.

Question   Inventory control

Edgington Co uses 4,000 kg of a raw material in a year. It costs $10 to hold 1 kg for one year, and the costs of ordering each consignment of raw materials are $200.

Edgington Co uses between 100 kg and 600 kg a month, and the company's suppliers can take between 1 and 3 months to deliver materials that have been ordered.

Calculate the following.

(a)   The reorder quantity
(b)   The reorder level
(c)   The maximum level of inventory the company should hold

Answer

(a)   **Reorder quantity** = $\sqrt{\dfrac{2cd}{h}}$

   = $\sqrt{\dfrac{2 \times \text{ordering costs} \times \text{annual demand}}{\text{Inventory holding costs}}}$

   = $\sqrt{\dfrac{2 \times 200 \times 4,000}{10}}$

   =   400 kg

(b)   **Reorder level** = maximum usage × maximum lead time

   =   600 × 3
   =   1,800 kg

(c)   **Maximum inventory control level** = reorder level + reorder quantity − (minimum usage × minimum lead time)

   =   400 + 1,800 − (100 × 1)
   =   2,100 kg

xam focus
int

Make sure you show clear workings in calculations. This will help you to achieve 'own figures' marks for incorrect answers.

6 Computers and inventory control

Although the basic principles of inventory control are not difficult in themselves, you will appreciate by now that an effective system requires a good deal of administrative effort, even if only a few items of inventory are involved. There is therefore a good deal to be gained from computerisation of this function.

6.1 Computerised inventory files

A typical computerised **inventory** file would contain a record for each item, each record having fields (individual pieces of data) as follows.

(a) **Inventory code:** a unique inventory code to identify each item. This could be in bar code form for large organisations.

(b) **Description:** a brief description is helpful when perusing inventory records and probably essential when printing out lists of inventory for stocktaking purposes. Ideally the system will generate purchase orders which also require brief narrative details.

(c) **Supplier code:** this would match the code for the supplier in the purchase ledger.

(d) **Supplier's reference number:** again this information would be needed for purchase orders.

(e) **Quantity per unit:** this would specify how many individual items there were per 'unit'. This is sometimes called the 'factor'.

(f) **Cost price per item.**

(g) **Control levels:** there would be a field for each of the four control levels (minimum and maximum inventory, reorder level and reorder quantity).

(h) **Location:** a location code could be included if it were not part of the inventory code itself.

(i) **Movements history:** there could be fields for issues per day, per week, during the last month, in the last year and so on.

(j) **Job code:** there might be a field allowing costs to be linked to specific jobs. Inventories could be 'reserved' for jobs due to be started in the next week, say.

6.2 Inventory reports

A system with fields such as those above might be able to generate the following reports.

(a) **Daily listing:** a daily list of all items ordered, received, issued or placed on reserve. This might have 'exception reports' for unusual movements of inventory and for items that had reached the reorder level.

(b) **Inventory lists:** lists could be produced for stocktaking purposes, with inventory codes, descriptions and locations. This could be restricted to certain types of inventory, such as high value items or inventories with high turnover.

(c) **Inventory movements:** a report of inventory movements over time would help in setting control levels and in identifying 'slow-moving inventory' that is not really required.

(d) **Inventory valuations:** this would show current balances and place a value on inventories according to which calculation method (FIFO, LIFO, and so on) was in use.

(e) **Supplier analysis:** this would list all the items of inventory purchased from the same supplier, and might be useful for placing orders (several items could be ordered at the same time, cutting delivery costs).

6.3 Bill of materials

Many computerised inventory control systems have a **bill of materials facility**. This allows assembly records (sometimes called explosion records) to be compiled, containing details of the various assemblies that make up the final product. A tape deck, for example may have three main assemblies - the motor mechanism, the electronics and the outer casing.

Each individual assembly could be further broken down into its constituent materials and components.

6.4 A common fallacy

It is sometimes assumed that computerising inventory records will guarantee they are 100% accurate. In fact the discrepancies listed in Section 4.9 are just as likely to occur in a computerised as a non-computerised system. Stocktaking is thus equally important in a computerised inventory system as it is in a manual system.

Chapter Roundup

- Materials can be **classified** according to the substances that make them up, how they are measured, or their physical properties.

- Procedures and documentation are required for material purchases.

- Materials issued from inventory can be valued using FIFO, LIFO and weighted average methods.

- **Inventory control** is the regulation of inventory levels, which includes putting a value to the amounts of inventory issued and remaining. Inventory control also includes ordering, purchasing, receiving and storing goods.

- **Inventory control levels** can be calculated in order to maintain inventories at the optimum level. The four critical control levels are **reorder level, reorder quantity, minimum inventory control level** and **maximum inventory control level.**

Quick Quiz

1   What are the three main ways of classifying materials?

2   What are raw materials?

3   What is work in progress?

4   Generally, are items which are ready for sale or despatch known as work in progress?

5   List the five documents which you are likely to use when buying materials.

6   The goods received note is matched with two other documents in the buying process. What are they?

7   How would you calculate the cost of a unit of material using cumulative weighted average pricing?

8   What are the advantages of FIFO?

9   What is a bin in warehouse terms?

10   Which documents are used to update the stores ledger account?

11   What is the main point of holding inventories?

12   What does stocktaking involve?

13   What are the two methods of stocktaking that are commonly used?

14   What are the main reasons for a company setting control levels with regard to inventory?

15   What is the formula for the economic order quantity?

16   How would you calculate the minimum and maximum inventory control levels?

Answers to Quick Quiz

1   According to the substances that make them up, how they are measured and their physical properties.

2   Goods purchased for incorporation into products for sale.

3   A term used to represent an intermediate stage between the purchase of raw materials and the completion of the finished product.

4   No. Finished goods.

5
- Purchase requisition form
- Order form
- Despatch note
- Delivery note
- Goods received note (GRN)

6   The purchase order and the supplier's invoice.

7    $\dfrac{\text{Total cost of units in inventory}}{\text{Number of units in inventory}}$

8
- It is a logical pricing method
- It is easy to understand
- The closing inventory can be near to a valuation based on the cost of replacing the inventory

9   A division of shelving or some other container which can be located by a code letter or number.

10   Goods received notes and materials requisition notes.

11   In order for them to be used to make products.

12   Counting physical inventory on hand at a certain date, and checking this against the accounting records.

13   Periodic stocktaking and continuous stocktaking.

14   To ensure it doesn't run out of inventory, and to ensure that it does not carry too much inventory.

15    $Q = \sqrt{\dfrac{2cd}{h}}$

16   Minimum inventory control level = reorder level − (average usage × average lead time)

Maximum inventory control level = reorder level + reorder quantity − (minimum usage × minimum lead time)

Now try the questions below from the Exam Question Bank

Number	Level	Marks	Time
Q5	Examination	N/A	20 mins

Labour

Chapter topic list

Study guide reference

			Syllabus reference
2	(b)	Describe the process of accounting for input costs and relating them to work done	1(c)
2	(c)	Identify the documentation required, and the flow of documentation, for different cost accounting transactions	1(c)
2	(d)	Explain the use of codes in categorising and processing transactions, and the importance of correct coding	1(c)(iii)
6	(a)	Explain, illustrate and evaluate labour remuneration methods	3(b)(ii)
6	(b)	Describe the operation of a payroll accounting system	3(b)(ii)
6	(d)	Describe the procedures and documentation required to ensure the correct coding, analysis and recording of direct and indirect labour	3(b)(i),(ii)
6	(e)	Describe and illustrate the accounting for labour costs	3(b)(ii)
6	(f)	Discuss the relationship between the labour costing system and the payroll accounting system	3(b)(iii)
6	(g)	Explain the causes and costs of, and calculate, labour turnover	3(b)
6	(h)	Describe and illustrate measures of labour efficiency and utilisation	3(b)

1 Labour costs

FAST FORWARD

Labour costs can be determined according to some prior agreement, the amount of time worked or the quality of work done.

1.1 What are labour costs?

Labour costs could be said to include any or all of the following items.

- The gross amount due to an employee
- Employer's national insurance
- Amounts paid to recruit labour
- Amounts paid for staff welfare
- Training costs
- The costs of benefits like company cars

The list could be extended, but we shall not go any further because in this chapter we are only concerned with the first item, the employee's gross salary.

The word **labour** is generally associated with strenuous physical effort but in the context of cost accounting it is not confined to manual work. **Labour costs** are the amounts paid to any employee, including supervisors, office staff, managers and tea ladies. We shall distinguish between **direct labour** and **indirect labour**, but even then you must not assume that this is necessarily a manual/clerical distinction (hopefully you are beginning to realise that direct costs and indirect costs differ in that they are accounted for differently). We are not making a political or social statement but simply a statement of fact. For example, most or all of the 'direct labour cost' of an audit is the result of its being done by highly paid and highly qualified pen-pushers (accountants)!

1.2 Determining labour costs

There are three ways in which labour costs can be determined.

    (a)   According to some prior agreement.

    (b)   According to the amount of time worked.

    (c)   According to the amount and/or quality of work done (piecework or performance based remuneration).

Payment for most jobs is by a combination of methods (a) and (b). There will be a **basic wage** or **salary** which is agreed when the appointment is made. There will be a set number of hours per week during which the employee is expected to be available for work. There will be extra payments for time worked over and above the set hours, or deductions for time when the employee is not available beyond an agreed limit.

2 The payroll accounting system

ST FORWARD

Labour attendance time is recorded on an attendance record or a clockcard. **Jobtime** may be recorded on daily time sheets, weekly time sheets, jobcards or route cards depending on the circumstances.

You can see from the previous section that records of labour costs fall into three categories.

- Records of agreed basic wages and salaries
- Records of time spent working
- Records of work done

There are a number of ways in which this can be organised, but basically the information flow will be as follows.

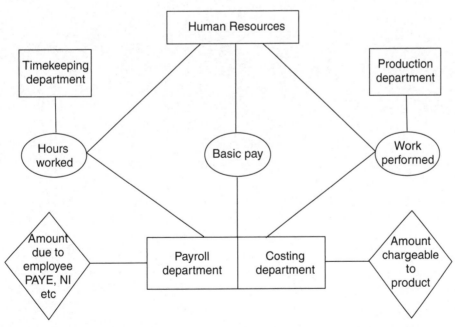

In practice, timekeeping would probably be a sub-function of production or of Human Resources. Alternatively, Human Resources may keep records of hours spent on the premises and available for work, while the production department keeps records of time spent doing different tasks. The system used will depend upon the nature of the job and the bases chosen for paying employees on the one hand and for costing products on the other.

Information flows back to the Human Resources department so that employees can be considered for promotion or disciplined if appropriate.

All the information may, in practice, be given first to payroll, who would then pass it on for costing analysis, or vice versa. (Remember that in some organisations payroll administration is contracted out to a third party.) The main point is that both payroll and costing need the same information, but they analyse it differently: payroll asks **who**, and costing asks **what**.

2.1 Basic pay

Levels of basic pay are ultimately decided by senior management who will take into account what other employers are paying for similar work, what they consider the work to be worth, how easy it is to recruit labour and any agreements with trade unions.

The basic pay due to an individual worker will be mentioned in his or her **letter of appointment** and included in his or her **contract of employment**. The main on-going record, however, will probably be kept on an **employee record card** held in the personnel department. This will also show subsequent increases in the wage rate or salary level and much other information. An example of an employee record card is shown on the following page.

Much of the information on the employee record card is confidential and there is no need for staff in the payroll department or the costing department to know about it.

PERSONNEL RECORD CARD

NUMBER

NAME OTHER, A.N.

PERSONAL DETAILS

| SURNAME | OTHER |
| FORENAMES | ALBERT NEIL |

	SEX	Nationality	British
	(M) F	Social Security Number	WD 48 47 41C

Date of Birth	1 June 20X9
Marital Status	Single (Married) Separated Divorced Widowed
Dependants	None
Disabilities	None
Eligible	Pension Scheme 20X9 January
Joined	20X9 January

ADDRESS
94 Bootsale House
Antique Street
Old Salum
MERSEY ME5

Telephone 01973 89521

ADDRESS 1ST CHANGE
17 Newton Close
Brookeside
MERSEY ME1

Telephone 01973 12221

ADDRESS 2ND CHANGE

Telephone

Professional Qualifications
Certified Accountant 20X9

Educational Details

Higher Education

A levels	Economics (C)
BTec	Computer Services
GCSE	n/a
O levels	3
CSEs	4
Other	City & Guilds Photography

IN EMERGENCY CONTACT

Name Other, Noreen Olga   Wife

Address
17 Newton Close
Brookeside
MERSEY ME1

Telephone (h) 01973 12221
Telephone (wk) 01973 51443

EMPLOYMENT HISTORY

Years of Service (12 months to 31 December)
1 2 3 4 5 6 7 8 9 10 11 12 13 14 15 16 17 18 19 20 21 22

FROM	TO	TITLE	DEPT	REASON	PAY
1/1/X8	31/3/X8	Junior Clerk	Sls Ledger	1st job here	£6,500
1/4/X8	30/6/X8			Probation period over	£7,000
1/7/X8				Annual payrise 5%	£7,350
1/X9		Senior Clerk	Pur Ledger	Got ACCA Quals & promoted	£9,000
7/X9				10% pay rise	£9,900
7/Y0				10% (8% + 2% merit)	£10,890
12/Y0		Asst Technician	Pcyroll	Transfer	£10,890

Training History

Course Code			
0713/I		Induction to new employees	

Special Details

Leave Entitlement   20 days

Ideally, therefore, details of basic pay for all employees are compiled on separate lists which are given to payroll and costing. A fresh list should be issued whenever the pay rates are revised.

In a **computerised wage system**, the basic rates are usually part of a **database**, and payroll and costing are only able to access information that is relevant to their tasks. Costing, for example, does not need to know the names of individual employees: in fact it is more efficient for workers to be coded according to the department they work in and the type of work that they do.

2.2 Time records and performance records

2.2.1 Attendance time

The bare minimum record of employees' time is a **simple attendance record** showing days absent because of holiday, sickness or other reason. Such a system is usually used when it is assumed that all of the employees' time is taken up doing one job and no further analysis is required. A typical record of attendance is shown on the following page.

The next step up is to have some **record of time of arrival, time of breaks and time of departure**. The simplest form is a **'signing-in' book** at the entrance to the building with, say, a page for each employee. Unless someone is watching constantly, however, this system is open to abuse and many employers use a **time recording clock** which stamps the time on a **clock card** inserted by the employee. More modern systems involve the use of a plastic card like a credit card which is 'swiped' through a device which makes a computer record of the time of arrival and departure.

The next step is to analyse the hours spent at work according to what was done during those hours. The method adopted depends upon the size of the organisation and the nature of the work.

2.2.2 Detailed analysis of time: continuous production

Where routine, repetitive work is carried out it might not be practical to record the precise details. For example if a worker stands at a conveyor belt for seven hours his work can be measured by keeping a note of the number of units that pass through his part of the process during that time. If a group of employees all contribute to the same process, the total units processed per day (or week or whatever) can be divided by the number of employees.

RECORD OF ATTENDANCE

NAME: A.N. OTHER DEPT: 072 NI REF: WD 4847 41C LEAVE ENTITLEMENT: 20

	1	2	3	4	5	6	7	8	9	10	11	12	13	14	15	16	17	18	19	20	21	22	23	24	25	26	27	28	29	30	31
JAN																															
FEB																															
MAR																															
APR																															
MAY																															
JUNE																															
JULY																															
AUG																															
SEPT																															
OCT																															
NOV																															
DEC																															

Illness : I Leave : L Training : T
Industrial Accident : IA Unpaid Leave : UL Jury Service : J
Maternity : M Special Leave : SL

Note overleaf: (1) The reasons for special leave (eg bereavement).
(2) Ensure training is noted on personnel card.

No				Ending	
Name					

	HOURS	RATE	AMOUNT	DEDUCTIONS	
Basic				Income Tax	
O/T				NI	
Others				Other	
				Total deduction	
Total					
Less deductions					
Net due					

	Time	Day	Basic time	Overtime
	1230	T		
	0803	T		
	1700	M		
	1305	M		
	1234	M		
	0750	M		

Signature _____

2.2.3 Detailed analysis of time: job costing

When the work is not of a repetitive nature the records required might be one or more of the following.

(a) **Daily time sheets**. These are filled in by the employee to indicate the **time spent on each job**. The total time on the time sheet should correspond with the time shown on the attendance record. Times are recorded daily and so there is less risk that they will be forgotten. This system does produce considerable paperwork.

(b) **Weekly time sheets**. These are similar to daily time sheets but are passed to the cost office at the end of the week. Paperwork is reduced and weekly time sheets are particularly suitable where there are few job changes in a week.

(c) **Job cards**. Cards are prepared for each job (or operation forming part of a complete job) unlike time sheets which are made out for each employee. When an employee works on a job he or she records on the job card the time spent on that job. Job cards also carry instructions to the operator on how the job is to be carried out. Such records reduce the amount of writing to be done by the employee and therefore the possibility of error.

(d) **Route cards**. These are similar to job cards, except that they follow the product through the works and carry details of all operations to be carried out. They thus carry the cost of all operations involved in a job and are very useful for control purposes.

It is important to note the following.

- Wages are calculated on the basis of the hours noted on the attendance card
- Production costs are obtained from the time sheets/job cards/route cards

The manual recording of times on time sheets or job cards is, however, liable to error or even deliberate deception, and may be unreliable. A **time clock** or **automated time recording system** is more accurate.

Time sheets and job or route cards can take many different forms, some of which involve computerised systems of time recording. The following examples may help to indicate the basic principles of recording labour costs of production work.

		Time Sheet No.						
	Employee name...........................			Clock Code...........................			Dept............	
	Date...			Week No.				
Job No.	Start time	Finish time	Quantity	Checker	Hours	Rate	Extension	

JOB CARD			
Department _ _ _ _ _ _ _ _ _ _ _ _ _ _ _ _ _ _	Job no _		
Date _	Operation no _		
Time allowance _ _ _ _ _ _ _ _ _ _ _ _ _ _ _ _	Time started _		
	Time finished _ _ _ _ _ _ _ _ _ _ _ _ _ _ _ _ _ _ _		
	Hours on job _ _ _ _ _ _ _ _ _ _ _ _ _ _ _ _ _ _		
Description of job	Hours	Rate	Cost
Employee no _ _ _ _ _ _ _ _ _ _ _ _ _ _ _ _ _ _	Certified by _		
Signature _			

The **time sheet** will be filled in by the employee, for **hours worked** on each job (job code) or **area of work** (cost code). The cost of the hours worked will be entered at a later stage in the accounting department.

A **job card** will be given to the employee, showing the work to be done and the expected time it should take. The employee will record the time started and time finished for each job. Breaks for tea and lunch may be noted on the card, as standard times. The hours actually taken and the cost of those hours will be calculated by the accounting department.

2.2.4 Salaried labour

You might think there is little point in salaried staff filling in a detailed timesheet about what they do every hour of the day, as their basic pay is a flat rate every month but, in fact, in many enterprises they are required to do so. There are a number of reasons for this.

(a)   Such timesheets aid the creation of **management information** about product costs, and hence **profitability**.

(b)   The timesheet information may have a direct impact on the **revenue the enterprise receives** (see below).

(c)   Timesheets are used to record hours spent and so **support claims for overtime payments** by salaried staff.

Below is shown the type of time sheet which can be found in large firms in the service sector of the economy. Examples of such firms are solicitors, accountants, and management consultants.

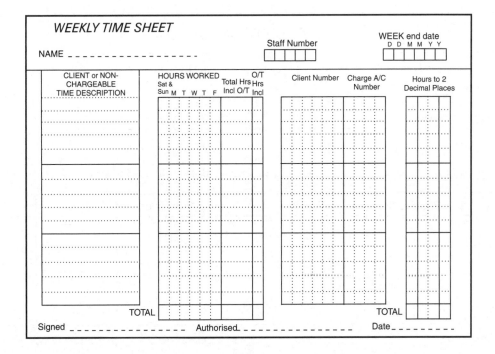

Service firms are chiefly in the business of selling the time and expertise of their employees to clients. This means that if an employee spends an hour working for a particular client, the client will be billed for one hour of the employee's time. A time sheet is necessary so that clients will be charged for the correct amount of time that has been spent doing their work.

2.2.5 Idle time

In many jobs there are times when, through no fault of their own, employees cannot get on with their work. A machine may break down or there may simply be a temporary shortage of work.

Idle time has a cost because employees will still be paid their basic wage or salary for these unproductive hours and so there should be a record of idle time. This may simply comprise an entry on time sheets coded to 'idle time' generally, or separate idle time cards may be prepared. A supervisor might enter the time of a stoppage, its cause, its duration and the employees made idle on an **idle time record card**. Each stoppage should have a separate reference number which can be entered on time sheets or job cards as appropriate.

2.2.6 Measurement by output

The labour cost of work done by pieceworkers is determined from what is known as a **piecework ticket** or an **operation card**. The card records the total number of items (or **pieces**) produced and the number of rejects. Payment is only made for 'good' production.

```
┌─────────────────────────────────────────────────────────────────────┐
│                         OPERATION CARD                                │
├─────────────────────────────────────────────────────────────────────┤
│ Operator's Name...................   Total Batch Quantity..........   │
│ Clock No .........................   Start Time ..................    │
│ Pay week No ........ Date .......    Stop Time ...................    │
├─────────────────────────────────────────────────────────────────────┤
│ Part No ..........................   Works Order No ..............    │
│ Operation ........................   Special Instructions ........    │
├──────────────┬─────────────┬──────────────────┬──────────┬───────────┤
│ Quantity     │ No Rejected │ Good Production  │  Rate    │    $      │
│ Produced     │             │                  │          │           │
│              │             │                  │          │           │
│              │             │                  │          │           │
│              │             │                  │          │           │
├──────────────┴─────────────┴──────────────────┴──────────┴───────────┤
│ Inspector.......................   Operative ....................     │
│ Supervisor......................   Date ........................      │
├─────────────────────────────────────────────────────────────────────┤
│   PRODUCTION CANNOT BE CLAIMED WITHOUT A PROPERLY SIGNED CARD          │
└─────────────────────────────────────────────────────────────────────┘
```

2.3 Coding of job costs

By now you will appreciate that to analyse labour costs effectively it is necessary to be able to link up different pieces of information in various ways. Most organisations therefore develop a series of codes to facilitate analysis for each of the following.

(a)   **Employee number** and perhaps a team number

(b)   **Pay rate**, for example 'A' for $5 per hour, 'B' for $6 per hour and so on

(c)   **Department** and/or **location** if the organisation has different branches or offices

(d)   **Job** or **batch type**, for example different codes for audit, accounts preparation and tax in a firm of accountants, or for bodywork and mechanical repairs in a garage

(e)   **Job** or **batch number** to enable each successive example of the same type of work to be allocated the next number in sequence

(f)   **Client number** so that all work done for the same client or customer can be coded to the same number

You might like to think of different ways in which different pieces of information could be grouped together. For example, combining (b), (c) and (d) would show you whether the workers in one location could do a certain type of work more cheaply than the workers in another location.

| Question | Labour costs of jobs |

Below are shown some extracts from the files of Penny Lane Co. You are required to calculate the labour cost of jobs 249 and 250.

Personnel files

	George	Paul	Ringo	John
Grade	A	B	C	D

Payroll - Master file

Grade	Basic rate per hour
A	$8.20
B	$7.40
C	$6.50
D	$5.30

Production report - labour

Job	Employee	Hours
249	George	14
249	Paul	49
250	George	2
250	John	107
250	Ringo	74

| Answer |

Job 249

Employee	Hours	Rate $	Total $
George	14	8.20	114.80
Paul	49	7.40	362.60
			477.40

Job 250

Employee	Hours	Rate $	Total $
George	2	8.20	16.40
John	107	5.30	567.10
Ringo	74	6.50	481.00
			1,064.50

3 Overtime, bonuses and absences

There are five main types of **incentive scheme,** piecework, time-saved bonus, discretionary bonus, group bonus scheme and profit-sharing scheme.

3.1 Overtime

If an employee works for more hours than the basic daily requirement many organisations pay an extra amount.

The overtime payment may simply be at the **basic rate**. If an employee earns $5 an hour he will get an extra $5 for every hour worked in addition to the basic hours. If he earns $10,000 a year an hourly rate can be calculated by multiplying the basic hours per day by the normal number of days worked per week by the 52 weeks in the year. For example 7 hours × 5 days × 52 weeks = 1,820 hours and the hourly rate is approximately $5.49.

Usually, however, overtime is paid at a **premium rate**. You will hear expressions like 'time and a third', 'time and a half' and so on. This means that the hourly rate for overtime hours is $(1 + \frac{1}{3})$ × basic rate or $(1 + \frac{1}{2})$ × basic rate.

3.1.1 Example: Overtime premium

Pootings Co pays overtime at time and a quarter. Jo's basic hours are 9 to 5 with an hour for lunch, but one particular Friday she worked until six o'clock. She is paid a basic wage of $5 per hour. How much did she earn on the Friday in question, and how much of this is overtime premium?

Solution

The most obvious way of calculating the amount earned is as follows.

	$
Basic time (7 × $5)	35.00
Overtime (11/4 × $5)	6.25
Total pay	41.25

It is wrong, however, to say that the overtime premium is $6.25. For costing purposes all of the hours worked, whether in basic time or outside it, are costed at the basic rate. The premium is the extra amount paid on top of the basic rate for the hours worked over and above the basic hours.

	$
Basic pay (8 × $5)	40.00
Overtime premium (1/4 × $5)	1.25
	41.25

The **overtime premium** is thus $1.25. This is an important point because overtime premium is usually treated as an **indirect cost**. This is quite reasonable if you think about it. If you and your colleague use identical calculators it is reasonable to suppose that they cost the same amount to produce. It might be that one was assembled at 10 o'clock in the morning and the other at 10 o'clock at night but this doesn't make the calculators different from each other. They should therefore have the same cost and so **most organisations treat overtime premium as an overhead** and do not allocate it to the products manufactured outside basic hours.

There are two exceptions to this rule.

(a) If overtime is worked at the specific request of a customer to get his order completed, the premium is a **direct cost of the order**.

(b) If overtime is worked regularly by a production department in the normal course of operations, the overtime paid to direct workers could be incorporated into an **average direct labour hourly rate** (though it does not need to be).

Exam focus point

If you have trouble remembering how to deal with overtime premiums, think how you would feel if you had to pay more for your new car radio than all of the others in the shop, simply because it was made after 5.30 pm.

3.2 Incentives and bonuses

Overtime premiums are paid to encourage staff to work longer hours than normal (or at least to recognise and reward the personal sacrifice of doing so). **Incentives and bonuses** are paid to encourage staff to work harder whatever the time of day.

Incentive schemes include the following.

- Piecework
- Time-saved bonus
- Discretionary bonus
- Group bonus scheme
- Profit-sharing scheme

3.2.1 Piecework

Pieceworking can be seen as an incentive scheme since the more output you produce the more you are paid. If you are paid 5c per unit produced and you want to earn $300 gross a week you know you have to produce 6,000 units that week.

The system can be further refined by paying a different rate for different levels of production (**differential piecework**). For example the employer could pay 3c per unit for output of up to 3,500 a week, 5c per unit for every unit over 3,500.

In practice, persons working on such schemes normally receive a guaranteed minimum wage because they may not be able to work because of problems outside their control.

3.2.2 Example: Piecework

An employee is paid $5 per piecework hour produced. In a 35 hour week he produces the following output.

	Piecework time allowed per unit
3 units of product A	2.5 hours
5 units of product B	8.0 hours

Required

Calculate the employee's pay for the week.

Solution

Piecework hours produced are as follows.

Product A	3 × 2.5 hours	7.5 hours
Product B	5 × 8 hours	40.0 hours
Total piecework hours		47.5 hours

Therefore employee's pay = 47.5 × $5 = $237.50 for the week.

3.2.3 Time-saved bonus

Suppose that a garage has calculated that it takes an average of 45 minutes for an engineer to perform an MOT test, but the job could be done competently in 30 minutes. It could encourage its engineers to do such work at the faster rate by paying **a bonus for every minute saved** on the job up to a maximum of 15 minutes.

There are problems with this approach. In the first place it is necessary to establish a standard time for all types of work, and this may not be easy. In the second place a less than competent engineer may rush the job and not do it properly.

3.2.4 Discretionary bonuses

It is not uncommon, especially in smaller businesses, for **employers to give their employees bonuses simply because they think they deserve one**. This is a possible approach if it is difficult to measure an employee's output. Many office workers fall into this category. If, however, there is no obvious connection between what a person does and whether or not a bonus is paid, the scheme is likely to be perceived as unfair.

3.2.5 Group bonus schemes

Sometimes it is not possible to measure individual effort because overall performance is not within any one person's control (for example railway workers). In such cases, however, it is possible to measure overall performance and **a bonus can therefore be paid to all those who contributed.**

3.2.6 Profit-sharing schemes

In a **profit-sharing scheme** employees receive **a certain proportion of their company's year-end profits** (the size of their bonus might also be related to level of responsibility and length of service).

3.3 Absence from work

An employee may be absent from work for a variety of reasons, the most usual being as follows.

- Holidays
- Sickness
- Maternity/paternity/adoption leave
- Training

The costs relating to absence through sickness, maternity/paternity/adoption leave and training are usually treated as an overhead rather than a direct cost of production. Although some organisations treat holiday pay as an overhead, the normal treatment is to regard it as a direct cost by charging an inflated hourly rate. Suppose an employee is normally paid $4 an hour for a 35 hour week and is entitled to four weeks annual holiday. He will therefore receive $560 ($4 × 35 × 4) holiday pay. Assuming that the employee works the remaining 48 weeks, his attendance time will total 1,680 (48 × 35) hours. Dividing $560 by 1,680 hours gives an addition of approximately 33c per hour to the employee's hourly rate to ensure that holiday pay is recovered.

Time absent because of holidays is paid at the normal basic rate, as is absence on training courses as a rule. There are statutory minimum levels for maternity pay and sickness pay, but above these employers can be as generous (or otherwise) as they wish.

Question	Labour cost classification (1)

Classify the following labour costs as either direct or indirect.

(a) The basic pay of direct workers (cash paid, tax and other deductions)
(b) The basic pay of indirect workers
(c) Overtime premium
(d) Bonus payments
(e) Employer's National Insurance contributions
(f) Idle time of direct workers

Answer

(a)   The basic pay of direct workers is a direct cost to the unit, job or process.

(b)   The basic pay of indirect workers is an indirect cost, unless a customer asks for an order to be carried out which involves the dedicated use of indirect workers' time, when the cost of this time would be a direct labour cost of the order.

(c)   Overtime premium paid to both direct and indirect workers is an indirect cost, except in two particular circumstances.

  (i)   If overtime is worked at the specific request of a customer to get his order completed, the overtime premium paid is a direct cost of the order.

  (ii)   If overtime is worked regularly by a production department in the normal course of operations, the overtime premium paid to direct workers could be incorporated into the (average) direct labour hourly rate.

(d)   Bonus payments are generally an indirect cost.

(e)   Employer's national insurance contributions (which are added to employees' total pay as a wages cost) are normally treated as an indirect labour cost.

(f)   Idle time is an overhead cost, that is an indirect labour cost.

Question   Labour cost classification (2)

A direct labour employee's wage in week 5 consists of the following.

		$
(a)	Basic pay for normal hours worked, 36 hours at $4 per hour	144
(b)	Pay at the basic rate for overtime, 6 hours at $4 per hour	24
(c)	Overtime shift premium, with overtime paid at time-and-a-quarter ¼ × 6 hours × $4 per hour	6
(d)	A bonus payment under a group bonus (or 'incentive') scheme - bonus for the month	30
Total gross wages in week 5 for 42 hours of work		204

Required

Establish which costs are direct costs and which are indirect costs.

Answer

Items (a) and (b) are direct labour costs of the items produced in the 42 hours worked in week 5.

Overtime premium, item (c), is usually regarded as an overhead expense, because it is 'unfair' to charge the items produced in overtime hours with the premium. Why should an item made in overtime be more costly just because, by chance, it was made after the employee normally clocks off for the day?

Group bonus scheme payments, item (d), are usually overhead costs, because they cannot normally be traced directly to individual products or jobs.

In this example, the direct labour employee costs were $168 in direct costs and $36 in indirect costs.

4 Labour turnover

FAST FORWARD

Labour turnover is the rate at which employees leave a company and this rate should be kept as low as possible. The cost of labour turnover can be divided into **preventative** and **replacement** costs.

4.1 The reasons for labour turnover

There are many reasons why employees will leave their job. It may be because they wish to go to work for another company or organisation. Alternatively it may be for one of the following unavoidable reasons.

- Illness or accidents
- A family move away from the locality
- Marriage, pregnancy or difficulties with child care provision
- Retirement or death

In addition to the above examples, other causes of labour turnover are as follows.

- Paying a lower wage rate than is available elsewhere
- Requiring employees to work in unsafe or highly stressful conditions
- Requiring employees to work unsociable hours
- Poor relationships between management and staff
- Lack of opportunity for career enhancement
- Requiring employees to work in inaccessible places
- Discharging employees for misconduct, bad timekeeping or unsuitability

4.2 Measuring labour turnover

Key term

- **Labour turnover** is a measure of the number of employees leaving/being recruited in a period of time (say one year) expressed as a percentage of the total labour force.

- Labour turnover rate = $\dfrac{\text{Replacements}}{\text{Average number of employees in period}} \times 100\%$

4.2.1 Example: Labour turnover

(a) Florence Co had a staff numbering 800 at the beginning of 20X1 and 1,200 at the end of that year. Four hundred employees resigned on 30 June, and were immediately replaced by 400 new employees on 1 July. 400 extra employees were also recruited at that time.

What is the labour turnover rate?

$$\text{Rate} = \frac{400}{(800 + 1{,}200) \div 2} \times 100\% = 40\%$$

(b) Rome Co had a staff of 2,000 at the beginning of 20X1 and, owing to a series of redundancies caused by the recession, 1,000 at the end of the year. Voluntary redundancy was taken by 1,500 staff at the end of June, 500 more than the company had anticipated, and these excess redundancies were immediately replaced by new joiners.

The labour turnover rate is calculated as follows.

$$\text{Rate} = \frac{500}{(2{,}000 + 1{,}000) \div 2} \times 100\% = 33\%$$

4.3 The costs of labour turnover

The costs of labour turnover can be large and management should attempt to keep labour turnover as low as possible so as to minimise these costs. The **cost of labour turnover** may be divided into the following.

- Preventative costs
- Replacement costs

4.3.1 Replacement costs

These are the costs incurred as a result of **hiring new employees** and they include the following.

(a) Cost of selection and placement.

(b) Inefficiency of new labour; productivity will be lower.

(c) Costs of training; training costs will include formal training courses plus the costs of on-the-job instructors diverted from their own work to teach new recruits.

(d) Loss of output due to delay in new labour becoming available.

(e) Increased wastage and spoilage due to lack of expertise among new staff.

(f) The possibility of more frequent accidents at work.

(g) Cost of tool and machine breakages.

4.3.2 Preventative costs

These are costs incurred in order to **prevent employees leaving** and they include the following.

(a) Cost of personnel administration incurred in maintaining good relationships.
(b) Cost of medical services including check-ups, nursing staff and so on.
(c) Cost of welfare services, including sports facilities, laundry services and canteen meals.
(d) Pension schemes providing security to employees.

4.4 The prevention of high labour turnover

Labour turnover will be reduced by the following actions.

- Paying satisfactory wages
- Offering satisfactory hours and conditions of work
- Creating good relations between fellow workers, supervisors and subordinates
- Offering good training schemes and a well-understood career or promotion ladder
- Improving the content of jobs to create job satisfaction
- Proper planning so as to avoid redundancies
- Investigating the cause of high labour turnover rates

Exam focus point

In December 2004, Question 1 in Section B required examples of replacement and preventative costs and the formula for the rate of labour turnover.

5 Measuring labour efficiency and utilisation

Labour efficiency and utilisation can be measured using ratios.

5.1 Labour efficiency

Labour costs are often a large proportion of the total costs incurred by many organisations. It is important therefore that the performance of the labour force is continually measured.

Labour efficiency is one such performance measurement. Labour efficiency is generally measured by comparing actual results for an organisation with budgets (for now you can think of a budget as a plan for the future (in money terms) and is therefore the result that we expect to get).

5.1.1 Efficiency, capacity and production volume ratios

Three ways of measuring labour efficiency include the following.

- Efficiency ratio (or productivity ratio)
- Capacity ratio
- Production volume ratio, or activity ratio

Key term

- **Efficiency ratio** $= \dfrac{\text{Expected hours to make actual output}}{\text{Actual hours taken}} \times 100\%$

- **Capacity ratio** $= \dfrac{\text{Actual hours worked}}{\text{Hours budgeted}} \times 100\%$

- **Production volume ratio** $= \dfrac{\text{Expected hours to make actual output}}{\text{Hours budgeted}} \times 100\%$

These ratios are usually expressed as percentages.

Efficiency ratio × Capacity ratio = Production volume ratio

5.1.2 Example: Ratios

Barney Rubble Co budgets to make 25,000 units of output (in four hours each) during a budget period of 100,000 hours.

Actual output during the period was 27,000 units which took 120,000 hours to make.

Required

Calculate the efficiency, capacity and production volume ratios.

Solution

(a) Efficiency ratio $\dfrac{(27,000 \times 4)\,\text{hours}}{120,000} \times 100\% = 90\%$

(b) Capacity ratio $\dfrac{120,000\,\text{hours}}{100,000\,\text{hours}} \times 100\% = 120\%$

(c) Production volume ratio $\dfrac{(27,000 \times 4)\,\text{hours}}{100,000} \times 100\% = 108\%$

These ratios may be used, therefore, to measure the performance of the labour force. At a later stage in your studies you will come across variances, in particular labour variances which are another means of measuring labour efficiency.

> The examiner commented in December 2004 that very few candidates were able to correctly apply the ratios.

5.2 Labour utilisation

It is possible to monitor the efficient use of labour by calculating **labour utilisation rates** or ratios. These ratios consider how actual working time is utilised, that is to say whether the time is **productive** or **non-productive**. We shall now consider some of the ways in which labour utilisation can be measured.

5.2.1 Idle time

We considered idle time earlier on in this chapter. A useful ratio for the control of idle time is the **idle time ratio**.

$$\textbf{Idle time ratio} = \frac{\text{Idle hours}}{\text{Total hours}} \times 100\%$$

This ratio is useful because it shows the proportion of available hours which were lost as a result of idle time.

5.2.2 Absenteeism

When staff are absent from work, this is another reason why productive time may be reduced. We can also calculate ratios which might provide useful measures of absenteeism. These ratios include the following.

(a) $\dfrac{\text{Number of hours/days absent from work (in a given period)}}{\text{Total number of hours/days paid (in a given period)}}$

(b) $\dfrac{\text{Number of hours/days absent from work (in a given period)}}{\text{Total number of hours/days worked (in a given period)}}$

It is important to keep a check on absenteeism and management should be aware of any patterns which may begin to emerge within an organisation.

5.2.3 Sickness

Similarly, levels of sickness may also be measured by means of ratios which are similar to those used for measuring absenteeism.

The types of ratios which might provide a useful measure of sickness within an organisation include the following.

(a) $\dfrac{\text{Number of days off work due to sickness (in a given period)}}{\text{Total number of days paid (in a given period)}}$

(b) $\dfrac{\text{Number of days off work due to sickness (in a given period)}}{\text{Total number of days worked (in a given period)}}$

As with absenteeism, it is important that sickness rates are monitored by management. It is possible that during the winter time sickness rates may seasonally be very high, possibly because of flu epidemics, colds or other illnesses which are rife during this period.

5.2.4 Overtime levels

The amount of overtime worked, and the costs of overtime to an organisation may also be measured by calculating ratios.

The management of an organisation may be interested to know whether the amount of overtime worked in an organisation occurs at any particular time of the year, and whether they may be justified in hiring extra staff during these periods.

The following ratios may be used to indicate the overtime levels in an organisation.

(a) $\dfrac{\text{Hours of overtime worked}}{\text{Total hours worked}}$

(b) $\dfrac{\text{Overtime labour costs}}{\text{Total labour costs}}$

It is worth noting that overtime levels may be seasonal. For example, staff working in department stores around Christmas may work many hours of overtime; many stores have late-night shopping and are generally open for longer hours than usual during this period.

Chapter Roundup

- **Labour costs** can be determined according to some prior agreement, the amount of time worked or the quality of work done.

- **Labour attendance time** is recorded on an attendance record or a clockcard. **Jobtime** may be recorded on daily time sheets, weekly time sheets, jobcards or route cards depending on the circumstances.

- There are five main types of **incentive scheme,** piecework, time-saved bonus, discretionary bonus, group bonus scheme and profit-sharing scheme.

- **Labour turnover** is the rate at which employees leave a company and this rate should be kept as low as possible. The cost of labour turnover can be divided into **preventative** and **replacement** costs.

- Labour efficiency and utilisation can be measured using ratios.

Quick Quiz

1   Name the three categories of labour cost records.

2   Which two documents are used to record attendance time?

3   Which four documents may be used to record the amount of time spent on a job?

4   Give three reasons why salaried staff may be required to fill in detailed timesheets.

5   What is idle time, and why may it occur?

6   List five types of incentive scheme.

7   What is the formula used to calculate the labour turnover rate?

8   List five methods used to reduce labour turnover.

Answers to Quick Quiz

1   Agreed basic wages and salaries, time spent, work done.

2   A record of attendance and a clockcard.

3   Daily time sheets, weekly time sheets, job cards and route cards.

4   • Timesheets assist in the creation of management information about product costs and profitability

    • Timesheet information may have a direct impact on the revenue an organisation receives (eg solicitors, accountants)

    • Timesheet information may support overtime claims made by salaried staff

5   Time during which employees cannot get on with their work (though it is not their fault). It occurs when a machine breaks down or when there is a temporary shortage of work.

6   Piecework, time-saved bonus, discretionary bonus, group bonus scheme, profit-sharing scheme.

7   Labour turnover rate = $\dfrac{\text{Replacements}}{\text{Average number of employees in period}} \times 100\%$

8   • Paying satisfactory wages
    • Offering satisfactory hours and conditions of work
    • Offering good training schemes
    • Improving job content to create job satisfaction
    • Proper staff planning so as to avoid redundancies

    (See Section 4.4 for full list)

Now try the questions below from the Exam Question Bank

Number	Level	Marks	Time
Q6	Examination	N/A	20 mins

7

Expenses

Chapter topic list

Study guide reference

			Syllabus reference
2	(b)	Describe the process of accounting for input costs and relating them to work done	1(c)
2	(c)	Identify the documentation required, and the flow of documentation, for different cost accounting transactions	1(c)
2	(d)	Explain the use of codes in categorising and processing transactions, and the importance of correct coding	1(c)(iii)
7	(b)	Describe the procedures and documentation required to ensure the correct authorisation, coding, analysis and recording of direct and indirect expenses	3(c)(ii)
7	(c)	Describe capital and revenue expenditure and the relevant accounting treatment	3(c)(i)
7	(d)	Calculate the explain depreciation charges using straight-line, reducing balance and machine hour methods	3(c)(i)
7	(e)	Discuss the relationship between the expenses costing system and the expense accounting system	3(c)(iii)

1 Expense distinctions

FAST FORWARD

- **Capital expenditure** is expenditure which results in the acquisition of non-current assets. Non-current assets are assets acquired to provide benefits in more than one accounting period. Capital expenditure is charged to the income statement via a depreciation charge over a period of time.

- **Revenue expenditure** is expenditure which is incurred for the purpose of the trade of the business, or in order to maintain the existing earning capacity of non-current assets. It is charged to the income statement in the period to which it relates.

We have now looked at materials costs and labour costs in some detail in Chapters 5 and 6. Any other costs that might be incurred by an organisation are generally known as **expenses.**

Like materials and labour costs, expenses can be also divided up into different categories. You should not find too much difficulty in distinguishing between the following.

- Direct expense costs
- Indirect expense costs
- Fixed expense costs
- Variable expense costs

1.1 Revenue and capital expenditure

Expenses may also be classified as either **revenue** expenditure or as **capital expenditure.**

Key term

- **Capital expenditure** is expenditure which results in the acquisition of non-current assets.

- **Non-current assets** are assets which are acquired to provide benefits in more than one accounting period and are not intended to be resold in the normal course of trade.

Capital expenditure is **not** charged to the income statement as an expense. A **depreciation charge** is instead charged to the income statement in order to write the capital expenditure off over a period of time. The depreciation charge is therefore an expense in the income statement.

For example, if an asset is bought for $20,000 and it is expected to last for 5 years, then for five years, $4,000 ($20,000 ÷ 5 years) will be charged to the income statement.

The costs incurred in purchasing non-current assets result in the non-current assets appearing in the balance sheet.

Revenue expenditure is expenditure which is incurred for one of the following reasons.

- For the purpose of the trade of the business, including administration expenses, selling and distribution expenses and finance charges.

- In order to maintain the existing earning capacity of non-current assets.

Revenue expenditure is charged to the income statement in the period to which it relates.

1.1.1 Example: Revenue and capital expenditure compared

Let us look at an example which should help you to distinguish between **revenue items** and **capital items.**

Suppose that Bevan Co purchases a building for $30,000. A few years later it adds an extension to the building at a cost of $10,000. The building needs to have a few broken windows mended, its floors polished, and some missing roof tiles replaced. These cleaning and maintenance jobs cost $900.

Which items of expenditure are revenue expenditure and which are capital expenditure?

Solution

The original purchase ($30,000) and the cost of the extension ($10,000) are capital expenditure because they are incurred to acquire and then improve a non-current asset. The other costs of $900 are revenue expenditure because they are maintaining the existing earning capacity of the building.

Revenue and capital items are therefore distinguished by the ways they are accounted for in the income statement and the balance sheet.

1.2 Revenue and capital expenditure and costing

Revenue expenditure is of more relevance to the costing of products than capital expenditure. Capital expenditure is only of relevance when it is turned into revenue expenditure in the form of depreciation.

It is important that you have a clear understanding of the differences between revenue and capital items of expenditure. In an examination, you may be asked to distinguish between these terms and to decide whether certain items are capital or revenue items.

Question   Capital and revenue expenditure

Distinguish between capital expenditure and revenue expenditure and give an example of each.

Answer

Capital expenditure is expenditure which results in the acquisition of non-current assets or an improvement in their ability to earn income. **Revenue expenditure** is expenditure which is incurred either for the purpose of the trade or to maintain the **existing** earning capacity of non-current assets.

For example:

Expense	Cost	Capital/revenue
Ford Transit van	$8,000	Capital
Sign-painting of company name, logo and telephone number on van	$500	Capital
Petrol for van	$500	Revenue
New engine, replacing old one which blew up	$1,000	Revenue

1.3 Direct expenses and indirect expenses

A second major distinction that must be made is between **direct** and **indirect** expenses.

Key term

- A **direct cost** is a cost that can be traced in full to the product or service that is being costed.

- **Direct material** is all material becoming part of the product (unless used in negligible amounts and/or having negligible cost).

- **Direct wages** are all wages paid for labour (either as basic hours or as overtime) expended on work on the product itself.

- **Direct expenses** are any expenses which are incurred on a specific product other than direct material cost and direct wages.

Direct expenses are charged to the product as part of the **prime** cost. Examples of direct expenses are as follows.

- The cost of **special** designs, drawings or layouts
- The **hire of tools** or equipment for a particular job

Direct expenses are also referred to as **chargeable expenses.**

Indirect expenses are also known as overheads and are studied in detail in the next chapter.

2 Types of expense

Revenue expenditure other than materials and labour costs can arise for a number of different reasons.

(a) **Buildings costs**. The main types are rent, business rates and buildings insurance.

(b) **The costs of making buildings habitable**. Gas and electricity bills and water rates, repairs and maintenance costs and cleaning costs.

(c) **People-related costs**. These include expenditure on health and safety, the cost of uniforms, and the cost of staff welfare provisions like tea and coffee, canteen costs and staff training.

(d) **Machine operating costs**. Machines need fuel or power and they need to be kept clean and properly maintained. Machines also need to be insured. A proportion of the capital cost of the machines becomes revenue expenditure in the form of depreciation. Some machines are hired.

(e) **Information processing costs**. Associated with information processing are the costs of telephone, postage, fax, computer disks and stationery, as well as subscriptions to information sources, like trade journals.

(f) **Finance costs**. If there is a bank loan there will be interest and bank charges to pay, and if equipment is leased there will be lease interest. Dividends paid to shareholders, however, are not a cost, they are an appropriation of some of the income earned in excess of all costs.

(g) **Selling and distribution costs**. Selling expenses include advertising, the salaries and commissions of salesmen, and the costs of providing consumer service and after sales service. The organisation's finished product also has to be stored and then delivered to customers. Distribution expenses would therefore include warehouse charges, upkeep and running of delivery vehicles and carriage outwards.

(h) Finally there are the **costs of dealing with the outside world**. Fees paid to professionals like external auditors, surveyors or solicitors and the costs of marketing (such as market research) would all be collected under this heading.

A typical detailed income statement might, therefore, have the following headings.

	$	$
Sales		X
Less cost of sales:		
Opening inventory	X	
Materials	X	
Labour	X	
Depreciation	X	
Power and fuel	X	
	X	
Less closing inventory	(X)	
Cost of sales		(X)
Gross profit		X
Less costs of administration, distribution and selling:		
Wages and salaries	X	
Rent and rates	X	
Insurance	X	
Heat and light	X	
Depreciation of office equipment	X	
Repairs and maintenance	X	
Cleaning	X	
Telecommunications	X	
Printing, postage and stationery	X	
Hire of computer equipment	X	
Advertising	X	
Warehouse charges	X	
Carriage outwards	X	
Audit and accountancy fees	X	
Bank charges	X	
Interest	X	
		(X)
Profit before tax		X

The following paragraphs describe some of these expenses in more detail.

2.1 Rent

Rent is usually an annual charge payable quarterly in advance.

Rent is normally subject to a tenancy agreement and it may be fixed for a period of so many years, or reviewable annually, or there may be some other agreement.

2.2 Business rates

These are charges levied by local authorities in Britain, on non-domestic properties in their area. They are based upon a rateable value multiplied by a uniform rate. They are usually payable in two instalments in April and October each year. Most countries have expenses which are similar to business rates, though they may have different names.

2.3 Insurance costs

These comprise **premiums** paid to an insurance company to cover the risk, say, of damage to buildings or their contents by fire, flood, explosions, theft and so on. Buildings insurance is usually based on the cost of rebuilding the property with adjustments to take account of the property's particular location. It is an annual sum, payable either whenever the renewal date occurs or in instalments.

Other types of insurance are charged on a similar basis. Examples include employer's liability insurance (against the risk of harming employees), and vehicle insurance.

2.4 Electricity, gas and telecommunications

Electricity, gas and telecommunications charges normally have two elements, a fixed amount called a standing charge, generally payable quarterly, and a variable amount based on consumption. There are a number of rates depending on the status of the user (domestic/commercial/industrial) and the time of day the power is consumed or the calls are made.

2.5 Subscriptions

Subscriptions are generally paid annually, though not necessarily by calendar year. This category includes both subscriptions to publications like trade journals or information services and subscriptions for membership of Chambers of Commerce or professional or trade bodies and the like.

2.6 Professional fees

Such charges are usually made on the basis of time spent attending to the client's business.

2.7 Hire charges

Hire charges are sometimes payable on a time basis. For example a cement mixer may be hired for, say, $10 a day. Sometimes an additional charge is made for usage. A photocopier, for example, might have a meter on it showing how many copies had been made. The meter would be read periodically by the hire company and the invoice would include a charge for the number of copies made in the period.

2.8 Discretionary costs

Discretionary costs are, as you might expect, costs that are incurred at somebody's discretion. Whereas an organisation has to pay a certain amount for, say, electricity simply so that the business can function, other costs are not crucial to the short-term continuance of operations. The main examples are research and development costs, staff training and advertising.

Before we go on to consider the way in which expenses are recorded for cost accounting purposes, we are going to look at one further type of expense.

3 Depreciation and obsolescence

Depreciation is a method of writing off capital expenditure. There are two methods used, **straight-line** and **reducing balance**.

3.1 Depreciation

We mentioned depreciation at the beginning of this chapter and described it as a method of writing off capital expenditure.

There are two principal methods of depreciating an asset, the **straight line method** and the **reducing balance method**.

(a)   The **straight line method** charges an equal amount of depreciation each period.

(b)   The **reducing balance method** charges the largest amount of depreciation at the beginning of an asset's life. As the asset grows older the amount charged each period gets steadily smaller.

3.1.1 Example: Depreciation methods

Two assets are purchased for $8,000 each. One is depreciated over four years using the straight line method and the other is depreciated at the rate of 25% per annum on the reducing balance. What is the value of each asset after four years and how much per year is charged to the income statement?

Solution

	Asset A		Asset B	
	Balance sheet	IS	Balance sheet	IS
	$	$	$	$
Capital cost	8,000		8,000	
Year 1 charge	(2,000)	2,000	(2,000)	2,000
c/f	6,000		6,000	
Year 2 charge	(2,000)	2,000	1,500	1,500
c/f	4,000		4,500	
Year 3 charge	(2,000)	2,000	(1,125)	1,125
c/f	2,000		3,375	
Year 4 charge	(2,000)	2,000	(844)	844
Value after four years	-		2,531	

The income statement charge for asset A is calculated by splitting the $8,000 capital cost into four. For asset B it is calculated by taking 25% of the opening balance each year. In theory asset B could continue to be depreciated for evermore.

In order to decide which method is most appropriate we need to think a little more about why we are depreciating the asset at all.

3.2 The objectives of depreciation accounting

If an asset is purchased for $8,000 at the beginning of the year and sold for $6,000 at the end of the year then it is reasonable to conclude that the cost of owning the asset for a year is $2,000. This $2,000 is a real cost and it is in addition to the costs of using the asset, like fuel and repairs costs.

If the business had not owned the asset it would not have been able to make its product. It is therefore reasonable that the $2,000 cost should be charged as a cost of the product (although we won't say how to do this, for now).

One of the objectives of depreciation accounting is therefore **to find some way of calculating this cost of ownership.**

Consider, however, the use of a machine that is constructed to do a specific job for a specific firm. It may last 20 years and yet be of no use to anybody else at any time in which case its resale value would be nil on the same day that it was bought. It is, however, hardly fair to charge the whole cost of the machine to the first product that it makes, or even to the first year's production. Very probably the products it is making in year 19 will be just as well made as the products made in year 1.

Thus a second objective of depreciation accounting is **to spread out the capital cost of the asset over as long a period as the asset is used.** In the example given there is a good case for spreading this cost in equal proportions over the whole 20 years.

The answer to the question 'which method is best?' therefore depends upon the following.

- The asset in question
- The way it is used
- The length of time it is used
- Its useful life in the light of changes in production methods, technology and so on

3.3 Depreciation in practice

This sounds as if there are a lot of things to take into account, but in practice you may find that the method most often used is the straight line method because it is simple and gives a reasonable approximation (given that depreciation is at best an estimate).

Typical depreciation rates under the straight line method are as follows.

Freehold land	Not depreciated
Freehold buildings	2% per annum (50 years)
Leasehold buildings	Over the period of the lease
Plant and machinery	10% per annum (10 years)
Fixtures and fittings	10% per annum (10 years)
Motor vehicles	25% per annum (4 years)

Note that these are not rules. Businesses can choose whatever method or rate they think is most appropriate. Motor vehicles, for example, are often depreciated using the reducing balance method since it is well known that in reality they lose the largest proportion of their value in their first few years.

3.4 Obsolescence

Key term

Obsolescence is the loss in value of an asset because it has been superseded, for example due to the development of a technically superior asset or changes in market conditions.

As the loss in value is due to quite another reason than the **wear and tear** associated with depreciation and because obsolescence may be rapid and difficult to forecast, it is not normal practice to make regular charges relating to obsolescence. Instead, **the loss resulting from the obsolescence should be charged direct to the costing income statement.**

 Question   Depreciation

(a)   It has been calculated that a fork-lift truck is used 65% of the time in the warehouse and the rest of the time in the production department.

Does this have any significance for costing purposes?

(b)   At the end of its first year of use the meter on a leather stamping machine read 9728. It cost $4,000 and the suppliers are willing to buy it back for 20% of its cost at any time so that it can be used for parts. The sales literature claimed that it was capable of producing at least 100,000 stampings. The machine is used exclusively on one product, which will be discontinued in three years' time.

     (i)   Is the depreciation charge for the machine a direct expense or an indirect expense?
     (ii)   What is the depreciation charge for the first year?

Answer

(a)   Yes. The annual depreciation charge for the fork-lift truck is an indirect revenue expense to be shared (65:35) between the warehouse and the production department. In other words it is a *cost* of these departments.

(b)   (i)   The machine is used exclusively for one product and therefore the whole of the depreciation charge is traceable *directly* to that product. Depreciation is thus a direct expense in this case.

     (ii)   At the current rate of usage it looks as though the machine will last ten years but it will not be needed after the fourth year of its life and so straight line depreciation over four years seems the most appropriate charge.

$$\text{Depreciation charge} = \frac{\text{Cost - residual value}}{\text{Useful life}} = \frac{\$4,000 - \$800}{4}$$

$$= \$800$$

4 Recording expenses

AST FORWARD

- **Direct expenses** are recorded by coding them to the appropriate job or client.

- **Indirect expenses** are initially **allocated** to appropriate cost centres and then spread out or **apportioned** to the cost centres that have benefited from the expense.

- In **responsibility accounting,** cost centres collect the costs that are the responsibility of the cost centre manager, and hence may be known as **responsibility centres.**

In this chapter we are only going to deal with the initial stages of recording expenses. Much more detail will be found in the following chapter which explains how overhead costs are attributed to the total costs of individual units of product.

4.1 Direct expenses

Direct expenses (such as plant hire for a specific job or solicitor's fees for drawing up a contract to provide a service) can simply be coded to the appropriate job or client when the bill arrives and recorded together with other direct costs.

4.2 Indirect expenses

Key term

> **Allocation** is the process by which whole cost items are charged to a cost centre.

Indirect expenses are initially allocated to the appropriate cost centres. We met cost centres briefly in Chapter 3 but in case you have forgotten a cost centre is something (location, function, activity or item of equipment, say) which incurs costs that can be attributed to units of production (cost units). That something may be any of the following.

Cost centre type	Examples	
	Production	Service
Location	Factory A	Top floor
Function	Finishing department	Accounts department
Activity	Painting	Invoicing
Item of equipment	Spray-gun	Computer

The decision as to which cost centre is the appropriate one for an expense depends upon the type of expense. Some expenses will be solely related to production or to administration or to selling and distribution and can easily be allocated to the appropriate cost centre. Other costs, however, will be shared between these various functions and so such costs cannot be allocated directly to one particular cost centre. Cost centres therefore have to be established for the **initial allocation** of such shared expenses. Examples of shared expenses include: rent, rates, heating and lighting, buildings maintenance and so on.

4.2.1 Example: Overhead allocation

The coding, analysis and recording of indirect expenses and other overheads at the initial stage may be demonstrated by the following example.

The weekly costs of Medlycott Co include the following.

Wages of foreman of Department A	$1,000
Wages of foreman of Department B	$1,200
Indirect materials consumed in Department A	$400
Rent of premises shared by Departments A and B	$1,500

Medlycott Co's cost accounting system includes the following cost centres.

Code	
101	Department A
102	Department B
201	Rent

Show how the costs will be initially coded.

Solution

(a)

	$	Code
Wages of foreman of Department A	1,000	101
Wages of foreman of Department B	1,200	102
Indirect materials consumed in Department A	400	101
Rent of premises shared by Departments A and B	1,500	201

(b)   You may think that this is so obvious as not to be worth explaining. You will certainly not be surprised to be told that the next stage is to share the rent paid between the two departments. Why, you might ask, do we not split the cost of rent straightaway and not bother with cost centre 201?

(c) To answer this question consider the following extract from the cost accounts of Medlycott Co, several months after the previous example. Cost centre 201 is no longer used because nobody could see the point of it.

	Cost centre	
	101	102
	$	$
Wages	1,172.36	1,415.00
Materials	73.92	169.75
Rent	638.25	1,086.75

You have just received a memo telling you that starting from this month (to which the above figures relate), Department A is to pay 25% of the total rent for the premises shared with Department B and Department B is to be split into 2 departments, with the new department (C) paying 37% of the remaining rent charge. The manager of Department B is standing over you asking you how much his department's new monthly rent charge will be.

(d) The answer is $815.06. More importantly the first thing you have to do to calculate the answer is to recreate the total cost information that used to be allocated to cost centre 201. This is not very difficult in the present example, but imagine that there were 10 cost centres sharing premises and the cost information was recorded in a bulky ledger. Do you think it would have been easy to spot that the monthly rent had increased to $1,725?

4.3 Documentation

There are several ways in which this initial allocation could be documented. A common method is to put a stamp on the invoice itself with boxes to fill in, as appropriate.

%	A/C	$	P
25.00%	101	431	25
47.25%	102	815	06
27.75%	103	478	69
TOTAL	201	1,725	00

Approved		Date	
Authorised		Date	
Posted		Date	

The dividing up of the total cost into portions (**apportionment**) is described in more detail in the next chapter.

4.4 Apportionment and responsibility accounting

The last point raises another important question. It is unlikely that the managers of departments A, B and C have any control over the amount of rent that is paid for the building. They need to be made aware that their part of the building is not free but they are not responsible for the cost. The person responsible for controlling the amount of a cost such as this is more likely to be a separate manager, who looks after the interests of all of the company's buildings.

If cost centre 201 is maintained it can therefore be used to collect all the costs that are the responsibility of the premises manager. This approach is known as **responsibility accounting** (we looked at this briefly in Chapter 3) and such cost centres can be called **responsibility centres**.

Chapter Roundup

- **Capital expenditure** is expenditure which results in the acquisition of non-current assets. Non-current assets are assets acquired to provide benefits in more than one accounting period. Capital expenditure is charged to the income statement via a depreciation charge over a period of time.

- **Revenue expenditure** is expenditure which is incurred for the purpose of the trade of the business, or in order to maintain the existing earning capacity of non-current assets. It is charged to the income statement in the period to which it relates.

- Depreciation is a method of writing off capital expenditure. There are two methods used, **straight-line** and **reducing balance**.

- **Direct expenses** are recorded by coding them to the appropriate job or client.

- **Indirect expenses** are initially **allocated** to appropriate cost centres and then spread out or **apportioned** to the cost centres that have benefited from the expense.

- In **responsibility accounting**, cost centres collect the costs that are the responsibility of the cost centre manager, and hence may be known as **responsibility centres**.

Quick Quiz

1   What is capital expenditure?

2   What is revenue expenditure?

3   What is the main distinguishing feature of capital and revenue expenditure?

4   What are the two main methods of depreciating an asset?

5   What are the two main objectives of depreciation accounting?

6   What is obsolescence?

7   What is responsibility accounting?

Answers to Quick Quiz

1   Expenditure resulting in the acquisition of non-current assets. It is not charged to the income statement as an expense. Instead a depreciation charge is made to the income statement which writes off the capital expenditure over a period of time.

2   Revenue expenditure is expenditure incurred for the purpose of the trade of the business, or in order to maintain the existing earning capacity of non-current assets. It is charged to the income statement in the period to which it relates.

3   The way that they are accounted for in the income statement (see answers 1 and 2).

4   Straight line method and reducing balance method.

5   To find a way of calculating the cost of ownership of non-current assets and to spread out the capital cost of the asset over its lifetime.

6   The loss in value of an asset because it has been superseded.

7   When cost centre managers have responsibility for controlling the amount of the cost collected within certain cost centres, such cost centres are called responsibility centres.

Now try the questions below from the Exam Question Bank

Number	Level	Marks	Time
Q7	Examination	N/A	20 mins

Overheads and absorption costing

Chapter topic list

Study guide reference

			Syllabus reference
8	(a)	Explain the rationale for absorption costing	4(b)
8	(b)	Describe the nature of production and service cost centres and their significance for production overhead allocation, apportionment and absorption	4(b)
8	(c)	Discuss the process of allocating, apportioning and absorbing production overheads to establish product costs	4(b)
8	(d)	Apportion overheads to cost centres using appropriate bases	4(b)
8	(e)	Re-apportion service cost centre overheads to production cost centres using direct and step down methods	4(b)
9	(a)	Justify, calculate and apply production cost centre overhead absorption rates using labour hour and machine hour methods	4(b)
9	(b)	Explain the relative merits of actual and pre-determined absorption rates	4(b)
9	(c)	Describe and illustrate the accounting for production overhead costs, including the analysis and interpretation of over/under absorption	4(b)
9	(d)	Describe and apply methods of attributing non-production overheads to cost units	4(b)
9	(e)	Calculate product costs using the absorption costing method	4(b)

1 What are overheads?

Overhead is part of the cost incurred in the course of making a product, providing a service or running a department, which cannot be traced directly and in full to the product, service or department.

Now that we have completed our detailed study of direct materials, direct labour and direct expenses, we can move on to look in more depth at **indirect costs,** or **overheads.** Overheads may be dealt with in a number of different ways. In this chapter we will be looking at **traditional absorption costing**. The only other method that you need to have knowledge of is **marginal costing**. We will be looking at marginal costing in detail in the next chapter.

1.1 General overheads

Key term

An **overhead** is the cost incurred in the course of making a product, providing a service or running a department, but which cannot be traced directly and in full to the product or service.

Overheads are the total of the following.

- Indirect materials
- Indirect labour
- Indirect expenses

(Note that in the previous chapter we were looking at **expenses**, and whether they were direct or indirect.)

One common way of categorising overheads is as follows.

- Production overhead
- Administration overhead
- Selling overhead
- Distribution overhead

You will remember that we looked at overheads briefly in Chapter 3 when we were studying cost classification.

2 What is absorption costing?

Absorption costing is a method of sharing overheads between a number of different products or services on a fair basis. It involves **allocation**, **apportionment** and **absorption**.

2.1 The objective of absorption costing

The objective of absorption costing is to include in the total cost of a product or service an appropriate **share** of the organisation's total overhead. By an appropriate share we mean an amount that reflects the amount of time and effort that has gone into producing the unit of product or service.

If an organisation had only one production department and produced identical units then the total overheads would be divided among the total units produced. Life is, of course, never that simple. Absorption costing is a method of sharing overheads between a number of different products or services on a fair basis.

2.2 Absorption costing procedures

The three steps involved in calculating the costs of overheads to be charged to cost units are

- Allocation
- Apportionment
- Absorption

Allocation is the process of assigning whole items of cost to cost centres. We studied the process of allocation in the previous chapter.

We shall now begin our study of absorption costing by looking at the first stage of **overhead apportionment**.

Question   Absorption costing

(a) What is absorption costing?
(b) What are the three stages of absorption costing?

Answer

(a) **Absorption costing** is a method of determining a product cost that includes a proportion of all production overheads incurred in the making of the product and possibly a proportion of other overheads such as administration and selling overheads.

(b)
- **Allocation** of costs to cost centres
- **Apportionment** of costs between cost centres
- **Absorption** of costs into cost units

3 Overhead apportionment – Stage 1

FAST FORWARD

The first stage of overhead apportionment is to **identify** all overhead costs.

Key term

> **Apportionment** is a procedure whereby indirect costs (overheads) are spread fairly between cost centres.

3.1 Sharing out common costs

Overhead apportionment follows on from overhead allocation. The first stage of overhead apportionment is to **identify all overhead costs** as production, administration, selling and distribution overhead. This means that the shared costs (such as rent and rates, heat and light and so on) initially allocated to a single cost centre must now be **shared out** between the other (functional) cost centres.

3.2 Bases of apportionment

It is important that overhead costs are shared out on a **fair basis** using appropriate bases of apportionment. The bases of apportionment for the most usual cases are given below.

Overhead	Basis of apportionment
Rent, rates, heating and light, repairs and depreciation of buildings	Floor area occupied by each cost centre
Depreciation, insurance of equipment	Cost or book value of equipment
Personnel office, canteen, welfare, wages and cost office, first aid	Number of employees, or labour hours worked in each cost centre
Heating, lighting (see above)	Volume of space occupied by each cost centre

Don't forget that some overhead costs can be **allocated directly** to the user cost centre without having to be apportioned. For example indirect wages can be directly allocated because they relate solely to an individual cost centre.

Exam focus point

> Question 2 in December 2005 required you to state appropriate bases of apportionment for factory rent and staff canteen overheads.

3.2.1 Example: Bases of apportionment

Bravo Co incurred the following overhead costs.

	$
Depreciation of factory	1,000
Factory repairs and maintenance	600
Factory office costs (treat as production overhead)	1,500
Depreciation of equipment	800
Insurance of equipment	200
Heating	390
Lighting	100
Canteen	900
	5,490

Information relating to the production and service departments in the factory is as follows.

	Cost centre			
	Production A	Production B	Service X	Service Y
Floor space (m²)	1,200	1,600	800	400
Volume (m³)	3,000	6,000	2,400	1,600
Number of employees	30	30	15	15
Book value of equipment	$30,000	$20,000	$10,000	$20,000

On what bases should the overhead costs be apportioned between the four departments? How much overhead would be apportioned to each department?

Solution

Item of cost	Basis of apportionment	Total cost	To Cost centre			
			A	B	X	Y
		$	$	$	$	$
Factory depreciation	floor area	1,000	300	400	200	100
Factory repairs	floor area	600	180	240	120	60
Factory office	no. of employees	1,500	500	500	250	250
Equipment depn	book value	800	300	200	100	200
Equipment insurance	book value	200	75	50	25	50
Heating	volume	390	90	180	72	48
Lighting	floor area	100	30	40	20	10
Canteen	no. of employees	900	300	300	150	150
Total		5,490	1,775	1,910	937	868

Workings

Factory depreciation

Total floor space = (1,200 + 1,600 + 800 + 400)m²
= 4,000 m²

Factory depreciation is apportioned to the different cost centres as follows.

Production department A $= \dfrac{1,200}{4,000} \times \$1,000 = \$300$

Production department B $= \dfrac{1,600}{4,000} \times \$1,000 = \$400$

Service department X $= \dfrac{800}{4,000} \times \$1,000 = \$200$

Service department Y $= \dfrac{400}{4,000} \times \$1,000 = \$100$

The same method can be applied in order to calculate the apportionments of the other overheads.

Question

Baldwin Co is preparing its production overhead budgets. Cost centre expenses and related information have been budgeted as follows.

	Total $	Machine shop A $	Machine shop B $	Assembly $	Canteen $	Maintenance $
Indirect wages	78,560	8,586	9,190	15,674	29,650	15,460
Consumable materials (inc. maintenance)	16,900	6,400	8,700	1,200	600	–
Rent and rates	16,700					
Buildings insurance	2,400					
Power	8,600					
Heat and light	3,400					
Depreciation of machinery	40,200					
Value of machinery	402,000	201,000	179,000	22,000	–	–
Other information:						
Power usage – technical estimates (%)	100	55	40	3	–	2

	Total $	Machine shop A $	Machine shop B $	Assembly $	Canteen $	Maintenance $
Direct labour (hours)	35,000	8,000	6,200	20,800	–	–
Machine usage (hours)	25,200	7,200	18,000	–	–	–
Area (square metres)	45,000	10,000	12,000	15,000	6,000	2,000

Required

Calculate the overheads to be apportioned to the five cost centres.

Answer

	Total $	A $	B $	Assembly $	Canteen $	Maintenance $	Basis o apportionmer
Indirect wages	78,560	8,586	9,190	15,674	29,650	15,460	Actual
Consumable materials	16,900	6,400	8,700	1,200	600		Actual
Rent and rates	16,700	3,711	4,453	5,567	2,227	742	Area
Insurance	2,400	533	640	800	320	107	Area
Power	8,600	4,730	3,440	258		172	Usage
Heat and light	3,400	756	907	1,133	453	151	Area
Depreciation	40,200	20,100	17,900	2,200	–	–	Value
	166,760	44,816	45,230	26,832	33,250	16,632	

Workings

(1) **Rent and rates, insurance, heat and light**

Floor area is a sensible measure to use as the basis for apportionment.

	Area	Proportion total area	Share of rent & rates	Share of insurance	Share of heat & light
	Sq metres		$	$	$
Machine shop A	10,000	10/45	3,711	533	756
Machine shop B	12,000	12/45	4,453	640	907
Assembly	15,000	15/45	5,567	800	1,133
Canteen	6,000	6/45	2,227	320	453
Maintenance	2,000	2/45	742	107	151
	45,000		16,700	2,400	3,400

(2) **Power**

	Percentage	Share of cost
	%	$
Machine shop A	55	4,730
Machine shop B	40	3,440
Assembly	3	258
Maintenance	2	172
		8,600

(3) **Depreciation**

In the absence of specific information about the non-current assets in use in each department and the depreciation rates that are applied, this cost is shared out on the basis of the **relative value of each department's machinery** to the total. In practice more specific information would (or should) be available.

4 Overhead apportionment – Stage 2

ST FORWARD

The second stage of apportionment is to **reapportion service centre costs.**

4.1 Reapportionment of service cost centre costs

The second stage of overhead apportionment concerns the treatment of **service cost centres**.

A factory is usually divided into **several production cost centres** and also **many service cost centres**. Service cost centres might include the **stores** or the **canteen**.

Only the production cost centres are **directly involved** in the manufacture of the units. In order to be able to add production overheads to unit costs, it is necessary to have all the overheads charged to the production cost centres only.

The next stage in absorption costing is therefore to **apportion the overheads of service cost centres to the production cost centres**. This is sometimes called **reapportionment**.

4.2 Methods of reapportionment

The reapportionment of service cost centre costs can be done by a number of methods. You only need to know about the following two methods.

- Direct method of reapportionment
- Step down method of reapportionment

Whichever method of reapportionment is used, **the basis of apportionment must be fair**. A different apportionment basis may be applied for each service cost centre. This is demonstrated in the following table.

Service cost centre	Possible basis of apportionment
Stores	Number or cost value of material requisitions
Maintenance	Hours of maintenance work done for each cost centre
Production planning	Direct labour hours worked in each production cost centre

4.2.1 Direct method of reapportionment

The **direct method of reapportionment** involves apportioning the costs of each service cost centre **to production cost centres only**.

This method is most easily explained by working through the following example.

4.2.2 Example: Direct method of reapportionment

Baldwin Co incurred the following overhead costs.

	Production departments		Stores	Maintenance
	P	Q	department	department
	$	$	$	$
Allocated costs	6,000	4,000	1,000	2,000
Apportioned costs	2,000	1,000	1,000	500
	8,000	5,000	2,000	2,500

Production department P requisitioned materials to the value of $12,000. Department Q requisitioned $8,000 of materials. The maintenance department provided 500 hours of work for department P and 750 hours for department Q.

Required

Calculate the total production overhead costs of Departments P and Q.

Solution

Service department	Basis of apportionment	Total cost	Dept P	Dept Q
		$	$	$
Stores	Value of requisitions (W1)	2,000	1,200	800
Maintenance	Maintenance hours (W2)	2,500	1,000	1,500
		4,500	2,200	2,300
Previously allocated and apportioned costs		13,000	8,000	5,000
Total overhead		17,500	10,200	7,300

Workings

(1) **Stores department overheads**

These are reapportioned as follows.

Total value of materials requisitioned   = $12,000 + $8,000

     = $20,000

Reapportioned to Department P $= \dfrac{\$12,000}{\$20,000} \times \$2,000 = \$1,200$

Reapportioned to Department Q $= \dfrac{\$8,000}{\$20,000} \times \$2,000 = \$800$

(2) **Maintenance department overheads**

These are reapportioned as follows.

Total hours worked = 500 + 750 = 1,250 hours

Reapportioned to Department P $= \dfrac{500}{1,250} \times \$2,500 = \$1,000$

Reapportioned to Department Q $= \dfrac{750}{1,250} \times \$2,500 = \$1,500$

The total overhead has now been shared, on a fair basis, between the two production departments.

Question   Apportionment (2)

The following information also relates to Baldwin Co.

	Total $	Machine shop A $	Machine shop B $	Assembly $	Canteen $	Mainten-ance $
Indirect wages	78,560	8,586	9,190	15,674	29,650	15,460
Consumable materials	16,900	6,400	8,700	1,200	600	–
Rent and rates	16,700	3,711	4,453	5,567	2,227	742
Insurance	2,400	533	640	800	320	107
Power	8,600	4,730	3,440	258	–	172
Heat and light	3,400	756	907	1,133	453	151
Depreciation	40,200	20,100	17,900	2,200	–	–
	166,760	44,816	45,230	26,832	33,250	16,632

Other information:

	Total	Machine shop A	Machine shop B	Assembly	Canteen	Mainten-ance
Power usage – technical estimates (%)	100	55	40	3	–	2
Direct labour (hours)	35,000	8,000	6,200	20,800	–	–
Machine usage (hours)	25,200	7,200	18,000	–	–	–
Area (square metres)	45,000	10,000	12,000	15,000	6,000	2,000

Required

Using the bases which you consider to be the most appropriate, calculate overhead totals for Baldwin Co's three production departments, Machine Shop A, Machine Shop B and Assembly.

Answer

	Total	A	B	Assembly	Canteen	Mainten-ance	Basis appo. tionme
	$	$	$	$	$	$	
Total overheads	166,760	44,816	45,230	26,832	33,250	16,632	
Reapportion (W1)	–	7,600	5,890	19,760	(33,250)	–	Dir labc
Reapportion (W2)	–	4,752	11,880	–	–	(16,632)	Mac usi
Totals	166,760	57,168	63,000	46,592	–	–	

Workings

(1)   **Canteen overheads**

Total direct labour hours = 35,000

Machine shop A $= \dfrac{8,000}{35,000} \times \$33,250 = \$7,600$

Machine shop B $= \dfrac{6,200}{35,000} \times \$33,250 = \$5,890$

Assembly $= \dfrac{20,800}{35,000} \times \$33,250 = \$19,760$

(2)   **Maintenance overheads**

Total machine hours   = 25,200

Machine shop A $= \dfrac{7,200}{25,200} \times \$16,632 = \$4,752$

Machine shop B $= \dfrac{18,000}{25,200} \times \$16,632 = \$11,880$

The total overhead has now been shared, on a fair basis, between the three production departments.

4.2.3 Step down method of reapportionment

This method works as follows.

Step 1   Reapportion one of the service cost centre's overheads to all of the other centres which make use of its services (production and service).

Step 2   Reapportion the overheads of the remaining service cost centre to the production departments only. The other service cost centre is ignored.

4.2.4 Example: Step down method of reapportionment

A company has two production departments and two service departments (stores and maintenance). The following information about activity in a recent costing period is available.

	Production departments		Stores department	Maintenance department
	1	2		
Overhead costs	$10,030	$8,970	$10,000	$8,000
Value of material requisitions	$30,000	$50,000	–	$20,000
Maintenance hours used	8,000	1,000	1,000	–

The stores and maintenance departments do work for each other as shown in the table below

	Production departments		Stores department	Maintenance department
	1	2		
Stores work done (100%)	30%	50%	–	20%
Maintenance work done (100%)	80%	10%	10%	–

Required

Using the information given above, apportion the service department overhead costs using the step down method of apportionment, **starting with the stores department**.

Solution

	Production departments		Stores department	Maintenance department
	1	2		
	$	$	$	$
Overhead costs	10,030	8,970	10,000	8,000
Apportion stores (30%/50%/20%)	3,000	5,000	(10,000)	2,000
				10,000
Apportion maintenance ($^8/_9/^1/_9$)	8,889	1,111	–	(10,000)
	21,919	15,081	–	–

If the first apportionment had been the maintenance department, then the overheads of $8,000 would have been apportioned as follows.

	Production departments		Stores department	Maintenance department
	1	2		
	$	$	$	$
Overhead costs	10,030	8,970	10,000	8,000
Apportion maintenance (80%/10%/10%)	6,400	800	800	(8,000)
			10,800	–
Apportion stores ($^3/_8/^5/_8$)	4,050	6,750	(10,800)	
	20,480	16,520	–	–

Note. Notice how the final results differ, depending upon whether the stores department or the maintenance department is apportioned first.

If one service cost centre, compared with the other(s), has higher overhead costs and carries out a bigger proportion of work for the other service cost centre(s), then the overheads of this service centre should be reapportioned first.

Question	Reapportionment

Elm Co has two service departments serving two production departments. Overhead costs apportioned to each department are as follows.

Production 1	Production 2	Service 1	Service 2
$	$	$	$
97,428	84,947	9,384	15,823

Service 1 department is expected to work a total of 40,000 hours for the other departments, divided as follows.

	Hours
Production 1	20,000
Production 2	15,000
Service 2	5,000

Service 2 department is expected to work a total of 12,000 hours for the other departments, divided as follows.

	Hours
Production 1	3,000
Production 2	8,000
Service 1	1,000

Required

The finance director has asked you to reapportion the costs of the two service departments using the direct method of apportionment.

Answer

Direct apportionment method	Production 1	Production 2	Service 1	Service 2
	$	$	$	$
	97,428	84,947	9,384	15,823
Apportion Service 1 costs (20:15)	5,362	4,022	(9,384)	–
	102,790	88,969	–	15,823
Apportion Service 2 costs (3:8)	4,315	11,508	–	(15,823)
	107,105	100,477	–	–

Question

Stepdown method

When you show the finance director how you have reapportioned the costs of the two service departments, he says 'Did I say that we used the direct method? Well, I meant to say the step down method.'

Required

Prove to the finance director that you know how to use the step down method. (**Note.** Apportion the overheads of service department 1 first.)

Answer

Step down method	Production 1	Production 2	Service 1	Service 2
	$	$	$	$
	97,428	84,947	9,384	15,823
Apportion Service 1 costs (20:15:5)	4,692	3,519	(9,384)	1,173
	102,120	88,466	–	16,996
Apportion Service 2 costs (3:8)	4,635	12,361	–	(16,996)
	106,755	100,827	–	–

5 Overhead absorption

Overheads are **absorbed** into cost units using a predetermined overhead absorption rate.

5.1 Overhead absorption rate

term

Overhead absorption is the process whereby overhead costs allocated and apportioned to production cost centres are added to unit, job or batch costs. Overhead absorption is sometimes called **overhead recovery**.

Having allocated and apportioned all overheads, the next stage in the costing treatment of overheads is to add them to, or **absorb them into, cost units.**

Overheads are usually added to cost units using a **predetermined overhead absorption rate**, which is calculated using figures from the budget.

An overhead absorption rate for the forthcoming accounting period is calculated and used as follows.

Step 1   **Estimate the overhead** likely to be incurred during the coming period.

Step 2   **Estimate the activity level for the period.** This could be **total hours, units, or direct costs** or whatever measure of activity upon which the overhead absorption rates are to be based.

Step 3   **Divide the estimated overhead by the budgeted activity level.** This produces the predetermined overhead absorption rate.

Step 4   **Absorb** or **recover** the overhead into the cost unit by multiplying the calculated absorption rate by the actual activity.

5.1.1 Example: Overhead absorption rates

Channel Co makes two products, the Jersey and the Guernsey. Jerseys take 2 labour hours each to make and Guernseys take 5 labour hours.

Required

Calculate the overhead cost per unit for Jerseys and Guernseys respectively if overheads are absorbed on the basis of labour hours.

Solution

Step 1   Estimate the overhead likely to be incurred during the coming period

Channel Co estimates that the total overhead will be $50,000

Step 2   Estimate the activity level for the period

Channel Co estimates that a total of 100,000 direct labour hours will be worked

Step 3   Divide the estimated overhead by the budgeted activity level

Overhead absorption rate = $\dfrac{\$50,000}{100,000\,hrs}$ = $0.50 per direct labour hour

Step 4   Absorb the overhead into the cost unit by applying the calculated absorption rate

	Jersey	Guernsey
Labour hours per unit	2	5
Absorption rate per labour hour	$0.50	$0.50
Overhead absorbed per unit	$1	$2.50

5.2 Possible bases of absorption

The most common absorption bases (or **'overhead recovery rates'**) are as follows.

- A rate per machine hour
- A rate per direct labour hour
- A percentage of direct labour cost
- A percentage of direct materials cost
- A percentage of total direct cost (prime cost)
- A rate per unit
- A percentage of factory cost (for administration overhead)
- A percentage of sales value or factory cost (for selling and distribution overhead)

The most appropriate basis for production overhead depends largely on the organisation concerned. As with apportionment it is a matter of being fair.

Many factories tend to use the **direct labour hour rate** or **machine hour rate** in preference to a rate based on a percentage of direct materials cost, wages or prime cost.

A **machine hour rate** would be used in departments where production is controlled or dictated by machines. A **direct labour hour basis** is more appropriate in a labour intensive environment.

Exam focus point

Only labour hour and machine hour absorption methods are examinable in this paper.

5.2.1 Example: Bases of absorption

The budgeted production overheads and other budget data of Bases Co are as follows.

Budget	Production dept X
Production overhead cost	$36,000
Direct materials cost	$32,000
Direct labour cost	$40,000
Machine hours	10,000
Direct labour hours	18,000
Units of production	

Required

Calculate the overhead absorption rate per machine hour and per labour hour for department X.

Solution

Rate per machine hour = $\dfrac{\$36,000}{10,000 \text{ hrs}}$ = $3.60 per machine hour

Rate per direct labour hour = $\dfrac{\$36,000}{18,000 \text{ hrs}}$ = $2 per direct labour hour

Question   Overhead absorption rate

(a)   If production overheads in total are expected to be $108,000 and direct labour hours are planned to be 90,000 hours costing $5 per hour, what is the overhead absorption rate per **direct labour hour**?

(b)   If production overheads in total are expected to be $720,000 and direct machine hours are planned to be 50,000 hours, what is the overhead absorption rate per **direct machine hour**?

Answer

(a) **Overhead absorption rate** = $\dfrac{\text{Expected overheads}}{\text{Planned direct labour hours}}$

$\dfrac{\$108,000}{90,000}$ = $1.20 per direct labour hour

(b) **Overhead absorption rate** = $\dfrac{\text{Expected overheads}}{\text{Planned direct machine hours}}$

$\dfrac{\$720,000}{50,000}$ = $14.40 per direct machine hour

5.3 The arbitrary nature of absorption costing

It should be obvious to you that, even if a company is trying to be 'fair', there is a great **lack of precision** about the way an absorption base is chosen.

This arbitrariness is one of the main criticisms of absorption costing, and if absorption costing is to be used then it is important that **the methods used are kept under regular review.** Changes in working conditions should, if necessary, lead to changes in the way in which work is accounted for.

For example, a **labour intensive department** may become **mechanised**. If a direct labour hour rate of absorption had been used previous to the mechanisation, it would probably now be more appropriate to change to the use of a machine hour rate.

6 Over and under absorption

ST FORWARD

Under or **over absorption** of overheads occurs because the predetermined overhead absorption rates are based on forecasts (estimates).

- If actual overheads are greater than absorbed overheads, then overheads are **under absorbed**.
- If actual overheads are less than absorbed overheads, then overheads are **over absorbed**.

6.1 Predetermined recovery rates

It was stated earlier that the usual method of accounting for overheads is to add overhead costs on the basis of a **predetermined recovery rate**. This rate is a sort of **expected cost** since it is based on figures representing what is supposed to happen (that is, figures from the budget). Using the **predetermined overhead absorption rate**, the actual cost of production can be established as follows.

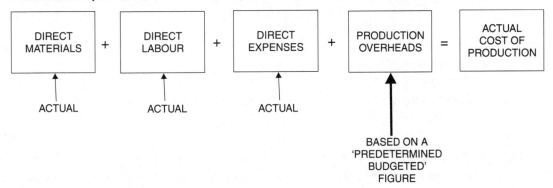

Many students become seriously confused about what can appear to be a very unusual method of costing (**actual cost** of production including a figure based on the **budget**). Study the following example. It will help to clarify this tricky point.

6.1.1 Example: Under/over absorption of overheads

The estimated overhead in a production department is $80,000 and the estimated activity is 40,000 direct labour hours. The overhead recovery rate (using a direct labour hour basis) would be $2 per direct labour hour ($80,000 ÷ 40,000 direct labour hours).

Actual overheads in the period are, say $84,000 and 45,000 direct labour hours are worked.

	$
Overhead incurred (actual)	84,000
Overhead absorbed (45,000 × $2)	90,000
Over absorption of overhead	6,000

In this example, the cost of units produced has been charged with $6,000 more than was actually spent. An adjustment to reconcile the overheads charged to the actual overhead is necessary and the over-absorbed overhead will be **written off as a credit in the income statement** at the end of the accounting period.

6.2 Under/over absorption of overheads

The discrepancy between actual overheads incurred, and the overheads absorbed is the **under absorption** or **over absorption** of overhead. This under/over absorption is an inevitable feature of absorption costing.

The overhead absorption rate is predetermined from estimates of overhead cost and the expected volume of activity. It is quite likely, therefore, that either one or both of the estimates will not agree with what actually occurs. When this happens, under or over absorption of overheads will arise.

Question	Overhead absorption

The actual total production overhead expenditure of Nuthatch Co, was $176,533. Its actual activity, and the predetermined overhead absorption rates were as follows.

	Machine shop A	Machine shop B	Assembly
Direct labour hours	8,200	6,500	21,900
Machine usage hours	7,300	18,700	–
Predetermined overhead absorption rates	$7.94 per machine hr	$3.50 per machine hr	$2.24 per direct labour hr

Required

Calculate the under or over absorption of overheads.

Answer

		$	$
Actual expenditure			176,533
Overhead absorbed			
Machine shop A	7,300 hrs × $7.94	57,962	
Machine shop B	18,700 hrs × $3.50	65,450	
Assembly	21,900 hrs × $2.24	49,056	
			172,468
Under-absorbed overhead			4,065

The following equation should help you to calculate the under/over absorption of overheads quickly and easily.

ACTUAL OVERHEADS – ABSORBED OVERHEADS = POSITIVE / NEGATIVE VALUE

- If the result is NEGATIVE (N), there is OVER ABSORPTION (O)
- If the result is POSITIVE (P), there is UNDER ABSORPTION (U)

Remember **NOPU!**

7 Non-production overheads

ST FORWARD

For **internal reporting** purposes and for organisations which base the selling prices of their products on estimates of total cost, a **total cost per unit of output** may be required.

For **external reporting** (eg statutory accounts) it is not necessary to allocate non-production overheads to products.

For **internal reporting** purposes and for organisations which base the selling price of their product on estimates of **total** cost or even actual cost (such industries usually use a job costing system), a total cost per unit of output may be required. Builders, law firms and garages often charge for their services by adding a percentage profit margin to actual cost. For product pricing purposes and for internal management reports it may therefore be appropriate to allocate non-production overheads to units of output.

7.1 Bases for apportioning

Two possible methods of allocating such non-production overheads are as follows.

(a) **Choose a basis for the overhead absorption rate** which most closely matches the non-production overhead such as direct labour hours, direct machine hours and so on.

(b) **Allocate non-production overheads on the ability of the products to bear such costs**. One possible approach is to use the production cost as the basis for allocating non-production costs to products.

The **overhead absorption rate** is calculated as follows.

$$\text{Overhead absorption rate} = \frac{\text{Estimated non-production overheads}}{\text{Estimated production costs}}$$

If, for example, budgeted distribution overheads are $200,000 and budgeted production costs are $800,000, the predetermined distribution overhead absorption rate will be 25% of production cost.

Other bases for absorbing overheads are as follows.

Types of overhead	Possible absorption base
Selling and marketing	Sales value
Research and development	Consumer cost (= production cost minus cost of direct materials) or added value (= sales value of product minus cost of bought in materials and services)
Distribution	Sales values
Administration	Consumer cost or added value

7.2 Administration overheads

The administration overhead usually consists of the following.

- Executive salaries
- Office rent and rates
- Lighting
- Heating and cleaning the offices

In cost accounting, administration overheads are regarded as periodic charges which are charged against the gross costing profit for the year (as in financial accounting).

7.3 Selling and distribution overheads

Selling and distribution overheads are often considered collectively as one type of overhead but they are actually quite different forms of expense.

(a) **Selling costs** are incurred in order to obtain sales.

(b) **Distribution costs** begin as soon as the finished goods are put into the warehouse and continue until the goods are despatched or delivered to the customer.

Selling overhead is therefore often absorbed on the basis of sales value so that the more profitable product lines take a large proportion of overhead.

Distribution overhead is more closely linked to production than sales and from one point of view could be regarded as an extra cost of production. It is, however, more usual to regard production cost as ending on the factory floor and to deal with distribution overhead separately. It is generally absorbed on a percentage of production cost but special circumstances, such as size and weight of products affecting the delivery charges, may cause a different basis of absorption to be used.

Exam focus point

> Overheads and absorption costing are examined frequently in this examination. It is vital that you are happy with the contents of this chapter as it covers one of the most important topics in the Accounting for Costs syllabus.

Chapter Roundup

- **Overhead** is part of the cost incurred in the course of making a product, providing a service or running a department, which cannot be traced directly and in full to the product, service or department.

- Absorption costing is a method of sharing overheads between a number of different products or services on a fair basis. It involves **allocation, apportionment** and **absorption**.

- The first stage of apportionment is to **identify** all overhead cost.

- The second stage of apportionment is to **reapportion service centre costs**.

- Overheads are **absorbed** into cost units using a predetermined overhead absorption rate.

- **Under** or **over absorption** of overheads occurs because the predetermined overhead absorption rates are based on forecasts (estimates).

    - If actual overheads are greater than absorbed overheads, then overheads are **under absorbed**.

    - If actual overheads are less than absorbed overheads, then overheads are **over absorbed**.

- For **internal reporting** purposes and for organisations which base the selling prices of their products on estimates of total cost, a **total cost per unit of output** may be required.

Quick Quiz

1   What is allocation?

2   Match the following overheads with the most appropriate basis of apportionment.

Overhead	Basis of apportionment
(a) Depreciation of equipment	(1) Direct machine hours
(b) Heat and light costs	(2) Number of employees
(c) Canteen	(3) Book value of equipment
(d) Insurance of equipment	(4) Floor area

3   Which of the following departments are directly involved in production?

Department	Involved in production (✓)
Finished goods warehouse	
Canteen	
Machining department	
Offices	
Assembly department	

4   In relation to calculating total absorption cost, label the following descriptions in the correct order as Steps 1 – 5.

Description	Step
A Apportion overhead costs between departments	
B Establish the overhead absorption rate	
C Choose fair methods of apportionment	
D Apply the overhead absorption rate to products	
E Reapportion service department costs	

5   How do the direct and step down methods of service cost centre apportionment differ?

6   A direct labour hour basis of overhead absorption is most appropriate in which of the following environments?

A   Machine-intensive
B   Labour-intensive
C   When all units produced are identical
D   None of the above

7   Does over absorption occur when absorbed overheads are greater than or less than actual overheads?

☐   Greater than

☐   Less than

8   Bridge Co has a budgeted production overhead of $214,981 and a budgeted activity of 35,950 hours of direct labour. Before settling on these estimates the company's accountant had a number of other possibilities for each figure, as shown below. Determine (preferably by inspection rather than full calculation) whether overheads will be over or under absorbed in each case if the alternatives turn out to be the actual figures.

Over or under absorption

(a) $\dfrac{\$215,892}{35,950}$ ☐

(b) $\dfrac{\$214,981}{36,005}$ ☐

(c) $\dfrac{\$213,894}{36,271}$ ☐

(d) $\dfrac{\$215,602}{35,440}$ ☐

Answers to Quick Quiz

1   The process whereby whole cost items are charged direct to a cost unit or cost centre.

2   (a)   (3)
     (b)   (4)
     (c)   (2)
     (d)   (3)

3

Department	Involved in production (✓)
Finished goods warehouse	
Canteen	
Machining department	✓
Offices	
Assembly department	✓

4   A   =   2
     B   =   4
     C   =   1
     D   =   5
     E   =   3

5   The **direct method** is generally used when inter-service department work is not taken into account, ie the costs of each service cost centre are apportioned to production cost centres only. The **step down method** involves the following.

- Apportioning one of the service cost centre's overheads to the cost centres using its services (production and service).

- Apportioning the overheads of the remaining service cost centre to the **production departments only.**

6   B

7   ✓   Greater than

8   **Helping hand.** You could try to answer this activity by considering how the value of a simple fraction like 4 divided by 2 would increase or decrease as the value of the denominator or numerator varied. Remember that if the actual rate is more than the estimated rate there will be under absorption and vice versa.

     (a)   Under (because actual production overheads are higher than estimated).
     (b)   Over (because actual hours are higher than estimated).
     (c)   Over (because actual production overheads are lower than estimated and actual hours are higher).
     (d)   Under (because actual hours are lower than estimated and actual hours are higher).

     Helping hand. If you find it difficult to do this by inspection, there is nothing wrong with calculating the estimated rate ($214,981 ÷ 35,950 hours = $5.98) and then the actual rate in each case ($6.00; $5.97; $5.90; $6.08), but having done this make sure that you can explain in non-numerical terms what has happened. For example, in (c) lower overheads and a higher number of active hours have led to over absorption.

Now try the questions below from the Exam Question Bank

Number	Level	Marks	Time
8	Examination	N/A	20 mins

Marginal costing and absorption costing

Chapter topic list

Study guide reference

			Syllabus reference
10	(a)	Prepare profit statements using the absorption costing method	4(b)
10	(b)	Explain and illustrate the concept of contribution	4(b)
10	(c)	Prepare profit statements using the marginal costing method	4(a)
10	(d)	Compare and contract the use of marginal costing for period profit reporting and inventory valuation	4(c)
10	(e)	Reconcile the profits reported by absorption and marginal costing	4(c)
10	(f)	Discuss the usefulness of profit and contribution information respectively	4(c)

1 Marginal costing

FAST FORWARD

Marginal costing is an alternative method of costing to absorption costing. In marginal costing, only variable costs are charged as a cost of sale and a contribution is calculated which is sales revenue minus the variable cost of sales.

1.1 Marginal cost

Key term

Marginal cost is the cost of a unit of a product or service which would be avoided if that unit were not produced or provided.

The marginal production cost per unit of an item usually consists of the following.

- Direct materials
- Direct labour
- Variable production overheads

Direct labour costs might be excluded from marginal costs when the work force is a given number of employees on a fixed wage or salary. Even so, it is not uncommon for direct labour to be treated as a variable cost, even when employees are paid a basic wage for a fixed working week. If in doubt, you should treat direct labour as a variable cost unless given clear indications to the contrary.

The **marginal cost of sales** usually consists of the marginal cost of production adjusted for inventory movements plus the variable selling costs, which would include items such as sales commission, and possibly some variable distribution costs.

1.2 Contribution

Key term

Contribution is the difference between sales value and the marginal cost of sales.

Contribution is of fundamental importance in marginal costing, and the term 'contribution' is really short for 'contribution towards covering fixed overheads and making a profit'.

2 The principles of marginal costing

2.1 Principle 1

Period fixed costs are the same for any volume of sales and production (provided that the level of activity is within the 'relevant range'). Therefore, by selling an extra item of product or service the following will happen.

- Revenue will increase by the sales value of the item sold
- Costs will increase by the variable cost per unit
- Profit will increase by the amount of contribution earned from the extra item

2.2 Principle 2

Profit measurement should be based on an analysis of total contribution. Since fixed costs relate to a period of time, and do not change with increases or decreases in sales volume, it is misleading to charge units of sale with a share of fixed costs. Absorption costing is therefore misleading, and it is more appropriate to deduct fixed costs from total contribution for the period to derive a profit figure.

2.3 Principle 3

When a unit of product is made, the **extra costs incurred in its manufacture are the variable production costs.** Fixed costs are unaffected, and no extra fixed costs are incurred when output is increased. It is therefore argued that the valuation of closing inventories should be at variable production cost (direct materials, direct labour, direct expenses (if any) and variable production overhead) because these are the only costs properly attributable to the product.

Before explaining marginal costing principles any further, it will be helpful to look at a numerical example.

2.4 Example: Marginal costing principles

Bain Painkillers Co makes a drug called 'Relief', which has a variable production cost of $6 per unit and a sales price of $10 per unit. At the beginning of June 20X1, there were no opening inventories and production during the month was 20,000 units. Fixed costs for the month were $45,000 (production, administration, sales and distribution). There were no variable marketing costs.

Required

Calculate the contribution and profit for June 20X1, using marginal costing principles, if sales were as follows.

(a) 10,000 Reliefs
(b) 15,000 Reliefs
(c) 20,000 Reliefs

Solution

The first stage in the profit calculation must be to identify the variable cost of sales, and then the contribution. Fixed costs are deducted from the total contribution to derive the profit. All closing inventories are valued at marginal production cost ($6 per unit).

	10,000 Reliefs		15,000 Reliefs		20,000 Reliefs	
	$	$	$	$	$	$
Sales (at $10)		100,000		150,000		200,000
Opening inventory	0		0		0	
Variable production cost	120,000		120,000		20,000	
	120,000		120,000		20,000	
Less value of closing inventory (at marginal cost)	60,000		30,000		-	
Variable cost of sales		60,000		90,000		120,000
Contribution		40,000		60,000		80,000
Less fixed costs		45,000		45,000		45,000
Profit/(loss)		(5,000)		15,000		35,000
Profit/(loss) per unit		$(0.50)		$1		$1.75
Contribution per unit		$4		$4		$4

The conclusions which may be drawn from this example are as follows.

(a)   The **profit per unit varies** at differing levels of sales, because the average fixed overhead cost per unit changes with the volume of output and sales.

(b)   The **contribution per unit is constant** at all levels of output and sales. Total contribution, which is the contribution per unit multiplied by the number of units sold, increases in direct proportion to the volume of sales.

(c)   Since the **contribution per unit does not change**, the most effective way of calculating the expected profit at any level of output and sales would be as follows.

(i)   First calculate the total contribution.
(ii)   Then deduct fixed costs as a period charge in order to find the profit.

(d)   In our example the expected profit from the sale of 17,000 Reliefs would be as follows.

	$
Total contribution (17,000 × $4)	68,000
Less fixed costs	45,000
Profit	23,000

2.5 Summary

(a)   If total contribution exceeds fixed costs, a profit is made.

(b)   If total contribution **exactly equals fixed costs**, no profit and no loss is made. This is known as the **breakeven point**.

(c)   If total contribution is **less than fixed costs**, there will be a loss.

Question	Marginal costing principles

Wong Co makes two products, the Ping and the Pong. Information relating to each of these products for August 20X1 is as follows.

	Ping	Pong
Opening inventory	nil	nil
Production (units)	15,000	6,000
Sales (units)	10,000	5,000
Sales price per unit	$20	$30
Unit costs	$	$
Direct materials	8	14
Direct labour	4	2

	Ping	Pong
Variable production overhead	2	1
Variable sales overhead	2	3
Fixed costs for the month	$	
Production costs	40,000	
Administration costs	15,000	
Sales and distribution costs	25,000	

Required

(a)   Using marginal costing principles, calculate the profit in August 20X1.

(b)   Calculate the profit if sales had been 15,000 units of Ping and 6,000 units of Pong.

Answer

(a)

	$
Contribution from Pings (unit production = $20 – $(8 + 4 + 2 + 2) = $4 × 10,000)	40,000
Contribution from Pongs (unit production = $30 – $(14 + 2 + 1 + 3) = $10 × 5,000)	50,000
Total contribution	90,000
Fixed costs for the period ($40,000 + $15,000 + $25,000)	80,000
Profit	10,000

(b)   At a higher volume of sales, profit would be as follows.

	$
Contribution from sales of 15,000 Pings (× $4)	60,000
Contribution from sales of 6,000 Pongs (× $10)	60,000
Total contribution	120,000
Less fixed costs	80,000
Profit	40,000

2.6 Usefulness of profit and contribution information

The main advantage of **contribution information** (rather than profit information) is that it allows an easy calculation of profit if sales increase or decrease from a certain level.

By comparing total contribution with fixed overheads, it is possible to determine whether profits or losses will be made at certain sales levels.

Profit information, on the other hand, does not lend itself to easy manipulation but note how easy it was to calculate profits using contribution information in the question above.

3 Marginal costing and absorption costing and the calculation of profit

3.1 Introduction

FAST FORWARD

In **marginal costing**, fixed production costs are treated as **period costs** and are written off as they are incurred. In **absorption costing**, fixed production costs are absorbed into the cost of units and are carried forward in inventory to be charged against sales for the next period. Inventory values using absorption costing are therefore greater than those calculated using marginal costing.

Marginal costing as a cost accounting system is significantly different from absorption costing. It is an **alternative method** of accounting for costs and profit, which rejects the principles of absorbing fixed overheads into unit costs.

Marginal costing	Absorption costing
Closing inventories are valued at marginal production cost.	Closing inventories are valued at full production cost.
Fixed costs are period costs.	Fixed costs are absorbed into unit costs.
Cost of sales does not include a share of fixed overheads.	Cost of sales does include a share of fixed overheads (see note below).

Note. The share of fixed overheads included in cost of sales are from the previous period (in opening inventory values). Some of the fixed overheads from the current period will be excluded by being carried forward in closing inventory values.

In **marginal costing**, it is necessary to identify the following.

- Variable costs
- Contribution
- Fixed costs

In **absorption costing** (sometimes known as **full costing**), it is not necessary to distinguish variable costs from fixed costs.

3.2 Example: Marginal and absorption costing compared

Look back at the information contained in the question entitled Marginal costing principles. Suppose that the budgeted production for August 20X1 was 15,000 units of Ping and 6,000 units of Pong, and production overhead is absorbed on the basis of budgeted direct labour costs.

Required

Calculate the profit if production was as budgeted, and sales were as follows.

- (a)   10,000 units of Ping and 5,000 units of Pong
- (b)   15,000 units of Ping and 6,000 units of Pong

Administration, sales and distribution costs should be charged as a period cost against profit.

Solution

Budgeted production overhead is calculated as follows.

		$
Fixed		40,000
Variable:	Pings (15,000 × $2)	30,000
	Pongs (6,000 × $1)	6,000
Total		76,000

The production overhead absorption rate would be calculated as follows.

$$\frac{\text{Budgeted production overhead}}{\text{Budgeted direct labour cost}} = \frac{\$76,000}{(15,000 \times \$4) + (6,000 \times \$2)} \times 100\%$$

$$= 105.56\% \text{ of direct labour cost}$$

(a) If sales are 10,000 units of Ping and 5,000 units of Pong, profit would be as follows.

Absorption costing

	Pings $	Pongs $	Total $
Costs of production			
Direct materials	120,000	84,000	204,000
Direct labour	60,000	12,000	72,000
Overhead (105.56% of labour)	63,333	12,667	76,000
	243,333	108,667	352,000
Less closing inventories	(1/3) 81,111	(1/6) 18,111	99,222
Production cost of sales	162,222	90,556	252,778
Administration costs			15,000
Sales and distribution costs			
Variable			35,000
Fixed			25,000
Total cost of sales			327,778
Sales	200,000	150,000	350,000
Profit			22,222

Note. There is no under/over absorption of overhead, since actual production is the same as budgeted production.

The profit derived using absorption costing techniques is different from the profit ($10,000) using marginal costing techniques at this volume of sales (see earlier question).

(b) If production and sales are exactly the same, (15,000 units of Ping and 6,000 units of Pong) profit would be $40,000.

	$
Sales (300,000 + 180,000)	480,000
Cost of sales (352,000* + 15,000 + 48,000 + 25,000)	440,000
Profit	40,000

* No closing inventory if sales and production are equal.

This is the same as the profit calculated by marginal costing techniques in the earlier question.

3.3 Marginal costing versus absorption costing

(a) In **marginal costing**, it is necessary to identify the following. ⎯⎯ Variable costs ⎯⎯ Contribution ⎯⎯ Fixed costs

(b) In **absorption costing** it is not necessary to distinguish variable costs from fixed costs.

(c) Marginal costing and absorption costing are different techniques for assessing profit in a period.

(d) If there are changes in inventories during a period, so that opening inventory volumes are different to closing inventory volumes, marginal costing and absorption costing give different results for profit obtained.

(e) If the opening and closing inventory volumes are the same, marginal costing and absorption costing will give the same profit figure. This is because the total cost of sales during the period would be the same, no matter how calculated.

3.4 The long-run effect on profit

In the long run, total profit for a company will be the same whether marginal costing or absorption costing is used. Different accounting conventions merely affect the profit of individual accounting periods.

3.4.1 Example: Comparison of total profits

To illustrate this point, let us suppose that a company makes and sells a single product. At the beginning of period 1, there are no opening inventories of the product, for which the variable production cost is $4 and the sales price $6 per unit. Fixed costs are $2,000 per period, of which $1,500 are fixed production costs.

	Period 1	Period 2
Sales	1,200 units	1,800 units
Production	1,500 units	1,500 units

Required

Determine the profit in each period using the following methods of costing.

(a)   Absorption costing. Assume normal output is 1,500 units per period.
(b)   Marginal costing.

Solution

It is important to notice that although production and sales volumes in each period are different (and therefore the profit for each period by absorption costing will be different from the profit by marginal costing), over the full period, total production equals sales volume, the total cost of sales is the same, and therefore the profit is the same by either method of accounting.

(a)   **Absorption costing**

The absorption rate for fixed production overhead is $\dfrac{\$1,500}{1,500 \text{ units}}$ = $1 per unit.

Total unit cost for inventory valuation = $4 + $1 = $5

	Period 1		Period 2		Total	
	$	$	$	$	$	$
Sales		7,200		10,800		18,000
Production costs						
Variable	6,000		6,000		12,000	
Fixed	1,500		1,500		3,000	
	7,500		7,500		15,000	
Add opening inventory b/f	–		1,500			
	7,500		9,000			
Less closing inventory c/f						
(300 × $5)	1,500		–		–	
Production cost of sales	6,000		9,000		15,000	
Other costs	500		500		1,000	
Total cost of sales		6,500		9,500		16,000
Unadjusted profit		700		1,300		2,000
(Under-)/over-absorbed overhead		–		–		–
Profit		700		1,300		2,000

(b) Marginal costing

	Period 1		Period 2		Total	
	$	$	$	$	$	$
Sales		7,200		10,800		18,000
Variable production cost	6,000		6,000		12,000	
Add opening inventory b/f	–		1,200			
	6,000		7,200			
Less closing inventory c/f						
(300 × $4)	1,200		–		–	
Variable production cost						
of sales		4,800		7,200		12,000
Contribution		2,400		3,600		6,000
Fixed costs		2,000		2,000		4,000
Profit		400		1,600		2,000

Notes

(a) The total profit over the two periods is the **same** for each method of costing, but the profit in each period is different.

(b) In absorption costing, fixed production overhead of $300 is carried forward from period 1 into period 2 in inventory values, and becomes a charge to profit in period 2. In marginal costing all fixed costs are charged in the period they are incurred, therefore the profit in period 1 is $300 lower and in period 2 is $300 higher than the absorption costing profit.

4 Reconciling the profit figures given by the two methods

ST FORWARD

Reported profit figures using marginal costing or absorption costing will **differ** if there is any **change** in the level of inventories in the period. If production is **equal** to sales, there will be **no difference** in calculated profits using these costing methods.

4.1 Introduction

The difference in profits reported under the two costing systems is due to the different inventory valuation methods used.

If inventory levels increase between the beginning and end of a period, absorption costing will report the higher profit. This is because some of the fixed production overhead incurred during the period will be carried forward in closing inventory (which reduces cost of sales) to be set against sales revenue in the following period instead of being written off in full against profit in the period concerned.

If inventory levels decrease, absorption costing will report the lower profit because as well as the fixed overhead incurred, fixed production overhead which had been carried forward in opening inventory is released and is also included in cost of sales.

4.2 Example: Reconciling profits

The profits reported under absorption costing and marginal costing for period 1 in the example in Paragraph 3.4.1 would be reconciled as follows.

	$
Marginal costing profit [($2 × 1,200) – (2,000)]	400
Adjust for fixed overhead in inventory:	
Inventory increase of 300 units × $1 per unit	300
Absorption costing profit	700

Exam focus point

If you have trouble reconciling the different profits reported under absorption costing and marginal costing, remember the following formula.

Marginal costing profit	X
Increase/(decrease) in inventory units x fixed production overhead absorption rate	Y
Absorption costing profit	Z

Question   Profit reconciliation

Reconcile the profits reported under the two systems for period 2 of the example in Paragraph 3.4.1

Answer

	$
Marginal costing profit	1,600
Adjust for fixed overhead in inventory:	
Inventory decrease of 300 units × $1 per unit	(300)
Absorption costing profit	1,300

Question   Absorption v Marginal costing

The overhead absorption rate for product X is $10 per machine hour. Each unit of product X requires five machine hours. Inventory of product X on 1.1.X1 was 150 units and on 31.12.X1 it was 100 units. What is the difference in profit between results reported using absorption costing and results reported using marginal costing?

A   The absorption costing profit would be $2,500 less
B   The absorption costing profit would be $2,500 greater
C   The absorption costing profit would be $5,000 less
D   The absorption costing profit would be $5,000 greater

Answer

A   Difference in profit = **change** in inventory levels × fixed overhead absorption rate per unit = (150 – 100) × $10 × 5 = $2,500 **lower** profit, because inventory levels **decreased**. The correct answer is therefore option A.

The key is the change in the volume of inventory. Inventory levels have **decreased** therefore absorption costing will report a **lower** profit. This eliminates options B and D.

Option C is incorrect because it is based on the closing inventory only (100 units × $10 × 5 hours).

Question

When opening inventories are 8,500 litres and closing inventories 6,750 litres, a company reported a profit of $62,100 using marginal costing.

Assuming that the fixed overhead absorption rate was $3 per litre, what would be the profit using absorption costing?

A $41,850
B $56,850
C $67,350
D $82,350

Answer

B   Difference in profit = (8,500 – 6,750) × $3 = $5,250

Absorption costing profit = $62,100 – $5,250 = $56,850

The correct answer is B.

Since inventory levels reduced, the absorption costing profit will be lower than the marginal costing profit. You can therefore eliminate options C and D.

5 Marginal costing versus absorption costing - which is better?

ST FORWARD

Absorption costing is most often used for routine profit reporting and must be used for financial accounting purposes. **Marginal costing** provides better management information for planning and decision making.

The following diagram summarises the arguments in favour of both marginal and absorption costing.

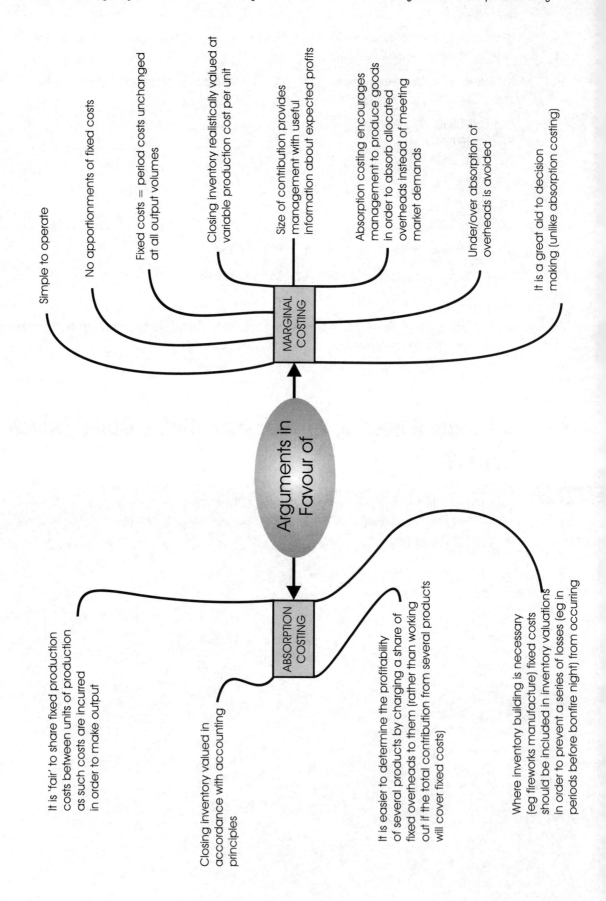

Chapter Roundup

- **Marginal costing** is an alternative method of costing to absorption costing. In marginal costing, only variable costs are charged as a cost of sale and a contribution is calculated which is sales revenue minus the variable cost of sales.

- **In marginal costing, fixed production costs are treated as period costs** and are written off as they are incurred. **In absorption costing, fixed production costs are absorbed into the cost of units** and are carried forward in inventory to be charged against sales for the next period. Inventory values using absorption costing are therefore greater than those calculated using marginal costing.

- **Reported profit figures** using marginal costing or absorption costing will **differ** if there is any change in the level of inventories in the period. If production is **equal** to sales, there will be **no difference** in calculated profits using these costing methods.

- **Absorption costing** is most often used for routine profit reporting and must be used for financial accounting purposes. **Marginal costing** provides better management information for planning and decision making.

Quick Quiz

1   What is marginal costing?

2   What is a period cost in marginal costing?

3   Sales value – marginal cost of sales = ...

4   What is a breakeven point?

5   Marginal costing and absorption costing are different techniques for assessing profit in a period. If there are changes in inventory during a period, marginal costing and absorption costing will report different profits.

  Which of the following statements are true?

  I   If inventory levels increase, marginal costing will report the higher profit.

  II   If inventory levels decrease, marginal costing will report the lower profit.

  III   If inventory levels decrease, marginal costing will report the higher profit.

  IV   If the opening and closing inventory volumes are the same, marginal costing and absorption costing will report the same profit figure.

  A   All of the above
  B   I, II and IV
  C   I and IV
  D   III and IV

6   Which of the following are arguments in favour of marginal costing? Tick as appropriate.

  ☐   (a)   Closing inventory is valued in accordance with accounting standards.

  ☐   (b)   It is simple to operate.

  ☐   (c)   There is no under or over absorption of overheads.

  ☐   (d)   Fixed costs are the same regardless of activity levels.

  ☐   (e)   The information from this costing method may be used for decision making.

Answers to Quick Quiz

1   An alternative method of costing to absorption costing. In marginal costing, a contribution is calculated (sales revenue minus the *variable* cost of sales), since only variable costs are charged as a cost of sales.

2   A fixed cost.

3   Contribution.

4   It is the point at which total contribution exactly equals fixed costs, and when no profit and no loss is made.

5   D

6   ☐ (a)

☑ (b)

☑ (c)

☑ (d)

☑ (e)

Now try the questions below from the Exam Question Bank

Number	Level	Marks	Time
Q9	Examination	N/A	30 mins

BPP
LEARNING MEDIA

Cost bookkeeping

Chapter topic list

1   Accounting for costs and ledger accounting
2   Getting costs into finished units
3   Control accounts
4   Cost bookkeeping
5   Interlocking systems: the cost ledger and financial ledger compared
6   Advantages and limitations of interlocking and integrated cost accounting systems

Study guide reference

			Syllabus reference
2	(b)	Describe the process of accounting for input costs and relating them to work done	1(c)
2	(d)	Explain the use of codes in categorising and processing transactions, and the importance of correct coding	1(c)(iii)
4	(d)	Describe and illustrate the accounting for material costs	3(a)
5	(e)	Discuss the relationship between the materials costing system and the inventory control system	3(a)(iii)
6	(e)	Describe and illustrate the accounting for labour costs	3(b)(ii)
6	(f)	Discuss the relationship between the labour costing system and the payroll accounting system	3(b)(iii)
7	(e)	Discuss the relationship between the expenses costing system and the expense accounting system	3(c)(iii)
9	(c)	Describe and illustrate the accounting for production overhead costs, including the analysis and interpretation of over/under absorption	4(b)

1 Accounting for costs and ledger accounting

> **FAST FORWARD**
>
> Cost records are a **detailed breakdown** of the information contained in the purchases account, the wages and salaries account and all the expense accounts in the nominal ledger.

1.1 Introduction

In previous chapters we have scrupulously avoided T accounts, debits and credits, ledgers and bookkeeping. The cost records we have described so far are quite adequate for individual products or jobs, and it is not essential to go beyond this.

However, unless records of **totals** are maintained and checks of these records are made, there is no way of knowing whether all the costs that should have been recorded really have been recorded. The solution to this problem is **to link the cost records to the cash and credit transactions that are summarised in the nominal ledger**. If you like you can think of accounting for costs as dealing with debits. Let us look at an example to illustrate what we mean.

1.2 Example: Cost information and ledger accounting

(a) Suppose you buy $100 of materials for cash and $100 on credit. What entries will you make in the ledgers?

(b) From the knowledge you have already acquired elsewhere you should have no difficulty in answering this question. The cash transaction will be recorded in the cash book, analysed as appropriate. It will also be recorded in the nominal ledger as follows.

		$	$
DEBIT	Purchases	100	
CREDIT	Cash		100

(c)   The credit transaction will be recorded in the purchase ledger under the name of the supplier in question. It will also be recorded in the nominal ledger as follows.

		$	$
DEBIT	Purchases	100	
CREDIT	Payables ledger control account		100

(d)   Now consider this transaction from the point of view of what you have learnt in this book. The appropriate stores ledger and bin card will have been updated to show the acquisition of $200 worth of inventory but the cash and credit side of the transactions have not entered any cost records. In other words, the cost records are only interested in the entry made in the nominal ledger under purchases.

We could go further and explain that just as the analysed cash book is a very detailed breakdown of the entries in the cash control account in the nominal ledger, and just as the payables ledger shows the detailed information behind the payables ledger control account, the cost records are a **detailed breakdown** of the information contained in the purchases account, the wages and salaries account, and all the expense accounts in the nominal ledger.

It is tempting to go no further than this. So long as you understand the basic principles of double entry bookkeeping, the cost accounting aspects of it should cause you no more difficulty than any other aspects.

All you really need to know, however, is the following.

(a)   How to turn purchases, wages and so on into finished units of production.
(b)   How to deal with under-/or over-absorbed overheads.

2 Getting costs into finished units

2.1 Introduction

In your studies for other papers you may have come across **inventory accounts**, and you may have got used to the idea that entries are only made in these accounts at the year end (the opening inventory balance is written off to the income statement and the closing inventory balance is carried forward in its place). The following layout should be very familiar.

	IS	
	$	$
Sales		3,600
Opening inventory	500	
Materials	500	
Labour	500	
Production overheads	500	
	2,000	
Closing inventory	(200)	
Cost of sales		(1,800)
Gross profit		1,800

The confusing thing here is that there are three figures that represent inventory, but only two that are bold enough to advertise the fact! The figure called **cost of sales** is, of course, inventory that has been sold.

We shall demonstrate how a single purchase of materials works through into the final accounts. The relevant double entries are:

			$	$
(a)	DEBIT	Materials	X	
	CREDIT	Cash		X

Being the buying of materials which are put into raw materials inventory

			$	$
(b)	DEBIT	Work in progress	X	
	CREDIT	Materials		X

Being the issue of materials to production for use in work in progress

			$	$
(c)	DEBIT	Finished goods	X	
	CREDIT	Work in progress		X

Being the issue of units that are now finished to finished goods inventory

			$	$
(d)	DEBIT	Cost of sales	X	
	CREDIT	Finished goods		X

Being the taking of units out of finished goods inventory and selling them

			$	$
(e)	DEBIT	Income statement	X	
	CREDIT	Cost of sales		X

Being the closing off of ledger accounts and the drawing up of financial statements

Entry (e) would only be made at the end of a period.

2.2 Example: Basic cost accounting entries

Fred Flintstone Co begins trading with $200 cash. $200 is initially spent on timber to make garden furniture. $100 worth of timber is left in store, whilst the other $100 is worked on to make garden chairs and tables. Before long, $50 worth of timber has been converted into garden furniture and this furniture is sold for $150. How will these events and transactions be reflected in the books?

Solution

CASH ACCOUNT

	$		$
Cash - opening balance	200	Purchase of materials	200
Sale of finished goods	150	Closing balance	150
	350		350

MATERIALS ACCOUNT

	$		$
Cash purchase	200	Transfer to WIP	100
		Closing balance	100
	200		200

WORK IN PROGRESS ACCOUNT

	$		$
Transfer from materials	100	Transfer to finished goods	50
		Closing balance	50
	100		100

FINISHED GOODS ACCOUNT

	$		$
Transfer from WIP	50	Transfer to cost of sales	50
	50		50

COST OF SALES ACCOUNT

	$		$
Transfer from finished goods	50	Shown in income statement	50
	50		50

SALES ACCOUNT

	$		$
Shown in income statement	150	Cash	150
	150		150

FRED FLINTSTONE CO
INCOME STATEMENT

	$
Sales	150
Cost of sales	50
Profit	100

FRED FLINTSTONE CO
BALANCE SHEET

	$	$
Cash		150
Inventories: materials	100	
WIP	50	
		150
		300
Capital: b/f		200
profit		100
		300

The principle, as you can see, is very straightforward. We have not included entries for labour costs or direct expenses to keep things simple, but these are treated in the same way. Instead of amounts being debited initially to the materials account, they would be debited to the labour costs or direct expenses accounts (with cash being credited). They would then be transferred to work in progress and the other entries would be as for materials.

2.3 Accounting for labour costs

We will use an example to briefly review the principal bookkeeping entries for wages.

The following details were extracted from a weekly payroll for 750 employees at a factory in Trinidad.

Analysis of gross pay

	Direct workers $	Indirect workers $	Total $
Ordinary time	36,000	22,000	58,000
Overtime: basic wage	8,700	5,430	14,130
premium	4,350	2,715	7,065
Shift allowance	3,465	1,830	5,295
Sick pay	950	500	1,450
Idle time	3,200	–	3,200
	56,665	32,475	89,140
Net wages paid to employees	$45,605	$24,220	$69,825

Required

Prepare the wages control account for the week.

Solution

(a)   **The wages control account** acts as a sort of **collecting place** for net wages paid and deductions made from gross pay. The gross pay is then analysed between direct and indirect wages.

(b)   The first step is to determine which wage costs are **direct** and which are **indirect**. The direct wages will be debited to the **work in progress account** and the indirect wages will be debited to the **production overhead control account**.

(c)   There are in fact only two items of direct wages cost in this example, the ordinary time ($36,000) and the basic overtime wage ($8,700) paid to direct workers. All other payments (including the overtime premium) are indirect wages.

(d)   The net wages paid are debited to the control account, and the balance then represents the deductions which have been made for income tax, national insurance, and so on.

WAGES CONTROL ACCOUNT

	$		$
Bank: net wages paid	69,825	Work in progress - direct labour	44,700
Deductions control accounts*		Production overhead control:	
($89,140 – $69,825)	19,315	Indirect labour	27,430
		Overtime premium	7,065
		Shift allowance	5,295
		Sick pay	1,450
		Idle time	3,200
	89,140		89,140

* In practice there would be a separate deductions control account for each type of deduction made (for example, PAYE and National Insurance).

3 Control accounts

FAST FORWARD

A **control account** is an account which records total cost, unlike an individual ledger account which records individual debits and credits.

3.1 Introduction

Key term

> A **control account** is an account which records total cost. In contrast, individual ledger accounts record individual debits and credits.

Obviously the previous section is highly simplified. This is to avoid obscuring the basic principles. For example, we have until now assumed that if $200 of materials are purchased the only entries made will be Dr Materials, Cr Cash. In practice, of course, this $200 might be made up of 20 different types of material, each costing $10, and if so each type of material is likely to have its own sub-account. These sub-accounts would be exactly like individual personal accounts in the payables' ledger or the receivables' ledger. You have probably guessed that we need to use **control accounts** to summarise the detailed transactions (such as how the $200 of materials is made up) and to maintain the double entry in the nominal ledger.

terms

- A **materials control account** (or **stores control account**) records the total cost of invoices received for each type of material (purchases) and the total cost of each type of material issued to various departments (the sum of the value of all materials requisition notes).

- A **wages control account** records the total cost of the payroll (plus employer's national insurance contributions) and the total cost of direct and indirect labour as recorded in the wages analysis sheets and charged to each production job or process.

- A **production overhead control account** is a total record of actual expenditure incurred and the amount absorbed into individual units, jobs or processes. Subsidiary records for actual overhead expenditure items and cost records which show the overheads attributed to individual units or jobs must agree with or reconcile to the totals in the control account.

- A **work in progress control account** records the total costs of direct materials, direct wages and production overheads charged to units, jobs or processes, and the cost of finished goods which are completed and transferred to the distribution department. Subsidiary records of individual job costs and so on will exist for jobs still in production and for jobs completed.

The precise level of detail depends entirely upon the individual organisation. For example an organisation that makes different products might want a hierarchy of materials accounts as follows.

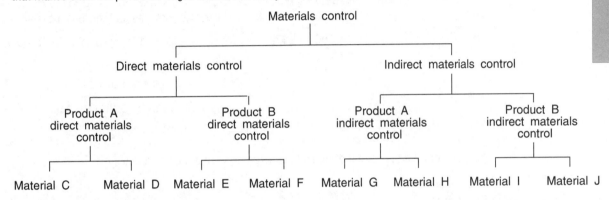

3.2 Coding

Each account in use needs to be classified by the use of coding. A suggested computer-based four-digit numerical coding account system is set out as follows.

Basic structure		Code number	Allocation
(a)	First division	1000 – 4999	This range provides for cost accounts and is divided into four main departmental sections with ten cost centre subsections in each department, allowing for a maximum of 99 accounts in each cost centre
	Second division	1000 – 1999	Departments 1 to 4
		2000 – 2999	
		3000 – 3999	
		4000 – 4999	
	Third division	000 – 099	Facility for ten cost centres in each department
		100 – 199	
		200 – 299	
		and so on	

Basic structure		Code number	Allocation
	Fourth division		Breakdown of costs in each cost centre
		01 – 39	direct costs
		40 – 79	indirect costs
		80 – 99	spare capacity
(b)		5000 – 5999	This range provides for the following.
			(i) Revenue accounts
			(ii) Work in progress accounts
			(iii) Finished goods accounts
			(iv) Cost of sales accounts
			(v) General expenses accounts
			(vi) Income statement
(c)		6000 – 6999	This range provides for individual stores items
(d)		7000 – 7999	This range provides for individual receivable accounts
(e)		8000 – 8999	This range provides for individual payable accounts
(f)		9000 – 9999	This range is used for balance sheet accounts including the following.
			(i) Stores control account
			(ii) Receivables' control account
			(iii) Payables' control account

An illustration of the coding of direct labour (grade T) might be as follows.

Department 2

Cost centre	1	2	3	4
Direct labour (grade T)	2009	2109	2209	2309

The four digit code is explained as follows.

    (a)   The first digit, 2, refers to department 2.
    (b)   The second digit 0, 1, 2 or 3 refers to the cost centre which incurred the cost.
    (c)   The last two digits, 09, refer to 'direct labour costs, grade T'.

Obviously systems that you come across in practice will exhibit different features. The above describes only broad characteristics that are likely to be typical of all such systems.

Question   **Stores Ledger Control**

The following data relate to the stores ledger control account of Fresh Co, an air freshener manufacturer, for the month of April 20X2.

	$
Opening inventory	18,500
Closing inventory	16,100
Deliveries from suppliers	142,000
Returns to suppliers	2,300
Cost of indirect materials issued	25,200

Required

(a)   Calculate the value of the issue of direct materials during April 20X2.
(b)   State the double entry to record the issue of direct materials in the cost accounts.

Answer

(a)   Since we are given no information on the issue of direct materials we need to construct a stores ledger control account.

STORES LEDGER CONTROL ACCOUNT

	$		$
Balance b/f	18,500	Payables/cash (returns)	2,300
Payables/cash	142,000	Overhead accounts	25,200
		WIP (balancing figure)	116,900
		Balance c/f	16,100
	160,500		160,500

The value of the issue of direct materials during April 20X2 was $116,900.

(b)   The issue of direct materials would therefore be recorded as follows.

DR	WIP control account	$116,900
CR	Stores ledger control account	$116,900

4 Cost bookkeeping systems

FAST FORWARD

There are two main cost bookkeeping systems, **interlocking systems** and **integrated systems.**

4.1 Introduction

There are two types of cost bookkeeping system, the **interlocking** and **integrated.** The main difference between the two systems is that interlocking systems require separate ledgers to be kept for the cost accounting function and the financial accounting function, which means that the cost accounting profit and financial accounting profit have to be reconciled. Integrated systems, on the other hand, combine the two functions in one set of ledger accounts.

Modern cost accounting systems (computerised) integrate cost accounting information and financial accounting information and are known as **integrated systems.** You are much more likely to deal with integrated systems in practice.

4.2 Dealing with overheads

We have already mentioned that the bookkeeping entries for overheads are not as straight forward as those for materials, labour and expenses. We shall now consider the way in which overheads are dealt with in a cost accounting system.

When an absorption costing system is in use we now know that the amount of overhead included in the cost of an item is absorbed at a predetermined rate. The entries made in the cash book and the nominal ledger, however, are the actual amounts.

As we saw in an earlier chapter, it is highly unlikely that the actual amount and the predetermined amount will be the same. The difference is called **under- or over-absorbed overhead**. To deal with this in the cost accounting books, therefore, we need to have an account to collect under- or over-absorbed amounts for each type of overhead.

4.3 Example: the under-/over-absorbed overhead account

Gnocci Co absorbs production overheads at the rate of $0.50 per operating hour and administration overheads at 20% of the production cost of sales. Actual data for one month was as follows.

Administration overheads	$32,000
Production overheads	$46,500
Operating hours	90,000
Production cost of sales	$180,000

What entries need to be made for overheads in the ledgers?

Solution

	Dr	Cr
	$	$
	Production overheads	
Cash	46,500	
Absorbed into WIP (90,000 × $0.50)		45,000
Under-absorbed overhead		1,500
	46,500	46,500
	Administration overheads	
Cash	32,000	
To cost of sales (180,000 × 0.2)		36,000
Over-absorbed overhead	4,000	
	36,000	36,000
	Under-/over-absorbed overhead	
Production overhead	1,500	
Administration overhead		4,000
Balance to income statement	2,500	
	4,000	4,000

Less production overhead has been absorbed than has been spent so there is under-absorbed overhead of $1,500. More administration overhead has been absorbed (into cost of sales, note, not into WIP) and so there is over-absorbed overhead of $4,000. The net over-absorbed overhead of $2,500 is a credit in the income statement.

4.4 Interlocking systems

An **interlocking system** is a cost bookkeeping system where separate ledger accounts are kept for both the cost accounting function and the financial accounting function. Such a system necessitates the reconciliation of the profits produced by the separate income statements. The cost accounts use the same basic data (purchases, wages and so on) as the financial accounts, but frequently adopt different bases for matters such as depreciation and inventory valuation.

The principal accounts in a system of interlocking accounts

(a)   The resources accounts

- Materials control account or stores control account
- Wages (and salaries) control account
- Production overhead control account
- Administration overhead control account
- Selling and distribution overhead control account

(b)   Accounts which record the cost of production items from the start of production work through to cost of sales

- Work in progress control account
- Finished goods control account
- Cost of sales control account

(c)   Sales account

(d)   The costing income statement

(e)   The under-/ over-absorbed overhead account

(f)   Cost ledger control account (in the cost ledger)

(g)   Financial ledger control account (in the financial ledger)

4.4.1 How an interlocking system works

An **interlocking system** features two ledgers.

(a)   The **financial ledger** contains asset, liability, revenue, expense and appropriation (eg dividend) accounts. The trial balance of an enterprise is prepared from the financial ledger.

(b)   The **cost ledger** is where cost information such as the build-up of work in progress is analysed in more detail.

4.4.2 The cost ledger control account

There are certain items of cost or revenue which are of no interest to the cost accountant because they are **financial accounting items**. These include the following.

- Interest or dividends received
- Dividends paid
- Discounts allowed or received for prompt payment of invoices

Some financial accounting items are related to costs and profits such as:

- Cash
- Creditors
- Debtors
- Revenue reserves

The items listed are *not* included in the separate cost accounting books, but are held in a **cost ledger control account.**

The **financial ledger control account** is a sort of 'dustbin' account which is used to keep the double entry system working.

4.5 Accounting entries in a system of cost ledger accounts

The accounting entries in a system of cost ledger accounts can be confusing and it is important to keep in mind some general principles. The following points have already been made in this chapter.

(a)   When **expenditure** is incurred on materials, wages or overheads, the actual amounts paid or payable are debited to the appropriate resources accounts. The credit entries (which in a financial accounting ledger would be in the cash or creditors accounts) are in the cost ledger control account.

(b)   When production begins, **resources are allocated to work in progress**. This is recorded by crediting the resources accounts and debiting the work in progress account. In the case of production overheads, the amount credited to the overhead account and debited to work in progress should be the amount of overhead absorbed. If this differs from the amount of overhead incurred, there will be a difference on the overhead control account; this should be written off to an 'under-/over-absorbed overhead' account. (One other point to remember is that when indirect materials and labour are allocated to production, the entries are to credit the materials and wages accounts and debit production overhead account.)

(c) As **finished goods** are produced, work in progress is reduced. This is recorded by debiting the finished goods control account and crediting the work in progress control account.

(d) To establish the **cost of goods sold**, the balances on finished goods control account, administration overhead control account and selling and distribution overhead control account are transferred to cost of sales control account. For a company with a full absorption costing system, the transfers from administration overhead and selling and distribution overhead accounts would be the amounts absorbed, rather than the amounts incurred. Any difference would again be written off to an 'under-/over-absorbed overhead' account.

(e) **Sales** are debited to the cost ledger control account and credited to sales account.

(f) **Profit** is established by transferring to the cost income statement the balances on sales account, cost of sales account and under-/over-absorbed overhead accounts.

4.6 Accounting entries in absorption costing and marginal costing systems

The principles outlined above are illustrated for absorption costing and marginal costing systems in the diagrams on the following pages.

The following points should be noted:

(a) In both diagrams the direct and indirect materials figures, and the direct and indirect labour figures, are extracted from the materials and wages analyses respectively.

(b) In the diagram of an absorption costing system, the debit in respect of overheads to the WIP account is the absorbed overheads and is found by multiplying the total units of the basis for absorption (labour hours, machines hours and so on) for the period by the overhead absorption rate. For example, if 10,000 direct labour hours were booked to cost units and the overhead absorption rate was $2 per direct labour hour, then $20,000 would be debited to the WIP account for overheads.

(c) In the diagram of the marginal costing system, only the variable overheads are debited to the WIP account. Fixed overheads are debited direct to the costing income statement.

(d) The final balance on the overhead account of the absorption costing system is the under- or over-absorbed overhead. There will be no such balance under a marginal costing system.

(e) The closing balances on the WIP and finished goods accounts under absorption costing will be at absorbed cost, but will be at marginal cost under marginal costing.

(f) Our diagrams are highly simplified versions of the full set of cost accounts used in practice.

Cost bookkeeping using absorption costing

Cost bookkeeping using marginal costing

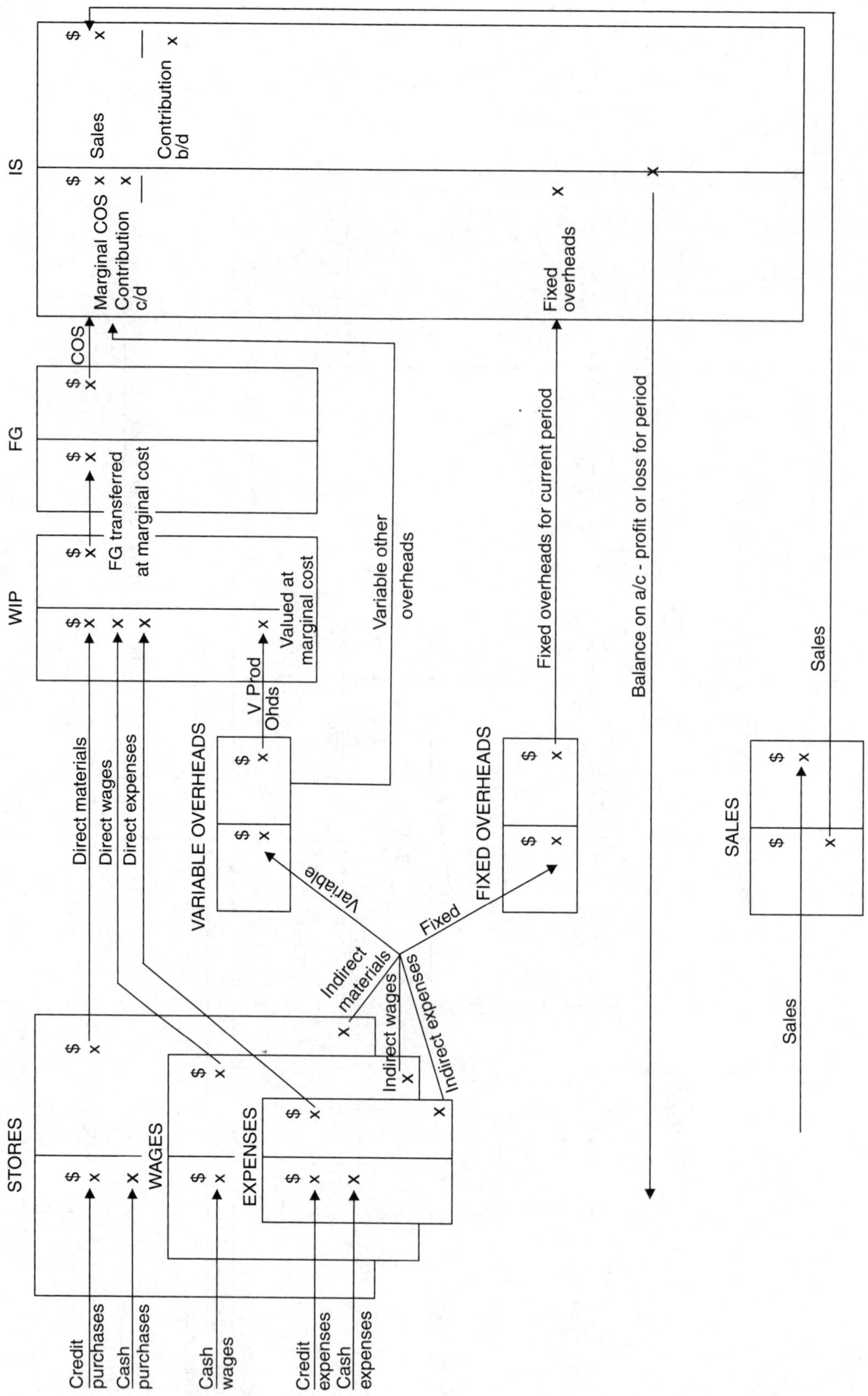

4.7 Example: interlocking accounts

Write up the cost ledger accounts of a manufacturing company for the latest accounting period. The following data is relevant.

(a)   There is no inventory on hand at the beginning of the period.

(b)   Details of the transactions for the period received from the financial accounts department include the following.

	$
Sales	420,000
Indirect wages:	
production	25,000
administration	15,000
sales and distribution	20,000
Materials purchased	101,000
Direct factory wages	153,200
Production overheads	46,500
Selling and distribution expenses	39,500
Administration expenses	32,000

(c)   Other cost data for the period includes the following.

Stores issued to production as indirect materials	$15,000
Stores issued to production as direct materials	$77,000
Cost of finished production	$270,200
Cost of goods sold at finished goods inventory valuation	$267,700
Standard rate of production overhead absorption	50c per operating hour
Rate of administration overhead absorption	20% of production cost of sales
Rate of sales and distribution overhead absorption	10% of sales revenue
Actual operating hours worked	160,000

Solution

The problem should be tackled methodically. The letters in brackets show the sequence in which the various entries are made. Any entries without a letter are merely transfers of closing balances.

COST LEDGER CONTROL (CLC)

	$		$
Sales (a)	420,000	Wages control (b)	213,200
Balance c/d	51,500	Materials control (c)	101,000
		Prod'n o'hd control (d)	46,500
		S & D o'hd control (e)	39,500
		Admin o'hd control (f)	32,000
		Cost income statement	39,300
	471,500		471,500
		Balance b/d	51,500

MATERIALS CONTROL

	$		$
CLC (c) - purchases	101,000	Prod'n o'hd control (k)(indirect materials)	15,000
		WIP control (l)(issues to production)	77,000
		∴Closing inventory c/d (balancing item)	9,000
	101,000		101,000
Closing inventory b/d	9,000		

WAGES CONTROL

	$		$
CLC (b)	213,200	Prod'n o'hd control (g)	25,000
		Admin o'hd control (h)	15,000
		S & D o'hd control (j)	20,000
		WIP control (m)(direct labour)	153,200
	213,200		213,200

PRODUCTION OVERHEAD CONTROL

	$		$
CLC (d)	46,500	WIP control (p)(160,000 × 50p)	
Wages control (g)	25,000	(overheads absorbed)	80,000
Materials control (k)	15,000	∴ O'hds under-absorbed	6,500
	86,500		86,500

ADMINISTRATION OVERHEAD CONTROL

	$		$
CLC (f)	32,000	Cost of sales control (q)	
Wages control (h)	15,000	(20% × $267,700)	53,540
∴ O'hds over-absorbed	6,540		
	53,540		53,540

SELLING AND DISTRIBUTION OVERHEAD CONTROL

	$		$
CLC (e)	39,500	Cost of sales control (r)(o/hds	
Wages control (j)	20,000	absorbed) (10% × $420,000)	42,000
		∴ O'hds under-absorbed	17,500
	59,500		59,500

WORK IN PROGRESS CONTROL

	$		$
Materials control (l)	77,000	Finished goods control (n)	270,200
Wages control (m)	153,200	(transfer of finished production)	
Prod'n o'hd control (p)	80,000	∴ Closing inventory of WIP c/d	40,000
	310,200		310,200
Balance b/d	40,000		

FINISHED GOODS CONTROL

	$		$
WIP control (n)	270,200	Cost of sales control (o)	267,700
		∴ Inventory of finished goods c/d	2,500
	270,200		270,200
Balance b/d	2,500		

COST OF SALES CONTROL

	$		$
Finished goods control (o)	267,700	Cost income statement	363,240
Admin o'hd control (q)	53,540		
S & D o'hd control (r)	42,000		
	363,240		363,240

SALES

	$		$
Cost income statement	420,000	CLC (a)	420,000

UNDER-/OVER-ABSORBED OVERHEAD

	$		$
Prod'n o'hd control	6,500	Admin o'hd control	6,540
S & D o'hd control	17,500	∴ Cost income statement	17,460
	24,000		24,000

COST INCOME STATEMENT

	$		$
Cost of sales control	363,240	Sales	420,000
Under-/over-absorbed o'hd	17,460		
CLC (profit for period)	39,300		
	420,000		420,000

Note how the trial balance can be extracted from the accounts.

TRIAL BALANCE

	Debit $	Credit $
Cost ledger control		51,500
Materials inventory	9,000	
Work in progress	40,000	
Finished goods inventories	2,500	
	51,500	51,500

5 Interlocking systems: the cost ledger and financial ledger compared

With interlocking systems, the cost accounting profit will not be the same as the financial accounting profit; these two profit figures need to be reconciled.

5.1 Introduction

If separate cost accounts and financial accounts are maintained, the cost profit will not be the same as the financial profit. This is because different income statements are prepared. Cost profit and financial profit will therefore need to be reconciled.

5.2 Items creating differences

Some examples of items creating differences between the cost accounting and financial accounting profits are listed as follows.

(a) **Items appearing in the financial accounts, but not in the cost accounts.**

    (i) Items of income which boost the financial accounts profit, but are excluded from the cost accounts.

- Interest or dividends received
- Discounts received (for early settlement of debts)
- Profits on disposal of non-current assets

    (ii) Items of expenditure which reduce the financial accounts profit, but which are excluded from the cost accounts.

- Interest paid
- Discounts allowed (for early settlement of debt)
- Losses on disposal of non-current assets
- Losses on investments
- Fines and penalties

    (iii) Appropriations of profit in the financial income statement.

- Donations
- Income tax
- Dividends paid and proposed
- Transfers to reserves
- Write-offs of goodwill, investments and other assets

(b) **Items appearing in the cost accounts, but not in the financial accounts** are infrequent, but usually relate to notional costs. These are charges made in the cost accounts in order to give a more realistic picture of the cost of an activity. There are two main types of notional cost.

    (i) **Interest on capital**. This represents the nominal cost of capital tied up in production and accounts for the cost of using the capital internally rather than investing it outside the business. The cost accountant makes the charge so that managers are fully aware of the true cost, for example, of holding inventories in the production process. The charge can also help to make the cost of items made with expensive capital equipment more comparable to the cost of items which are not.

    (ii) **Nominal rent charge**. This is a nominal charge raised for the use of premises which are owned. This enables a comparison to be made between the cost of production in a factory which is owned and the costs in one which is rented. The nominal rent charge makes managers more aware of the true cost of occupying the premises.

(c) **Differences may arise between the financial and cost accounts in the calculation of actual overhead costs incurred**. For example if the cost accounting books contain a provision for depreciation account, differences may arise in the choice of depreciation method (for example straight line method, reducing balance method, and so on) or in the expected life of the equipment.

(d) **Valuation of inventory on hand is likely to be made according to different bases for the respective accounts.** For the financial accounts the basis of **inventory** valuation will be the lower of FIFO or weighted average cost and net realisable value. For the cost accounts, the basis of **inventory** valuation might be any one of the following.

- LIFO cost
- FIFO cost
- Weighted average cost
- Standard cost
- Replacement cost

There will also be valuation differences if the cost accounts are based on the marginal costing method.

5.3 Differences in inventory valuations

Differences in inventory valuations should be studied carefully. Suppose the financial accounting profit of a company is $10,000, and that the only differences between the financial books and the cost books are the following inventory valuations.

	Financial accounts $	Cost accounts $
Opening inventory of WIP	4,000	5,000
Closing inventory of WIP	6,000	7,500
Opening inventory of finished goods	12,000	10,000
Closing inventory of finished goods	9,000	8,500

Opening and closing inventory value differences will affect profit, and it may be helpful to use the format of a trading account to work out what the effect of a difference is. Consider the following trading account.

TRADING ACCOUNT

	$		$
Opening inventory	10	Sales	100
Purchases	80	Closing inventory	20
	90		
Gross profit (balancing figure)	30		
	120		120

This account shows the following.

(a) A higher figure for opening inventory reduces profit.
(b) A higher figure for closing inventory increases profit.

If you are not sure about this point, re-calculate the profit in the following circumstances.

(a) Opening inventory is higher, say $15.
(b) Closing inventory is higher, say $30.
(c) Opening inventory is lower, say $8.
(d) Closing inventory is lower, say $16.

The resulting profits, all other items on the account being unchanged, would be $25 (lower), $40 (higher), $32 (higher) and $26 (lower) for (a), (b), (c) and (d) respectively.

Let us go back to our example above.

(a) Opening inventory of WIP: the cost accounts profit will be $1,000 less than the financial accounts profit (because the valuation is $1,000 higher).

(b) Closing inventory of WIP: the cost accounts profit will be $1,500 higher.

(c) Opening inventory of finished goods: the cost accounts profit will be $2,000 higher.

(d) Closing inventory of finished goods: the cost accounts profit will be $500 lower.

6 Advantages and limitations of interlocking and integrated cost accounting systems

6.1 Interlocking systems

The main advantages of interlocking systems is that they feature two ledgers, each of which fulfil different purposes. Having two sets of ledgers means that it is less likely that any conflict of needs will arise. This contrasts with integrated accounts, where one ledger is expected to fulfil two different purposes, and there may be conflicts between financial and cost accounting purposes, for example over valuation of inventory.

The main limitations of interlocking systems are as follows.

- Profits of separate cost and financial accounts must be reconciled
- They require more administration time
- They are more costly to run

6.2 Integrated systems

The main **advantage** of integrated systems is the saving in administration time and costs. This is because only one set of accounts needs to be maintained instead of two. There is also no need to reconcile the profits of the separate cost and financial accounts.

The main limitation of integrated accounts is that one set of accounts is expected to fulfil two different purposes, the cost accounts provide internal management information and the financial accounts are used for external reporting. At times external reporting and internal management information may conflict. For example, for external reporting, inventories will be valued in accordance with accounting standards. Cost accountants may however prefer to value inventories at marginal cost. It is clear therefore that in some circumstances it is more advantageous to have two separate systems.

Exam focus point

> The bookkeeping treatment of over-absorbed production overhead in the cost accounting ledger was examined in the Accounting for Costs pilot paper. Do you know what the correct treatment is?

Chapter Roundup

- Cost records are a **detailed breakdown** of the information contained in the purchases account, the wages and salaries account and all the expense accounts in the nominal ledger.

- A **control account** is an account which records total cost, unlike an individual ledger account which records individual debits and credits.

- There are two main cost bookkeeping systems, **interlocking systems** and **integrated systems.**

- With interlocking systems, the cost accounting profit will not be the same as the financial accounting profit; these two profit figures need to be reconciled.

Quick Quiz

1 What is a control account?

2 What are the two types of cost bookkeeping system?

3 Where are direct expenses and overheads collected?

4 List four financial accounting items which are of interest to the cost accountant.

5 Where are the items referred to in 4 held?

6 Are profits increased or reduced if the opening inventory figure is greater than the closing inventory figure?

7 What are the main limitations of interlocking systems?

Answers to Quick Quiz

1 An account which records total cost, as opposed to individual costs (which are recorded in individual ledger accounts).

2 Integrated and interlocking.

3 In the work in progress control account.

4 • Cash
  • Payables
  • Receivables
  • Revenue reserves

5 In the cost ledger control account.

6 Reduced.

7 • Profits of separate cost and financial accounts must be reconciled
  • They require more administration time
  • They are more costly to run

Now try the questions below from the Exam Question Bank

Number	Level	Marks	Time
Q10	Examination	N/A	30 mins

Part C
Product and service costs

11

Job, batch and service costing

Chapter topic list

Study guide reference

			Syllabus reference
2	(b)	Describe the process of accounting for input costs and relating them to work done	1(c)
2	(c)	Identify the documentation required, and the flow of documentation, for different cost accounting transactions	1(c)
2	(f)	Describe the different methods of costing final outputs and their appropriateness to different types of business organisation	1(c)
11	(a)	Describe the characteristics of job and batch costing respectively	5(a)
11	(b)	identify situations where the use of job or batch costing is appropriate	5(b)
11	(c)	Calculate unit costs using job and batch costing	5(b)
11	(d)	Discuss the control of costs in job and batch costing	5(b)
11	(e)	Apply cost plus pricing in job costing	5(b)
15	(a)	Describe the characteristics of service costing	5(c)
15	(b)	Describe the practical problems relating to the costing of services	5(c)
15	(c)	Identify situations (cost centres and industries) where the use of service costing is appropriate	5(c)
15	(d)	Illustrate suitable cost units that may be used for a variety of services	5(c)
15	(e)	Calculate service unit costs in a variety of situations	5(c)

1 Job costing

FAST FORWARD

Job costing is the costing method used where each cost unit is separately identifiable.

1.1 Introduction

In this chapter we will be looking at four important costing systems.

- Job costing
- Batch costing
- Unit costing
- Service costing

In the next chapter we will be looking at another important system, that of **process costing**.

Key term

> A **costing system** is a system of collecting costs which is designed to suit the way that goods are processed or manufactured or the way that services are provided.

Each organisation's costing system will have unique features but **costing systems of organisation's in the same line of business will have common aspects.** On the other hand, organisations involved in completely different activities, such as hospitals and car part manufacturers, will each use very different costing systems.

1.2 Aim of job costing

The aim of **job costing** is simply to collect the cost information shown below.

	$
Direct materials	X
Direct labour	X
Direct expenses	X
Direct cost	X
Production overhead	X
Total production cost	X
Administration overhead	X
Selling overhead	X
Cost of sales	X

To the final figure is added a profit **'mark-up'** and the total is the selling price of the job.

In other words, all we are doing is looking at one way of putting together the pieces of information that we have studied separately so far.

1.3 What is a job?

A **job** is a cost unit which consists of a single order or contract.

With other methods of costing it is usual to **produce for inventory**. Management therefore decide in advance how many units of each type, size, colour, quality and so on will be produced during the coming period. These decisions will all be taken without taking into account the identity of the individual customers who will eventually buy the products.

In job costing on the other hand, production is usually carried out in accordance with the **special requirements** of each customer. It is therefore usual for each job to **differ in one or more respects from every other job**, which means that a separate record must be maintained to show the details of a particular job.

The work relating to a job is usually carried out within a factory or workshop and moves through processes and operations as a **continuously identifiable unit**.

1.4 Procedure for the performance of jobs

The normal procedure in jobbing concerns involves the following.

(a) The prospective customer approaches the supplier and indicates the **requirements** of the job.

(b) A responsible official sees the prospective customer and agrees the **precise details of the items** to be supplied, for example the quantity, quality and colour of the goods, the date of delivery and any special requirements.

(c) The estimating department of the organisation then prepares an **estimate** for the job. The total of these items will represent the **quoted selling price**.

(d) At the appropriate time, the job will be **'loaded'** on to the factory floor. This means that as soon as all materials, labour and equipment are available and subject to the scheduling of other orders, the job will be started.

1.5 Collection of job costs

Each job will be given a **number** to identify it. A separate record must be maintained to show the details of individual jobs. The process of collecting job costs may be outlined as follows.

(a)   Materials requisitions are sent to stores.

(b)   The materials requisition note will be used to cost the materials issued to the job concerned, and this cost may then be recorded on a job cost sheet.

(c)   The job ticket is passed to the worker who is to perform the first operation.

(d)   When the job is completed by the worker who performs the final operation, the job ticket is sent to the cost office, where the time spent will be costed and recorded on the job cost sheet.

(e)   The relevant costs of materials issued, direct labour performed and direct expenses incurred as recorded on the job cost sheet are charged to the job account in the work in progress ledger.

(f)   The job account is debited with the job's share of the factory overhead, based on the absorption rate(s) in operation.

(g)   On completion of the job, the job account is charged with the appropriate administration, selling and distribution overhead, after which the total cost of the job can be ascertained.

(h)   The difference between the agreed selling price and the total actual cost will be the supplier's profit (or loss).

1.6 Job account

Here is a proforma job account, which will be one of the accounts in the work in progress control account.

JOB ACCOUNT

	$		$
Materials issued	X	Finished jobs	X
Direct labour	X		
Direct expenses	X		
Production overhead at predetermined rate	X		
Other overheads	X		
	X		X

1.7 Job cost sheet (or card)

When jobs are completed, **job cost sheets** are transferred from the **work in progress** category to **finished goods**. When delivery is made to the customer, the costs become a **cost of sale**.

1.7.1 Example: Job cost sheet

| JOB COST CARD | | | | | | | | | | | | Job No. | B641 | | |

Customer Mr J White **Customer's Order No.** **Vehicle make** Peugot 205 GTE

Job Description Repair damage to offside front door **Vehicle reg. no.** G 614 SOX

Estimate Ref. 2599 **Invoice No.**

Quoted price $338.68 **Invoice price** $355.05 **Date to collect** 14.6.X0

Material						Labour								Overheads			
Date	Req. No.	Qty.	Price	Cost $	Cost p	Date	Emp-loyee	Cost Ctre	Hrs.	Rate	Bonus	Cost $	Cost p	Hrs	OAR	Cost $	Cost p
12.6	36815	1	75.49	75	49	12.6	018	B	1.98	6.50	-	12	87	7.9	2.50	19	75
12.6	36816	1	33.19	33	19	13.6	018	B	5.92	6.50	-	38	48				
12.6	36842	5	6.01	30	05						13.65	13	65				
13.6	36881	5	3.99	19	95												
Total C/F				158	68	Total C/F						65	00	Total C/F		19	75

Expenses					Job Cost Summary	Actual		Estimate	
						$	p	$	p
Date	Ref.	Description	Cost $	Cost p	Direct Materials B/F	158	68	158	68
					Direct Expenses B/F	50	00		
					Direct Labour B/F	65	00	180	00
12.6	-	N. Jolley Panel-beating	50	-	Direct Cost	273	68		
					Overheads B/F	19	75		
						293	43		
					Admin overhead (add 10%)	29	34		
					= Total Cost	322	77	338	68
					Invoice Price	355	05		
Total C/F			50	-	Job Profit/Loss	32	28		

Comments

Job Cost Card Completed by _____

1.8 Job costing and computerisation

Job cost cards exist in **manual** systems, but it is increasingly likely that in large organisations the job costing system will be **computerised**, using accounting software specifically designed to deal with job costing requirements.

Job costing systems may also be used to control the costs of **internal service departments**, eg the maintenance department.

1.9 Example: Job costing

Pansy Co is a company that carries out jobbing work. One of the jobs carried out in May was job 2409, to which the following information relates.

Direct material Y:	400 kilos were issued from stores at a cost of $5 per kilo.
Direct material Z:	800 kilos were issued from stores at a cost of $6 per kilo. 60 kilos were returned to stores.
Department P:	300 labour hours were worked, of which 100 hours were overtime.
Department Q:	200 labour hours were worked, of which 100 hours were overtime.

Overtime work is not normal in Department P, where basic pay is $6 per hour plus an overtime premium of $1 per hour. Overtime work was done in Department Q in May because of a request by the customer of another job to complete his job quickly. Basic pay in Department Q is $8 per hour and overtime premium is $1.50 per hour. Overhead is absorbed at the rate of $3 per direct labour hour in both departments.

Required

(a)   Calculate the direct materials cost of job 2409
(b)   Calculate the direct labour cost of job 2409
(c)   Calculate the full production cost of job 2409 using absorption costing

Solution

(a)

	$
Direct material Y (400 kilos × $5)	2,000
Direct material Z (800 – 60 kilos × $6)	4,440
Total direct material cost	6,440

(b)

	$
Department P (300 hours × $6)	1,800
Department Q (200 hours × $8)	1,600
Total direct labour cost	3,400

Overtime premium will be charged to overhead in the case of Department P, and to the job of the customer who asked for overtime to be worked in the case of Department Q.

(c)

	$
Direct material cost	6,440
Direct labour cost	3,400
Production overhead (500 hours × $3)	1,500
	11,340

1.10 Cost plus pricing

Many organisations base the price of a product on simple **cost plus** rules which involves estimating costs and then adding a profit margin in order to set the price.

Key term

> **Cost plus pricing** is a method of determining the sales price by calculating the full cost of a product and adding a percentage mark-up for profit.

The full cost may be a fully absorbed production cost only, or it may include some absorbed administration, selling and distribution overhead (non-production overheads).

1.11 Example: Cost plus pricing

A company budgets to make 20,000 units which have a variable cost of production of $4 per unit. Fixed production costs are $60,000 per annum. The selling price is to be 40% higher than full cost.

Required

Calculate the selling price of the product using the cost plus pricing method.

Solution

Full cost per unit = variable cost + fixed cost

Variable cost = $4 per unit

Fixed cost = $\dfrac{\$60,000}{20,000}$ = $3 per unit

Full cost per unit   = $4 + $3
                  = $7

∴ Selling price   = $\dfrac{140}{100} \times \$7$
                  = $9.80

Exam focus point

An exam question about job costing may ask you to accumulate costs to arrive at a job cost, and then to determine a job price by adding a certain amount of profit. To do this, you need to remember the following crucial formula.

	%
Cost of job	100
+ profit	25
= price	125

Profit may be expressed either as a percentage of job cost (such as 25% 25/100 mark up) or as a percentage of price (such as 20% (25/125) margin).

Question   **Job costing**

A curtain-making business manufactures quality curtains to customers' orders. It has three production departments (X, Y and Z) which have overhead absorption rates (per direct labour hour) of $12.86, $12.40 and $14.03 respectively.

Two pairs of curtains are to be manufactured for customers. Direct costs are as follows.

	Job TN8	*Job KT2*
Direct material	$154	$108
Direct labour	20 hours dept X	16 hours dept X
	12 hours dept Y	10 hours dept Y
	10 hours dept Z	14 hours dept Z

Labour rates are as follows: $3.80(X); $3.50 (Y); $3.40 (Z)

The firm quotes prices to customers that reflect a required profit of 25% on selling price.

Required

Calculate the total cost and selling price of each job.

Answer

Helping hand. Note that the profit margin is given as a percentage on selling price. If profit is 25% on selling price, this is the same as $33\frac{1}{3}\%$ (25/75) on cost.

		Job TN8 $		Job KT2 $
Direct material		154.00		108.00
Direct labour: dept X	(20 × 3.80)	76.00	(16 × 3.80)	60.80
dept Y	(12 × 3.50)	42.00	(10 × 3.50)	35.00
dept Z	(10 × 3.40)	34.00	(14 × 3.40)	47.60
Total direct cost		306.00		251.40
Overhead: dept X	(20 × 12.86)	257.20	(16 × 12.86)	205.76
dept Y	(12 × 12.40)	148.80	(10 × 12.40)	124.00
dept Z	(10 × 14.03)	140.30	(14 × 14.03)	196.42
Total cost		852.30		777.58
Profit		284.10		259.19
Quoted selling price		1,136.40		1,036.77

2 Batch costing

FAST FORWARD

Batch costing is similar to job costing in that each batch of similar articles is separately identifiable. The **cost per unit** manufactured in a batch is the total batch cost divided by the number of units in the batch.

2.1 Introduction

Key term

A **batch** is a cost unit which consists of a separate, readily identifiable group of product units which maintains its separate identity throughout the production process.

The procedures for **costing batches** are very similar to those for costing jobs.

The batch is treated as a **job** during production and the costs are collected as described earlier in this chapter.

Once the batch has been completed, the **cost per unit** can be calculated as the total batch cost divided by the number of units in the batch.

Batches can be made to order and also produced for **inventory**.

2.2 Example: Batch costing

A company manufactures model cars to order and has the following budgeted overheads for the year, based on normal activity levels.

Department	Budgeted overheads $	Budgeted activity
Welding	6,000	1,500 labour hours
Assembly	10,000	1,000 labour hours

Selling and administrative overheads are 20% of production cost. An order for 250 model cars type XJS1, made as Batch 8638, incurred the following costs.

Materials $12,000
Labour   100 hours welding shop at $8/hour
               200 hours assembly shop at $9/hour

$500 was paid for the hire of special X-ray equipment for testing the welds.

Required

Calculate the cost per unit for Batch 8638.

Solution

The first step is to calculate the overhead absorption rate for the production departments.

$$\text{Welding} = \frac{\$6,000}{1,500} = \$4 \text{ per labour hour}$$

$$\text{Assembly} = \frac{\$10,000}{1,000} = \$10 \text{ per labour hour}$$

Total cost – Batch no 8638

	$	$
Direct material		12,000
Direct expense		500
Direct labour 100 × $8 =	800	
200 × $9 =	1,800	
		2,600
Prime cost		15,100
Overheads 100 × 4 =	400	
200 × 10 =	2,000	
		2,400
Production cost		17,500
Selling and administrative cost (20% of production cost)		3,500
Total cost		21,000

$$\text{Cost per unit} = \frac{\$21,000}{250} = \$84$$

Question   **Batch costing**

Lyfsa Kitchen Units Co crafts two different sizes of standard unit and a DIY all-purpose unit for filling up awkward spaces. The units are built to order in batches of around 250 (although the number varies according to the quality of wood purchased), and each batch is sold to NGJ Furniture Warehouses Co.

The costs incurred in May were as follows.

	Big unit	Little unit	All-purpose
Direct materials purchased	$5,240	$6,710	$3,820
Direct labour			
Skilled (hours)	1,580	1,700	160
Semi-skilled (hours)	3,160	1,900	300
Direct expenses	$1,180	$1,700	$250
Selling price of batch	$48,980	$43,125	$25,660
Completed at 31 May	100%	80%	25%

The following information is available.

All direct materials for the completion of the batches have been recorded. Skilled labour is paid $9 per hour, semi-skilled $7 per hour. Administration expenses total $4,400 per month and are to be allocated to the batches on the basis of direct labour hours. Direct labour costs, direct expenses and administration expenses will increase in proportion to the total labour hours required to complete the little units and the all-purpose units. On completion of the work the practice of the manufacturer is to divide the calculated profit on each batch 20% to staff as a bonus, 80% to the company. Losses are absorbed 100% by the company.

Required

(a)   Calculate the profit or loss made by the company on big units.
(b)   Project the profit or loss likely to be made by the company on little units and all-purpose units.

Answer

(a)   **Big units**

	$	$
Direct materials		5,240
Direct labour		
Skilled 1,580 hours at $9	14,220	
Semi-skilled 3,160 hours at $7	22,120	
		36,340
Direct expenses		1,180
Administrative expenses		
4,740 hours at $0.50 (see below)*		2,370
		45,130
Selling price		48,980
Calculated profit		3,850
Divided: Staff bonus 20%		770
Profit for company 80%		3,080

*Administrative expenses absorption rate $= \dfrac{\$4,400}{8,800}$ per labour hour

= $0.50 per labour hour

(b)

		Little units			All-purpose	
		$	$		$	$
Direct materials			6,710			3,820
Direct labour						
Skilled	1,700 hrs at $9	15,300		160 hrs at $9	1,440	
Semi-skilled	1,900 hrs at $7	13,300		300 hrs at $7	2,100	
Direct expenses		1,700			250	
Administration						
expenses:	3,600 hrs at $0.50	1,800		460 hrs at $0.50	230	
		32,100			4,020	
Costs to						
completion	20/80 × 32,100	8,025		75/25 × 4,020	12,060	
			40,125			16,080
Total costs			46,835			19,900
Selling price			43,125			25,660
Calculated						
profit/(loss)			(3,710)			5,760
Divided: Staff bonus 20%			-			1,152
(Loss)/profit for company			(3,710)			4,608

Note that whilst direct labour costs, direct expenses and administration expenses increase in proportion to the total labour hours required to complete the little units and the all-purpose units, there will be no further material costs to complete the batches.

3 Unit costing

Unit costing systems average the costs incurred in a period over all of the units of output in a period.

With batch costing and job costing, each cost unit is separately identifiable. The costs incurred could be traced to each table or to each batch of pens.

Some organisations may produce goods or services as a continuous stream of identical units which are not separately identifiable for costing purposes. For example:

- A sauce manufacturer produces a continuous stream of identical bottles of sauce
- A fast food restaurant serves a continuous supply of packets of chips with meals

In these types of environment the costing system averages the costs incurred over all of the units of output in a period.

$$\text{Cost per unit} = \frac{\text{Total cost for period}}{\text{number of units of output in the period}}$$

Question

Costing methods

Which method of costing (job, batch or unit costing) would be most appropriate for these businesses?

(a) A baker
(b) A transport company
(c) A plumber
(d) An accountancy firm
(e) A paint manufacturer

Answer

Helping hand. Think about the type of production process involved and how costs would be collected.

(a) **A baker** would probably use batch costing. The cost units (loaves, cakes) are identical but would be produced in separately identifiable batches.

(b) **A transport company** would use unit costing, probably using a cost unit such as the tonne-kilometre (the cost of carrying one tonne for one kilometre).

(c) **A plumber** would use job costing, since every plumbing job is a separately identifiable cost unit.

(d) **An accountancy firm** would use job costing, since each client would require a different amount of time from employees of different skills.

(e) **A paint manufacturer** would use unit costing since the total costs incurred would be averaged over all the tins of paint produced in a period.

We will go on to study a unit costing system known as **process costing** in detail in the next chapter.

4 Service costing

Service costing can be used by companies operating in a service industry or by companies wishing to establish the cost of services carried out by different departments.

Key term

Service costing is a method of accounting for services provided to internal customers (eg canteens, maintenance, personnel) and/or external customers (eg law firms, hospitals, schools). These may be referred to as service centres, service departments or service organisations.

4.1 What are service organisations?

Service organisations **do not make or sell tangible goods**. Profit-seeking service organisations include accountancy firms, law firms, transport companies, banks and hotels. Almost all not-for-profit organisations – hospitals, schools, libraries and so on – are also service organisations.

Service costing differs from the other costing methods in the following ways.

(a)   In general, with service costing, the cost of direct materials consumed will be relatively small compared to the labour, direct expenses and overheads cost.

(b)   Indirect costs tend to represent a higher proportion of total cost compared with product costing.

(c)   The output of most service organisations is often intangible and it is therefore difficult to establish a measurable unit cost.

4.2 Unit cost measures

A particular problem with service costing is the difficulty in defining a **realistic cost** unit that represents a suitable measure of the service provided. Frequently, a **composite cost unit** may be deemed more appropriate if the service is a function of two activity variables.

Typical composite cost units used by companies operating in a service industry are shown below.

Service	Cost unit
Road, rail and air transport services	Passenger-kilometre, tonne-kilometre
Hotels	Occupied room-night
Hospitals	Patient-day

Each organisation will need to ascertain the cost unit most appropriate to its activities. If a number of organisations within an industry use a common cost unit, valuable **comparisons** can be made between similar establishments. This is particularly applicable to hospitals, educational establishments and local authorities.

4.3 Example: Composite cost units

The following information is available for the Whiteley Hotel for the latest thirty day period.

Number of rooms available per night   40
Percentage occupancy achieved   65%
Room servicing cost incurred $3,900

Required

(a) Calculate the number of occupied room-nights.
(b) Calculate the room servicing cost per occupied room-night (to the nearest cent).

Solution

(a) Firstly, we need to calculate the number of occupied room-nights. We can do this as follows.

Number of occupied room-nights = 40 rooms × 30 nights × 65%

= 780

(b) In order to calculate the room servicing cost per occupied room-night we can use the following equation.

$$\text{Room servicing cost per occupied room-night} = \frac{\text{Total room servicing costs}}{\text{Number of occupied room-nights}}$$

$$= \frac{\$3,900}{780}$$

$$= \$5$$

mula to
rn

$\text{Cost per service unit} = \dfrac{\text{Total costs for period}}{\text{Number of service units in the period}}$	

4.4 Example: Composite cost units again

Carry Co operates a small fleet of delivery vehicles. Expected costs and activity details are as follows.

Loading	1 hour per tonne loaded
Loading costs:	
Labour (casual)	$6 per hour
Equipment depreciation	$80 per week
Supervision	$80 per week
Drivers' wages (fixed)	$100 per driver per week
Petrol	10c per kilometre
Repairs	5c per kilometre
Depreciation	$80 per week per vehicle
Supervision	$120 per week
Other general expenses (fixed)	$200 per week

There are two drivers and two vehicles in the fleet.

During a slack week, only six journeys were made.

Journey	Tonnes carried (one way)	One-way distance of journey Kilometres
1	5	100
2	8	20
3	2	60
4	4	50
5	6	200
6	5	300

Required

Calculate the expected average full cost per tonne-kilometre for the week.

Solution

Variable costs

Journey	1	2	3	4	5	6
	$	$	$	$	$	$
Loading labour	30	48	12	24	36	30
Petrol (both ways)	20	4	12	10	40	60
Repairs (both ways)	10	2	6	5	20	30
	60	54	30	39	96	120

Total costs

	$
Variable costs (total for journeys 1 to 6)	399
Loading equipment depreciation	80
Loading supervision	80
Drivers' wages	200
Vehicles depreciation	160
Drivers' supervision	120
Other costs	200
	1,239

Journey	Tonnes	One-way distance Kilometres	Tonne-kilometres
1	5	100	500
2	8	20	160
3	2	60	120
4	4	50	200
5	6	200	1,200
6	5	300	1,500
			3,680

$$\text{Cost per tonne-kilometre} = \frac{\$1,239}{3,680} = \$0.337$$

Note that the large element of fixed costs may distort this measure but that a variable cost per tonne-kilometre of $399/3,680 = $0.108 may be useful for budgetary planning and control.

Question   Cost units

Which of the following would be appropriate cost units for a passenger coach company?

(i)   Vehicle cost per passenger-kilometre

(ii)   Fuel cost for each vehicle per kilometre

(iii)   Fixed cost per kilometre

     A (i) only   B (i) and (ii) only   C (i) and (iii) only   D All of them

Answer

Answer: B

The vehicle cost per passenger-kilometre (i) is appropriate for cost control purposes because it **combines the distance travelled and the number of passengers carried, both of which affect cost.**

The fuel cost for each vehicle per kilometre (ii) can be useful for control purposes because it **focuses on a particular aspect** of the cost of operating each vehicle.

The fixed cost per kilometre (iii) is not particularly useful for control purposes because it **varies with the number of kilometres travelled.**

Chapter Roundup

- **Job costing** is the costing method used where each cost unit is separately identifiable.

- **Batch costing** is similar to job costing in that each batch of similar articles is separately identifiable. The **cost per unit** manufactured in a batch is the total batch cost divided by the number of units in the batch.

- **Unit costing systems** average the costs incurred in a period over all of the units of output in a period.

- **Service costing** can be used by companies operating in a service industry or by companies wishing to establish the cost of services carried out by different departments.

Quick Quiz

1   Which of the following are not characteristics of job costing?

    I   Customer driven production
    II   Complete production possible within a single accounting period
    III   Homogeneous products

    A   I and II only
    B   I and III only
    C   II and III only
    D   III only

2   The cost of a job is $100,000

    (a)   If profit is 25% of the job cost, the price of the job = $.................
    (b)   If there is a 25% margin, the price of the job = $....................

3   How would you calculate the cost per unit of a completed batch?

4   Match up the following services with their typical cost units

Service		Cost unit
Hotels		Patient-day
Education	?	Meal served
Hospitals		Full-time student
Catering organisations		Occupied bed-night

5   Cost per service unit = —————————

Answers to Quick Quiz

1   D

2   (a) $100,000 + (25% × $100,000) = $100,000 + $25,000 = $125,000

    (b)   Profit is 25 per cent of the selling price, therefore selling price should be written as 100%:

	%
Selling price	100
Profit	25
Cost	75

    ∴ Price = $100,000 × 100/75 = $133,333.

3    $$\frac{\text{Total batch cost}}{\text{Number of units in the batch}}$$

4
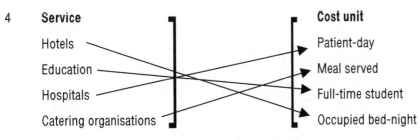

Service	Cost unit
Hotels	Patient-day
Education	Meal served
Hospitals	Full-time student
Catering organisations	Occupied bed-night

5   Cost per service unit = $\dfrac{\text{Total costs for period}}{\text{Number of service units in the period}}$

Now try the questions below from the Exam Question Bank

Number	Level	Marks	Time
Q11	Examination	N/A	30 mins

12

Process costing

Chapter topic list

Study guide reference

			Syllabus reference
2	(b)	Describe the process of accounting for input costs and relating them to work done	1(c)
2	(f)	Describe the different methods of costing final outputs and their appropriateness to different types of business organisation	1(c)
12	(a)	Describe the characteristics of process costing	5(b)
12	(b)	Identify situations where the use of process costing is appropriate	5(b)
12	(c)	Calculate unit costs and prepare process accounts where losses occur in process	5(b)
12	(d)	Explain and illustrate the nature of normal and abnormal losses/gains	5(b)
12	(e)	Calculate unit costs where losses are separated into normal and abnormal	5(b)
12	(f)	Prepare process accounts where losses are separated into normal and abnormal	5(b)
12	(g)	Account for scrap	5(b)
13	(a)	Describe and illustrate the concept of equivalent units	5(b)
13	(b)	Calculate unit costs where there is closing work in progress in a process	5(b)
13	(c)	Allocate process costs between finished output and work-in-progress	5(b)
13	(d)	Prepare process accounts where there is closing work-in-progress	5(b)
14	(a)	Distinguish between joint products and by products	5(b)
14	(b)	Explain the treatment of joint products and by-products at the point of separation	5(b)
14	(c)	Apportion joint process costs using net realisable values and weight/volume of output respectively	5(b)
14	(d)	Discuss the usefulness of product cost/profit data from a joint process	5(b)
14	(e)	Evaluate the benefit of further processing	5(b)

1 Process costing features

FAST FORWARD

Process costing is a costing method used where it is not possible to identify separate units of production usually because of the continuous nature of the production processes involved.

1.1 Introduction

We have now looked at three cost accounting methods: **job costing**, **batch costing,** and **service costing**. In this chapter we will consider another costing method, **process costing**. Process costing is applied when output consists of a continuous stream of **identical units**.

We will begin from basics and look at how to account for the most simple of processes. We will then move on to how to account for any **losses** which might occur, as well as what to do with any **scrapped units** which are sold. Next we will consider how to deal with **closing work in progress** before examining situations involving closing work in progress and losses.

Exam focus point

Process costing is frequently examined and it is very important you present your answers clearly.

1.2 Features of process costing

Process costing is a costing method used where it is not possible to identify separate units of production, usually because of the continuous nature of the production processes involved. It is common to identify process costing with **continuous production** such as the following.

- Oil refining
- The manufacture of soap
- Paint manufacture
- Food and drink manufacture

Features of process costing include the following.

(a) The continuous nature of production in process costing means that it is not possible to calculate the cost per unit of output or the cost per unit of closing inventory.

(b) There is often a **loss in process** due to spoilage, wastage, evaporation and so on.

(c) The **output** of one process becomes the **input** to the next until the finished product is made in the final process.

(d) Output from production may be a single product, but there may also be one or more **by-products** and/or **joint products**.

2 Basics of process costing

ST FORWARD

Use our suggested four-step approach when dealing with process costing questions.
Step 1 Determine output and losses
Step 2 Calculate cost per unit of output, losses and WIP
Step 3 Calculate total cost of output, losses and WIP
Step 4 Complete accounts

2.1 Basic techniques

Before tackling the more complex areas of process costing, we will begin by looking at a very simple process costing example which will illustrate the basic techniques which we will build upon in the remainder of this chapter.

2.1.1 Example: Basics of process costing

Suppose that Royal Oak Co makes coloured terracotta pots. Production of the pots involves two processes, shaping and colouring. During the year to 31 March 20X3, 1,000,000 units of material worth $500,000 were input to the first process, shaping. Direct labour costs of $200,000 and production overhead costs of $200,000 were also incurred in connection with the shaping process. There were no opening or closing inventories in the shaping department. The process account for shaping for the year ended 31 March 20X3 is as follows.

Process 1

PROCESS 1 (SHAPING) ACCOUNT

	Units	$		Units	$
Direct materials	1,000,000	500,000	Output to Process 2	1,000,000	900,000
Direct labour		200,000			
Production overheads		200,000			
	1,000,000	900,000		1,000,000	900,000

You will see that a **process account** is nothing more than a **ledger account** with debit and credit entries although it does have an additional column on both the debit and credit sides showing **quantity**. When preparing process accounts, perhaps as part of your workings, you are advised to include these memorandum quantity columns and to balance them off (ie ensure they total to the same amount on both sides) **before** attempting to complete the monetary value columns since they will help you to check that you have missed nothing out. This becomes increasingly important as more complications are introduced into questions.

Process 2

When using process costing, if a series of separate processes is needed to manufacture the finished product, the **output of one process becomes the input to the next until the final output is made in the final process**. In our example, all output from shaping was transferred to the second process, colouring, during the year to 31 March 20X3. Additional material costing $300,000 was input to the colouring process. Direct labour costs of $150,000 and production overhead costs of $150,000 were also incurred. There were no opening or closing inventories in the colouring department. The process account for colouring for the year ended 31 March 20X3 is as follows.

PROCESS 2 (COLOURING) ACCOUNT

	Units	$		Units	$
Materials from process 1	1,000,000	900,000	Output to finished		
Added materials		300,000	goods	1,000,000	1,500,00
Direct labour		150,000			
Production overhead		150,000			
	1,000,000	1,500,000		1,000,000	1,500,00

Added materials, labour and overhead in Process 2 are usually **added gradually** throughout the process. Materials from Process 1, in contrast, will often be **introduced in full at the start of the second process**.

2.2 Cost per unit

The main aim of process costing is to calculate a cost per unit that gives completed units and closing inventories a value.

$$\text{Cost per unit} = \frac{\text{Costs incurred}}{\text{Expected output}}$$

2.2.1 Example: Cost per unit

We can calculate a cost per unit for the earlier example (Royal Oak Co) as follows.

$$\text{Cost per unit} = \frac{\text{Costs incurred}}{\text{Expected output}}$$

$$\text{Process 1 cost per unit} = \frac{\$900,000}{1,000,000 \text{ units}}$$

$$= \$0.90 \text{ per unit}$$

$$\text{Process 2 cost per unit} = \frac{\$1,500,000}{1,000,000 \text{ units}}$$

$$= \$1.50 \text{ per unit}$$

Question

During a period, 50,000 units of material were input to Process 1 at the production plant of Jingles Co. The following costs were incurred.

Materials	$100,000
Direct labour	$200,000
Production overhead	$100,000

50,000 units were completed in Process 1 and transferred to Process 2. There were no opening or closing work in progress inventories.

Required

Calculate the cost per unit of Process 1 output.

Answer

$$\text{Cost per unit} = \frac{\text{Costs incurred}}{\text{Expected output}}$$

$$\text{Costs incurred} = \$100,000 + \$200,000 + \$100,000$$

$$= \$400,000$$

Expected output = Actual output = 50,000

$$\text{Cost per unit} = \frac{\$400,000}{50,000 \text{ units}}$$

$$= \$8 \text{ per unit}$$

2.3 Framework for dealing with process costing

Process costing is centred around **four key steps**. The exact work done at each step will depend on the circumstances of the question, but the approach can always be used. Don't worry about the terms used. We will be looking at their meaning as we work through the chapter.

Step 1 **Determine output and losses**

- Determine expected output
- Calculate normal loss and abnormal loss and gain
- Calculate equivalent units if there is closing work in progress

Step 2 **Calculate cost per unit of output, losses and WIP**

Calculate cost per unit or cost per equivalent unit.

Step 3 **Calculate total cost of output, losses and WIP**

In some examples this will be straightforward. In cases where there is work in progress, a statement of evaluation will have to be prepared.

Step 4 **Complete accounts**

- Complete the process account
- Write up the other accounts required by the question

Exam focus point

It always saves time in an exam if you don't have to think too long about how to approach a question before you begin. This four-step approach can be applied to any process costing question so it would be a good idea to memorise it now.

3 Losses and gains

FAST FORWARD

During a production process, a **loss** may occur due to wastage, spoilage, evaporation, and so on.

Key term

- **Normal loss** is the loss expected during a process. It is not given a cost.

- **Abnormal loss** is the extra loss resulting when actual loss is greater than normal or expected loss, and it is given a cost.

- **Abnormal gain** is the gain resulting when actual loss is less than the normal or expected loss, and it is given a 'negative cost'.

Since **normal loss is not given a cost**, the cost of producing these units is borne by the 'good' units of output.

Abnormal loss and gain units are valued at the same unit rate as 'good' units. Abnormal events do not therefore affect the cost of good production. Their costs are **analysed separately** in an **abnormal loss or abnormal gain account**.

3.1 Example: Normal loss

Suppose 2,000 units are input to a process. Normal loss is 5% of input and there are no opening or closing inventories.

Required

Calculate the normal loss.

Solution

Normal loss = 5% × 2,000 units
= 100 units

3.2 Example: Abnormal loss

Suppose 2,000 units are input to a process. Normal loss is 5% of input and there are no opening and closing inventories. Actual output was 1,800 units.

Required

Calculate the abnormal loss.

Solution

Normal loss = 5% × 2,000 units
= 100 units

Actual loss = 2,000 – 1,800
= 200 units

∴ Abnormal loss = Actual loss − normal loss
= 200 units − 100 units
= 100 units

3.3 Example: Abnormal gain

Suppose 2,000 units are input to a process. Normal loss is 5% of input and there are no opening or closing inventories. Actual output was 1,950 units.

Required

Calculate the abnormal gain.

Solution

Normal loss = 5% × 2,000 units
= 100 units

Actual loss = 2,000 units − 1,950 units
= 50 units

Abnormal gain = Actual loss − normal loss
= 50 units − 100 units
= 50 units

Question

Losses and gains

Jingles Co operates a single manufacturing process, and during March the following processing took place.

Opening inventory	nil	Closing inventory	nil
Units introduced	1,000 units	Output	900 units
Costs incurred	$4,500	Loss	100 units

Required

Determine the cost of output in the following circumstances.

(a) Expected or normal loss is 10% of input.
(b) There is no expected loss, so that the entire loss of 100 units was unexpected.

Answer

(a) **If loss is expected**, and is an unavoidable feature of processing, it is argued by cost accountants that there is no point in charging a cost to the loss. It is more sensible to accept that the loss will occur, and spread the costs of production over the expected units of output.

$$\frac{\text{Costs}}{\text{Expected output(90\% of 1,000)}} = \frac{\$4,500}{900 \text{ units}}$$

Cost per unit of output $= \dfrac{\$4,500}{900} = \$5$

Normal loss is not given any cost, so that the process account would appear as follows.

PROCESS ACCOUNT

	Units	$		Units	$
Costs incurred	1,000	4,500	Normal loss	100	0
			Output units	900	4,500
	1,000	4,500		1,000	4,500

It helps to enter normal loss into the process 'T' account, just to make sure that your memorandum columns for units are the same on the debit and the credit sides of the account.

(b) **If loss is unexpected** and occurred perhaps as a result of poor workmanship, poor quality materials, poor supervision, damage by accident, and so on, it is argued that it would be reasonable to charge a cost to the units of loss. The cost would then be transferred to an **'abnormal loss' account**, and eventually written off to the income statement as an item of loss in the period. Units of 'good output' would not be burdened with the cost of the loss, so that the cost per unit remains unaltered.

$$\frac{\text{Costs incurred}}{\text{Expected output}} = \frac{\$4,500}{1,000 \text{ units}}$$

Costs per unit $4.50

The process account and abnormal loss account would look like this.

PROCESS ACCOUNT

	Units	$		Units	$
Costs incurred	1,000	4,500	Abnormal loss	100	450
			Output units	900	4,050
	1,000	4,500		1,000	4,500

ABNORMAL LOSS ACCOUNT

	Units	$		Units	$
Process account	100	450	Income statement	100	450

3.4 Example: Losses and gains

Suppose 1,000 units at a cost of $4,500 are input to a process. Normal loss is 10% and there are no opening or closing inventories.

Required

(a) Complete the process account and the abnormal loss/gain account if actual output was 860 units (so that actual loss is 140 units).

(b) Complete the process account and the abnormal loss/gain account if actual output was 920 units (so that actual loss is 80 units).

Solution

Before we demonstrate the use of the 'four-step framework' we will summarise the way that the losses are dealt with.

- Normal loss is given no share of cost

- The cost of output is therefore based on the **expected** units of output, which in our example amount to 90% of 1,000 = 900 units

- **Abnormal loss** is given a cost, which is written off to the income statement via an abnormal loss/gain account

- **Abnormal gain** is treated in the same way, except that being a gain rather than a loss, it appears as a **debit** entry in the process account (whereas a loss appears as a **credit** entry in this account)

(a) **Output is 860 units**

Step 1 Determine output and losses

If actual output is 860 units and the actual loss is 140 units:

	Units
Actual loss	140
Normal loss (10% of 1,000)	100
Abnormal loss	40

Step 2 Calculate cost per unit of output and losses

The cost per unit of output and the cost per unit of abnormal loss are based on **expected** output.

$$\frac{\text{Costs incurred}}{\text{Expected output}} = \frac{\$4,500}{900 \text{ units}} = \$5 \text{ per unit}$$

Step 3 Calculate total cost of output and losses

Normal loss is not assigned any cost.

	$
Cost of output (860 × $5)	4,300
Normal loss	0
Abnormal loss (40 × $5)	200
	4,500

Step 4 Complete accounts

PROCESS ACCOUNT

	Units	$		Units	$
Cost incurred	1,000	4,500	Normal loss	100	0
			Output (finished goods a/c)	860	(× $5) 4,300
			Abnormal loss	40	(× $5) 200
	1,000	4,500		1,000	4,500

ABNORMAL LOSS/GAIN ACCOUNT

	Units	$		Units	$
Process a/c	40	200	Income statement	40	200

(b) **Output is 920 units**

Step 1 Determine output and losses

If actual output is 920 units and the actual loss is 80 units:

	Units
Actual loss	80
Normal loss (10% of 1,000)	100
Abnormal gain	20

Step 2 Calculate cost per unit of output and losses

The cost per unit of output and the cost per unit of abnormal gain are based on **expected** output.

$$\frac{\text{Costs incurred}}{\text{Expected output}} = \frac{\$4,500}{900 \text{ units}} = \$5 \text{ per unit}$$

(Whether there is abnormal loss or gain does not affect the valuation of units of output. The figure of $5 per unit is exactly the same as in the previous paragraph, when there were 40 units of abnormal loss.)

Step 3   Calculate total cost of output and losses

	$
Cost of output (920 × $5)	4,600
Normal loss	0
Abnormal gain (20 × $5)	(100)
	4,500

Step 4   Complete accounts

PROCESS ACCOUNT

	Units	$		Units	$
Cost incurred	1,000	4,500	Normal loss	100	0
Abnormal gain a/c	20	(× $5)100	Output (finished goods a/c)	920	(× $5) 4,600
	1,020	4,600		1,020	4,600

ABNORMAL LOSS/GAIN

	Units	$		Units	$
Income statement	20	100	Process a/c	20	100

If there is a closing balance in the abnormal loss or gain account when the profit for the period is calculated, this balance is taken to the income statement: an **abnormal gain** will be a **credit** and an **abnormal loss** will be a **debit** to the income statement.

Question

During period 3, costs of input to a process were $29,070. Input was 1,000 units, output was 850 units and normal loss is 10% of input.

During the next period, period 4, costs of input were again $29,070. Input was again 1,000 units, but output was 950 units.

There were no units of opening or closing inventory.

Required

Prepare the process account and the abnormal loss or gain account for each period.

Answer

Step 1   Determine output and losses

Period 3

	Units
Actual output	850
Normal loss (10% × 1,000)	100
Abnormal loss	50
Input	1,000

Period 4

	Units
Actual output	950
Normal loss (10% × 1,000)	100
Abnormal gain	(50)
Input	1,000

Step 2 **Calculate cost per unit of output and losses**

For each period the cost per unit is based on expected output.

$$\frac{\text{Cost of input}}{\text{Expected units of output}} = \frac{\$29,070}{900} = \$32.30 \text{ per unit}$$

Step 3 **Calculate total cost of output and losses**

Period 3

	$
Cost of output (850 × $32.30)	27,455
Normal loss	0
Abnormal loss (50 × $32.30)	1,615
	29,070

Period 4

	$
Cost of output (950 × $32.30)	30,685
Normal loss	0
Abnormal gain (50 × $32.30)	(1,615)
	29,070

Step 4 **Complete accounts**

PROCESS ACCOUNT

	Units	$		Units	$
Period 3					
Cost of input	1,000	29,070	Normal loss	100	0
			Finished goods a/c	850	27,455
			(× $32.30)		
			Abnormal loss a/c	50	1,615
			(× $32.30)		
	1,000	29,070		1,000	29,070
Period 4					
Cost of input	1,000	29,070	Normal loss	100	0
Abnormal gain a/c	50	1,615	Finished goods a/c	950	30,685
(× $32.30)			(× $32.30)		
	1,050	30,685		1,050	30,685

ABNORMAL LOSS OR GAIN ACCOUNT

	$		$
Period 3		*Period 4*	
Abnormal loss in process a/c	1,615	Abnormal gain in process a/c	1,615

A nil balance on this account will be carried forward into period 5.

(**Note**. It is considered more appropriate to value all units of output at a value based on expected loss ($32.30 per unit) rather than to have random fluctuations in the cost per unit each period due to variations in the loss. Period 3 output should therefore be costed at $29,070/850 = $34.20 per unit and period 4 output at $29,070/950 = $30.60 per unit.)

4 Accounting for scrap

FAST FORWARD

Loss may have a **scrap value**. Revenue from scrap is treated as a reduction in costs. It is conventional for the **scrap value of normal loss to be deducted from the cost of materials** before a cost per equivalent unit is calculated.

4.1 Basic rules

Loss may have a scrap value. The following basic rules are applied in accounting for this value in the process accounts.

(a) **Revenue from scrap** is treated, not as an addition to sales revenue, but as a **reduction in costs**.

(b) The scrap value of **normal loss** is therefore used to reduce the material costs of the process.

    DEBIT   Scrap account
    CREDIT   Process account

    with the scrap value of the normal loss.

(c) The scrap value of **abnormal loss** is used to reduce the cost of abnormal loss.

    DEBIT   Scrap account
    CREDIT   Abnormal loss account

    with the scrap value of abnormal loss, which therefore reduces the write-off of cost to the income statement at the end of the period.

(d) The scrap value of **abnormal gain** arises because the actual units sold as scrap will be less than the scrap value of normal loss. Because there are fewer units of scrap than expected, there will be less revenue from scrap as a direct consequence of the abnormal gain. The abnormal gain account should therefore be debited with the scrap value.

    DEBIT   Abnormal gain account
    CREDIT   Scrap account

    with the scrap value of abnormal gain.

(e) The **scrap account** is completed by recording the **actual cash received** from the sale of scrap.

    DEBIT   Cash received
    CREDIT   Scrap account

    with the cash received from the sale of the actual scrap.

The same basic principle therefore applies that only **normal losses** should affect the cost of the good output. The scrap value of **normal loss only** is credited to the process account. The scrap values of abnormal losses and gains are analysed separately in the abnormal loss or gain account.

4.1.1 Example: Scrap and abnormal loss or gain

A factory has two production processes. Normal loss in each process is 10% of input and scrapped units sell for $0.50 each from process 1 and $3 each from process 2. Relevant information for costing purposes relating to period 5 is as follows.

BPP
LEARNING MEDIA

Direct materials added:	Process 1	Process 2
Units	2,000	1,250
Cost	$8,100	$1,900
Direct labour	$4,000	$10,000
Production overhead	150% of direct labour cost	120% of direct labour cost
Output to process 2/finished goods	1,750 units	2,800 units
Actual production overhead	$17,800	

Required

Prepare the accounts for process 1, process 2, scrap, abnormal loss or gain and production overhead.

Solution

Step 1   **Determine output and losses**

	Process 1 Units	Process 2 Units
Output	1,750	2,800
Normal loss (10% of input)	200	300
Abnormal loss	50	–
Abnormal gain	–	(100)
	2,000	3,000*

* 1,750 units from Process 1 + 1,250 units input to process.

Step 2   **Calculate cost per unit of output and losses**

		Process 1 $		Process 2 $
Cost of input:				
Material		8,100		1,900
From Process 1		–	(1,750 × $10)	17,500
Labour		4,000		10,000
Overhead	(150% × $4,000)	6,000	(120% × 10,000)	12,000
		18,100		41,400
less: scrap value of **normal loss**	(200 × $0.50)	(100)	(300 × $3)	(900)
		18,000		40,500
Expected output:				
90% of 2,000		1,800		
90% of 3,000				2,700
Cost per unit:				
$18,000 ÷ 1,800		$10		
$40,500 ÷ 2,700				$15

Step 3   **Calculate total cost of output and losses**

	Process 1 $		Process 2 $
Output (1,750 × $10)	17,500	(2,800 × $15)	42,000
Normal loss (200 × $0.50)*	100	(300 × $3)*	900
Abnormal loss (50 × $10)	500		–
	18,100		42,900
Abnormal gain	–	(100 × $15)	(1,500)
	18,100		41,400

* Remember that normal loss is valued at scrap value only.

Step 4   Complete accounts

PROCESS 1 ACCOUNT

	Units	$		Units	$
Direct material	2,000	8,100	Scrap a/c (normal loss)	200	100
Direct labour		4,000	Process 2 a/c	1,750	17,500
Production overhead a/c		6,000	Abnormal loss a/c	50	500
	2,000	18,100		2,000	8,100

PROCESS 2 ACCOUNT

	Units	$		Units	$
Direct materials:					
From process 1	1,750	17,500	Scrap a/c (normal loss)	300	900
Added materials	1,250	1,900	Finished goods a/c	2,800	42,000
Direct labour		10,000			
Production overhead		12,000			
	3,000	41,400			
Abnormal gain	100	1,500			
	3,100	42,900		3,100	42,900

ABNORMAL LOSS ACCOUNT

	$		$
Process 1 (50 units)	500	Scrap a/c: sale of scrap of extra loss (50 units)	25
		Income statement	475
	500		500

ABNORMAL GAIN ACCOUNT

	$		$
Scrap a/c (loss of scrap revenue due to abnormal gain, 100 units × $3)	300	Process 2 abnormal gain (100 units)	1,500
Income statement	1,200		
	1,500		1,500

SCRAP ACCOUNT

	$		$
Scrap value of normal loss:		Cash a/c – cash received:	
Process 1 (200 units)	100	Loss in process 1 (250 units)	125
Process 2 (300 units)	900	Loss in process 2 (200 units)	600
Abnormal loss a/c (process 1)	25	Abnormal gain a/c (process 2)	300
	1,025		1,025

PRODUCTION OVERHEAD ACCOUNT

	$		$
Overhead incurred	17,800	Process 1 a/c	6,000
Over-absorbed overhead a/c (or IS)	200	Process 2 a/c	12,000
	18,000		18,000

Parks Co operates a processing operation involving two stages, the output of process 1 being passed to process 2. The process costs for period 3 were as follows.

Process 1

Material	3,000 kg at $0.25 per kg
Labour	$120

Process 2

Material	2,000 kg at $0.40 per kg
Labour	$84

General overhead for period 3 amounted to $357 and is absorbed into process costs at a rate of 375% of direct labour costs in process 1 and 496% of direct labour costs in process 2.

The normal output of process 1 is 80% of input and of process 2, 90% of input. Waste matter from process 1 is sold for $0.20 per kg and that from process 2 for $0.30 per kg.

The output for period 3 was as follows.

Process 1	2,300 kgs
Process 2	4,000 kgs

There was no inventory of work in progress at either the beginning or the end of the period and it may be assumed that all available waste matter had been sold at the prices indicated.

Required

Prepare the following accounts.

(a) Process 1 account
(b) Process 2 account
(c) Finished inventory account
(d) Scrap account
(e) Abnormal loss and gain account

Answer

Step 1   **Determine output and losses**

	Process 1 kgs		Process 2 kgs
Output	2,300		4,000
Normal loss (20% of 3,000 kgs)	600	(10% of 4,300)	430
Abnormal loss	100		–
Abnormal gain	–		(130)
	3,000		4,300*

* From process 1 (2,300 kgs) + 2,000 kgs added

Step 2   Determine cost per unit of output and losses

	Process 1 $		Process 2 $
Material (3,000 × $0.25)	750	(2,000 × $0.40)	800
From process 1	–	(2,300 × $0.50)	1,150
Labour	120		84
Overhead (375% × $120)	450	(496% × $84)	417
less: scrap value of **normal** loss			
(600 × $0.20)	(120)	(430 × $0.3)	(129)
	1,200		2,322
Expected output			
3,000 × 80%	2,400	4,300 × 90%	3,870
Cost per kg ($\frac{\$1,320 - \$120}{3,000 - 600}$)	$0.50	($\frac{\$2,451 - \$129}{4,300 - 430}$)	$0.60

Step 3   Determine total cost of output and losses

	Process 1 $		Process 2 $
Output (2,300 × $0.50)	1,150	(4,000 × $0.60)	2,400
Normal loss (scrap)			
(600 × $0.20)	120	(430 × $0.30)	129
Abnormal loss (100 × $0.50)	50		–
	1,320		2,529
Abnormal gain	–	(130 × $0.60)	(78)
	1,320		2,451

Step 4   Complete accounts

(a)

PROCESS 1 ACCOUNT

	kg	$		kg	$
Material	3,000	750	Normal loss to scrap a/c		
Labour		120	(20%)	600	1.
General overhead		450	Production transferred to		
			process 2	2,300	1,1!
			Abnormal loss a/c	100	!
	3,000	1,320		3,000	1,3!

(b)

PROCESS 2 ACCOUNT

	kg	$		kg	$
Transferred from					
process 1	2,300	1,150	Normal loss to scrap a/c		
Material added	2,000	800	(10%)	430	129
Labour		84	Production transferred to		
General overhead		417	finished inventory	4,000	2,400
	4,300	2,451			
Abnormal gain	130	78			
	4,430	2,529		4,430	2,529

(c)

FINISHED INVENTORY ACCOUNT

	kg	$
Process 2	4,000	2,400

(d)

SCRAP ACCOUNT

	kg	$		kg	$
Normal loss (process 1)	600	120	Abnormal gain (process 2)	130	39
Normal loss (process 2)	430	129	Cash	1,000	230
Abnormal loss					
(process 1)	100	20			
	1,130	269		1,130	269

(e)

ABNORMAL LOSS AND GAIN ACCOUNT

	kg	$		kg	$
Process 1 (loss)	100	50	Scrap value of		
Scrap value of abnormal			abnormal loss	100	20
gain	130	39	Process 2 (gain)	130	78
Income statement		9			
	230	98		230	98

Note. In this answer, a single account has been prepared for abnormal loss/gain. Your solution may have separated this single account into two separate accounts, one for abnormal gain and one for abnormal loss.

5 Closing work in progress

When units are partly completed at the end of a period (ie when there is **closing work in progress**) it is necessary to calculate the **equivalent units of production** in order to determine the cost of a completed unit.

In the examples we have looked at so far we have assumed that opening and closing inventories of work in process have been nil. We must now look at more realistic examples and consider how to allocate the costs incurred in a period between completed output (ie finished units) and partly completed closing inventory.

Some examples will help to illustrate the problem, and the techniques used to share out (apportion) costs between finished output and closing work in progress.

5.1 Example: Valuation of closing inventory

Trotter Co is a manufacturer of processed goods. In one process, there was no opening inventory, but 5,000 units of input were introduced to the process during the month, and the following costs were incurred.

	$
Direct materials	16,560
Direct labour	7,360
Production overhead	5,520
	29,440

Of the 5,000 units introduced, 4,000 were completely finished during the month and transferred to the next process. Closing inventory of 1,000 units was only 60% complete with respect to materials and conversion costs.

Solution

(a)   The problem in this example is to **divide the costs of production** ($29,440) between the finished output of 4,000 units and the closing inventory of 1,000 units.

(b)   To apportion costs fairly and proportionately, units of production must be converted into the equivalent of completed units, ie into **equivalent units of production**.

Key term

> **Equivalent units** are notional whole units which represent incomplete work, and which are used to apportion costs between work in process and completed output.

Step 1   **Determine output**

For this step in our framework we need to prepare a statement of equivalent units.

STATEMENT OF EQUIVALENT UNITS

	Total units	Completion	Equivalent units
Fully worked units	4,000	100%	4,000
Closing inventory	1,000	60%	600
	5,000		4,600

Step 2   **Calculate cost per unit of output, and WIP**

For this step in our framework we need to prepare a statement of costs per equivalent unit because equivalent units are the basis for apportioning costs.

STATEMENT OF COSTS PER EQUIVALENT UNIT

$$\frac{\text{Total cost}}{\text{Equivalent units}} = \frac{\$29,440}{4,600}$$

Cost per equivalent unit = $6.40

Step 3   **Calculate total cost of output and WIP**

For this stage in our framework a statement of evaluation may now be prepared, to show how the costs should be apportioned between finished output and closing inventory.

STATEMENT OF EVALUATION

	Equivalent units	Cost per equivalent unit	Valuation $
Fully worked units	4,000	$6.40	25,600
Closing inventory	600	$6.40	3,840
	4,600		29,440

Step 4   **Complete accounts**

The process account would be shown as follows.

PROCESS ACCOUNT

		Units	$		Units	$
(Stores a/c)	Direct materials	5,000	16,560	Output to next process	4,000	25,600
(Wages a/c)	Direct labour		7,360	Closing inventory c/f	1,000	3,840
(O'hd a/c)	Production o'hd		5,520			
		5,000	29,440		5,000	29,440

When preparing a process 'T' account, it might help to make the entries as follows.

(a)   **Enter the units first**. The units columns are simply memorandum columns, but they help you to make sure that there are no units unaccounted for (for example as loss).

(b)   Enter the costs of materials, labour and overheads next. These should be given to you.

(c)   Enter your valuation of finished output and closing inventory next. The value of the credit entries should, of course, equal the value of the debit entries.

5.2 Different rates of input

In many industries, materials, labour and overhead may be added at **different rates** during the course of production.

(a)   Output from a previous process (for example the output from process 1 to process 2) may be introduced into the subsequent process all at once, so that closing inventory is 100% complete in respect of these materials.

(b)   Further materials may be **added gradually** during the process, so that closing inventory is only **partially complete** in respect of these added materials.

(c)   Labour and overhead may be 'added' at yet another different rate. When production overhead is absorbed on a labour hour basis, however, we should expect the degree of completion on overhead to be the same as the degree of completion on labour.

When this situation occurs, equivalent units, and a cost per equivalent unit, should be **calculated separately for each type of material, and also for conversion costs**.

5.3 Example: Equivalent units and different degrees of completion

Suppose that Shaker Co is a manufacturer of processed goods, and that results in process 2 for a period were as follows.

Opening inventory	nil
Material input from process 1	4,000 units
Costs of input:	$
Material from process 1	6,000
Added materials in process 2	1,080
Conversion costs	1,720

Output is transferred into the next process, process 3. No losses occur in the process.

Closing work in process amounted to 800 units, complete as to:

Process 1 material	100%
Added materials	50%
Conversion costs	30%

Required

Prepare the process 2 account for the period.

Solution

Step 1   Determine output and losses

STATEMENT OF EQUIVALENT UNITS (OF PRODUCTION IN THE PERIOD)

| | | | Equivalent units of production | | | | | |
| | | | Process 1 material | | Added materials | | Labour and overhead | |
Input Units	Output	Total Units	Units	%	Units	%	Units	%
4,000	Completed Production	3,200	3,200	100	3,200	100	3,200	100
	Closing inventory	800	800	100	400	50	240	30
4,000		4,000	4,000		3,600		3,440	

Step 2   Calculate cost per unit of output and WIP

STATEMENT OF COST (PER EQUIVALENT UNIT)

Input	Cost $	Equivalent production in units	Cost per unit $
Process 1 material	6,000	4,000	1.50
Added materials	1,080	3,600	0.30
Labour and overhead	1,720	3,440	0.50
	8,800		2.30

Step 3   Calculate total cost of output and WIP

STATEMENT OF EVALUATION (OF FINISHED WORK AND CLOSING INVENTORIES)

Production	Cost element	Number of equivalent units	Cost per equivalent unit $	Total $	Cost $
Completed production		3,200	2.30		7,360
Closing inventory:	process 1 material	800	1.50	1,200	
	added material	400	0.30	120	
	labour and overhead	240	0.50	120	
					1,440
					8,800

Step 4   Complete accounts

PROCESS 2 ACCOUNT

	Units	$		Units	$
Process 1 material	4,000	6,000	Process 3 a/c	3,200	7,360
Added material		1,080	(finished output)		
Conversion costs		1,720	Closing inventory c/f	800	1,440
	4,000	8,800		4,000	8,800

Question

A chemical producer manufactures Product XK by means of two successive processes, Process 1 and Process 2. The information provided below relates to the most recent accounting period, period 10.

	Process 1	Process 2
Opening work in progress	Nil	Nil
Material input during period	2,400 units – cost $5,280	2,200 units (from Process 1)
Added material		$9,460
Direct labour	$2,260	$10,560
Factory overhead	100% of labour cost	2/3 of labour cost
Transfer to Process 2	2,200 units	
Transfer to finished goods		2,200 units
Closing work in progress	200 units	Nil
	100% complete with respect to materials and 30% complete with respect to labour and production overhead.	

Required

(a) Calculate the value of the goods transferred from Process 1 to Process 2 during period 10.

(b) Calculate the value of the closing work in progress left in Process 1 at the end of period 10.

(c) Calculate the value of the goods transferred from Process 2, to finished goods, during period 10, and the value of one unit of production.

Answer

(a) The value of goods transferred from Process 1 to Process 2 during period 10 was $9,240.

(b) The value of closing work in progress left in Process 1 at the end of Period 10 was $560.

Workings

Remember that when closing WIP is partly completed, it is necessary to construct a statement of equivalent units in order to apportion costs fairly and proportionately.

STATEMENT OF EQUIVALENT UNITS

			Process 1		
Input Units	Output	Total Units	material	Labour	Overheads
2,400	Completed production (transfer to Process 2)	2,200	2,200 (100%)	2,200 (100%)	2,200
	Closing work in progress	200	200 (100%)	60 (30%)	60 (30%)
2,400		2,400	2,400	2,260	2,260

STATEMENT OF COST PER EQUIVALENT UNIT

Input	Cost	Cost	Equivalent units produced	Cost per unit
	$	$		$
Process 1 materials		5,280	2,400	2.20
Labour	2,260			
Overhead	2,260	4,520	2,260	2.00
		9,800		4.20

STATEMENT OF EVALUATION

Output	Number of equivalent units	Cost per unit	Value $	Value $
Transfers to Process 2	2,200	4.20		9,240
Closing work in progress				
Process 1 materials	200	2.20	440	
Labour and overhead	60	2.00	120	
				560
				9,800

PROCESS 1 ACCOUNT

	Units	$		Units	$
Process 1	2,400	5,280	Transfers to Process 2	2,200	9,240
Labour and overheads		4,520	Closing WIP	200	560
	2,400	9,800		2,400	9,800

(c)   STATEMENT OF EQUIVALENT UNITS

Input Units	Output	Total	Materials	Labour and overhead
2,200	Transferred from Process 1	2,200	2,200 (100%)	2,200 (100%)
2,200		2,200	2,200	2,200

NB. No opening or closing WIP in Process 2.

STATEMENT OF COST PER EQUIVALENT UNIT

Input	Cost $	Cost $	Equivalent units produced	Cost per unit
Transfers from Process 1		9,240	2,200	4.20
Added materials		9,460	2,200	4.30
Labour	10,560			
Overhead	7,040	17,600	2,200	8.00
Value of one unit of production =				16.50

Value of goods transferred from Process 2 to finished goods = 2,200 units × $16.50 = $36,300.

6 Joint products and by-products

FAST FORWARD

> **Joint products** are two or more products separated in a process, each of which has a significant value compared to the other. A **by-product** is an incidental product from a process which has an insignificant value compared to the main product.

6.1 Introduction

We have studied process costing up to the point where we have calculated, say, output of process 3 as 50,000 units costing $400,000. This is all very well so long as the process produces 50,000 identical items, but what do we do if the next stage is to send some of the output through one kind of process and the rest through another, resulting in two different sorts of product? The end results may be of two basic types.

terms

> - **Joint products** are two or more products which are output from the same processing operation, but which are indistinguishable from each other (because they are the same commonly processed materials) up to their point of separation. Joint products have a substantial sales value (or a substantial sales value after further, separate processing has been carried out to make them ready for sale).
>
> - A **by-product** is a product which is similarly produced at the same time and from the same common process as the main product or joint products. The distinguishing feature of a by-product is its relatively low sales value.

The problem, if joint products or by-products are involved, is to split the common costs of processing between the various end products.

6.2 Problems in accounting for joint products

Joint products are not separately identifiable until a certain stage is reached in the processing operations. This stage is the **'split-off point'**, sometimes referred to as the **separation point**. Costs incurred prior to this point of separation are **common** or **joint costs**, and these need to be allocated (apportioned) in some manner to each of the joint products. In the following sketched example, there are two different split-off points.

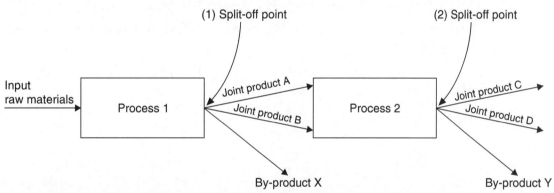

The **problems in accounting for joint products** are basically of two different sorts.

(a)   How common costs should be apportioned between products, in order to put a value to closing inventories and to the cost of sale (and profit) for each product.

(b)   Whether it is more profitable to sell a joint product at one stage of processing, or to process the product further and sell it at a later stage.

6.3 Dealing with common costs

The problem of costing for joint products concerns **common costs**, that is those common processing costs shared between the units of eventual output up to their 'split-off point'. Some method needs to be devised for sharing the common costs between the individual joint products for the following reasons.

(a)   To put a value to closing inventories of each joint product.
(b)   To record the costs and therefore the profit from each joint product.
(c)   Perhaps to assist in pricing decisions.

Here are some examples of the common costs problem.

(a)   How to spread the common costs of oil refining between the joint products made (petrol, naphtha, kerosene and so on).

(b)   How to spread the common costs of running the telephone network between telephone calls in peak and cheap rate times, or between local and long distance calls.

Methods that might be used to establish a basis for apportioning or allocating common costs to each product are as follows.

    (a)   Physical measurement

    (b)   Relative sales value apportionment method; sales value at split-off point

6.3.1 Dealing with common costs: physical measurement

With physical measurement, **the common cost is apportioned to the joint products on the basis of the proportion that the output of each product bears by weight or volume to the total output.** An example of this would be the case where two products, product 1 and product 2, incur common costs to the point of separation of $3,000 and the output of each product is 600 tons and 1,200 tons respectively.

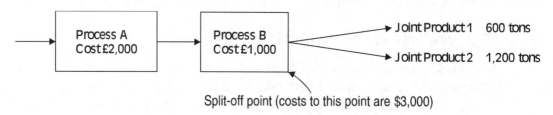

Split-off point (costs to this point are $3,000)

Product 1 sells for $4 per ton and product 2 for $2 per ton.

The division of the common costs ($3,000) between product 1 and product 2 could be based on the tonnage of output.

	Product 1		Product 2	Total
Output	600 tons	+	1,200 tons	1,800 tons
Proportion of common cost	$\left(\dfrac{600}{1,800}\right)$		$\left(\dfrac{1,200}{1,800}\right)$	
	$		$	$
Apportioned cost	1,000		2,000	3,000
Sales	2,400		2,400	4,800
Profit	1,400		400	1,800
Profit/sales ratio	58.3%		16.7% 37.5%	

Physical measurement has the following limitations.

    (a)   Where the products separate during the processes into different states, for example where one product is a gas and another is a liquid, this method is unsuitable.

    (b)   This method does not take into account the relative income-earning potentials of the individual products, with the result that one product might appear very profitable and another appear to be incurring losses.

6.3.2 Dealing with common costs: sales value at split-off point

With relative sales value apportionment of common cost, **the cost is allocated according to the product's ability to produce income**. This method is most widely used because the assumption that some profit margin should be attained for all products under normal marketing conditions is satisfied. The common cost is apportioned to each product in the proportion that the sales (market) value of that product bears to the sales value of the total output from the particular processes concerned. Using the previous example where the sales price per unit is $4 for product 1 and $2 for product 2.

    (a)   Common costs of processes to split-off point $3,000

    (b)   Sales value of product 1 at $4 per ton $2,400

    (c)   Sales value of product 2 at $2 per ton $2,400

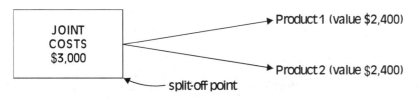

	Product 1	Product 2	Total
Sales	$2,400	$2,400	$4,800
Proportion of common cost apportioned	$\left(\dfrac{2,400}{4,800}\right)$	$\left(\dfrac{2,400}{4,800}\right)$	
	$	$	$
Apportioned cost	1,500	1,500	3,000
Sales	2,400	2,400	4,800
Profit	900	900	1,800
Profit/sales ratio	37.5%	37.5%	37.5%

A comparison of the gross profit margin resulting from the application of the above methods for allocating common costs will illustrate the greater acceptability of the relative sales value apportionment method. Physical measurement gives a higher profit margin to product 1, not necessarily because product 1 is highly profitable, but because it has been given a smaller share of common costs.

Question
Joint products

In process costing, a joint product is

A   A product which is produced simultaneously with other products but which is of lesser value than at least one of the other products

B   A product which is produced simultaneously with other products and is of similar value to at least one of the other products

C   A product which is produced simultaneously with other products but which is of greater value than any of the other products

D   A product produced jointly with another organisation

Answer

The correct answer is B, a product which is of similar value to at least one of the other products.

7 Joint products in process accounts

This example illustrates how joint products are incorporated into process accounts.

7.1 Example: joint products and process accounts

Three joint products are manufactured in a common process, which consists of two consecutive stages. Output from process 1 is transferred to process 2, and output from process 2 consists of the three joint products, Hans, Nils and Bumpsydaisies. All joint products are sold as soon as they are produced.

Data for period 2 of 20X6 are as follows.

	Process 1	Process 2
Opening and closing inventory	None	None
Direct material		
(30,000 units at $2 per unit)	$60,000	–
Conversion costs	$76,500	$226,200
Normal loss	10% of input	10% of input
Scrap value of normal loss	$0.50 per unit	$2 per unit
Output	26,000 units	10,000 units of Han
		7,000 units of Nil
		6,000 units of Bumpsydaisy

Selling prices are $18 per unit of Han, $20 per unit of Nil and $30 per unit of Bumpsydaisy.

Required

(a) Prepare the Process 1 account.
(b) Prepare the Process 2 account using the sales value method of apportionment.
(c) Prepare a profit statement for the joint products.

Solution

(a) **Process 1 equivalent units**

	Total units	Equivalent units
Output to process 2	26,000	26,000
Normal loss	3,000	0
Abnormal loss(balance)	1,000	1,000
	30,000	27,000

Costs of process 1

	$
Direct materials	60,000
Conversion costs	76,500
	136,500
Less scrap value of normal loss (3,000 × $0.50)	1,500
	135,000

Cost per equivalent unit $\dfrac{\$135,000}{27,000} = \$5$

PROCESS 1 ACCOUNT

	$		$
Direct materials	60,000	Output to process 2	
Conversion costs	76,500	(26,000 × $5)	130,000
		Normal loss (scrap value)	1,500
		Abnormal loss a/c	
		(1,000 × $5)	5,000
	136,500		136,500

(b) **Process 2 equivalent units**

	Total units	Equivalent units
Units of Hans produced	10,000	10,000
Units of Nils produced	7,000	7,000
Units of Bumpsydaisies produced	6,000	6,000
Normal loss (10% of 26,000)	2,600	0
Abnormal loss (balance)	400	400
	26,000	23,400

Costs of process 2

	$
Material costs - from process 1	130,000
Conversion costs	226,200
	356,200
Less scrap value of normal loss (2,600 × $2)	5,200
	351,000

Cost per equivalent unit $\dfrac{\$351,000}{23,400} = \$15$

Cost of good output (10,000 + 7,000 + 6,000) = 23,000 units × $15 = $345,000

The sales value of joint products, and the apportionment of the output costs of $345,000, is as follows.

	Sales value $	%	Costs (process 2) $
Hans (10,000 × $18)	180,000	36	124,200
Nils (7,000 × $20)	140,000	28	96,600
Bumpsydaisy (6,000 × $30)	180,000	36	124,200
	500,000	100	345,000

PROCESS 2 ACCOUNT

	$		$
Process 1 materials	130,000	Finished goods accounts	
Conversion costs	226,200	– Hans	124,200
		– Nils	96,600
		– Bumpsydaisies	124,200
		Normal loss (scrap value)	5,200
		Abnormal loss a/c	6,000
	356,200		356,200

(c) PROFIT STATEMENT

	Hans $'000	Nils $'000	Bumpsydaisies $'000
Sales	180.0	140.0	180.0
Costs	124.2	96.6	124.2
Profit	55.8	43.4	55.8
Profit/ sales ratio	31%	31%	31%

Question	Joint products process account

Prepare the Process 2 account and a profit statement for the joint products in the above example using the units basis of apportionment.

Answer

PROCESS 2 ACCOUNT

	$		$
Process 1 materials	130,000	Finished goods accounts	
Conversion costs	226,200	– Hans (10,000 × $15)	150,000
		– Nils (7,000 × $15)	105,000
		– Bumpsydaisies (6,000 × $15)	90,000
		Normal loss (scrap value)	5,200
		Abnormal loss a/c (400 × $15)	6,000
	356,200		356,200

PROFIT STATEMENT

	Hans	Nils	Bumpsydaisies
	$'000	$'000	$'000
Sales	180	140	180
Costs	150	105	90
Profit	30	35	90
Profit/ sales ratio	16.7%	25%	50%

Exam focus point

Remember to set out your workings clearly. The examiner has regularly commented that failure to do could lose valuable marks.

8 Accounting for by-products

FAST FORWARD

There are a number of methods to account for by-products and the choice of method will be influenced by the **circumstances of production** and **ease of calculation**.

8.1 Introduction

The by-product has some commercial value and its accounting treatment of income may be as follows.

(a) Income (minus any post-separation further processing or selling costs) from the sale of the by-product may be **added to sales of the main product**, thereby increasing sales turnover for the period.

(b) The sales of the by-product may be **treated as a separate, incidental source of income** against which are set only post-separation costs (if any) of the by-product. The revenue would be recorded in the income statement as 'other income'.

(c) The sales income of the by-product may be **deducted from the cost of production** or cost of sales of the main product.

(d) The **net realisable value of the by-product may be deducted from the cost of production of the main product**. The net realisable value is the final saleable value of the by-product minus any post-separation costs. Any closing inventory valuation of the main product or joint products would therefore be reduced.

The choice of method (a), (b), (c) or (d) will be influenced by the circumstances of production and ease of calculation, as much as by conceptual correctness. The method you are most likely to come across in examinations is method (d). An example will help to clarify the distinction between the different methods.

8.2 Example: Methods of accounting for by-products

During November 20X3, Splatter Co recorded the following results.

Opening inventory	Main product P, nil
	By-product Z, nil
Cost of production	$120,000

Sales of the main product amounted to 90% of output during the period, and 10% of production was held as closing inventory at 30 November.

Sales revenue from the main product during November 20X2 was $150,000.

A by-product Z is produced, and output had a net sales value of $1,000. Of this output, $700 was sold during the month, and $300 was still in inventory at 30 November.

Required

Calculate the profit for November using the four methods of accounting for by-products.

Solution

The four methods of accounting for by-products are shown below.

(a) **Income from by-product added to sales of the main product**

	$	$
Sales of main product ($150,000 + $700)		150,700
Opening inventory	0	
Cost of production	120,000	
	120,000	
Less closing inventory (10%)	12,000	
Cost of sales		108,000
Profit, main product		42,700

The closing inventory of the by-product has no recorded value in the cost accounts.

(b) **By-product income treated as a separate source of income**

	$	$
Sales, main product		150,000
Opening inventory	0	
Cost of production	120,000	
	120,000	
Closing inventory (10%)	12,000	
Cost of sales, main product		108,000
Profit, main product		42,000
Other income		700
Total profit		42,700

The closing inventory of the by-product again has no value in the cost accounts.

(c)   **Sales income of the by-product deducted from the cost of production in the period**

	$	$
Sales, main product		150,000
Opening inventory	0	
Cost of production (120,000 – 700)	119,300	
	119,300	
Less closing inventory (10%)	11,930	
Cost of sales		107,370
Profit, main product		42,630

Although the profit is different from the figure in (a) and (b), the by-product closing inventory again has no value.

(d)   **Net realisable value of the by-product deducted from the cost of production in the period**

	$	$
Sales, main product		150,000
Opening inventory	0	
Cost of production (120,000 – 1,000)	119,000	
	119,000	
Less closing inventory (10%)	11,900	
Cost of sales		107,100
Profit, main product		42,900

As with the other three methods, closing inventory of the by-product has no value in the books of accounting, but the value of the closing inventory ($300) has been used to reduce the cost of production, and in this respect it has been allowed for in deriving the cost of sales and the profit for the period.

Question   Joint products and by-products

Randolph Co manufactures two joint products, J and K, in a common process. A by-product X is also produced. Data for the month of December 20X2 were as follows.

Opening inventories	nil	
Costs of processing	Direct materials	$25,500
	Direct labour	$10,000

Production overheads are absorbed at the rate of 300% of direct labour costs.

		Production	Sales
		Units	Units
Output and sales consisted of:	Product J	8,000	7,000
	Product K	8,000	6,000
	By-product X	1,000	1,000

The sales value per unit of J, K and X is $4, $6 and $0.50 respectively. The saleable value of the by-product is deducted from process costs before apportioning costs to each joint product. Costs of the common processing are apportioned between product J and product K on the basis of sales value of production.

The individual profits for December 20X2 are:

	Product J	Product K
	$	$
A	5,250	6,750
B	6,750	5,250
C	22,750	29,250
D	29,250	22,750

Answer

The sales value of production was $80,000.

	$	
Product J (8,000 × $4)	32,000	(40%)
Product K (8,000 × $6)	48,000	(60%)
	80,000	

The costs of production were as follows.	$
Direct materials	25,500
Direct labour	10,000
Overhead (300% of $10,000)	30,000
	65,500
Less sales value of by-product (1,000 × 50c)	500
Net production costs	65,000

The profit statement would appear as follows (nil opening inventories).

		Product J		Product K	Total
		$		$	$
Production costs	(40%)	26,000	(60%)	39,000	65,000
Less closing inventory	(1,000 units)	3,250	(2,000 units)	9,750	13,000
Cost of sales		22,750		29,250	52,000
Sales	(7,000 units)	28,000	(6,000 units)	36,000	64,000
Profit		5,250		6,750	12,000

The correct answer is therefore A.

If you selected option B, you got the profits for each product mixed up.

If you selected option C or D, you calculated the cost of sales instead of the profit.

9 The further processing decision

ST FORWARD

A joint product should be processed further **only** if sales value minus further processing costs is greater than sales value at the split-off point.

The further processing decision problem is best explained by a simple example.

9.1 Example: further processing

Alice Co manufactures two joint products, A and B. The costs of common processing are $15,000 per batch, and output per batch is 100 units of A and 150 units of B. The sales value of A at split-off point is $90 per unit, and the sales value of B is $60 per unit. An opportunity exists to process product A further, at an extra cost of $2,000 per batch, to produce product C. One unit of joint product A is sufficient to make one unit of C which has a sales value of $120 per unit.

Should the company sell product A, or should it process A and sell product C?

Solution

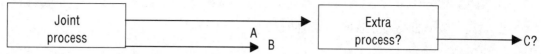

The problem is resolved on the basis that product C should be sold if the sales value of C minus its further processing costs exceeds the sales value of A.

	$
Sales value of C, per batch (100 × $120)	12,000
Sales value of A, per batch (100 × $90)	9,000
Incremental revenue from further processing	3,000
Further processing cost	2,000
Benefit from further processing in order to sell C	1,000 per batch

If the further processing cost had exceeded the incremental revenue from further processing, it would have been unprofitable to make and sell C. It is worth noting that the apportionment of joint processing costs between A and B is irrelevant to the decision, because the total extra profit from making C will be $1,000 per batch whichever method is used.

Question
Further processing decision

PCC Co produces two joint products, Pee and Cee, from the same process. Joint processing costs of $150,000 are incurred up to split-off point, when 100,000 units of Pee and 50,000 units of Cee are produced. The selling prices at split-off point are $1.25 per unit for Pee and $2.00 per unit for Cee.

The units of Pee could be processed further to produce 60,000 units of a new chemical, Peeplus, but at an extra fixed cost of $20,000 and variable cost of 30c per unit of input. The selling price of Peeplus would be $3.25 per unit.

Required

Ascertain whether the company should sell Pee or Peeplus.

Answer

The only relevant costs/incomes are those which compare selling Pee against selling Peeplus. Every other cost is irrelevant: they will be incurred regardless of what the decision is.

	Pee			Peeplus
Selling price per unit	$1.25			$3.25
	$		$	$
Total sales	125,000			195,000
Post-separation processing costs	–	Fixed	20,000	
	–	Variable	30,000	50,000
Sales minus post-separation	125,000			145,000
(further processing) costs				

It is $20,000 more profitable to convert Pee into Peeplus.

Chapter Roundup

- **Process costing** is a costing method used where it is not possible to identify separate units of production usually because of the continuous nature of the production processes involved.

- Use our suggested four-step approach when dealing with process costing questions.

  Step 1 Determine output and losses
  Step 2 Calculate cost per unit of output, losses and WIP
  Step 3 Calculate total cost of output, losses and WIP
  Step 4 Complete accounts

- During a production process, a **loss** may occur due to wastage, spoilage, evaporation, and so on.

- Loss may have a **scrap value**. Revenue from scrap is treated as a reduction in costs. It is conventional for the **scrap value of normal loss to be deducted from the cost of materials** before a cost per equivalent unit is calculated.

- When units are partly completed at the end of a period (ie when there is **closing work in progress**) it is necessary to calculate the **equivalent units of production** in order to determine the cost of a completed unit.

- **Joint products** are two or more products separated in a process, each of which has a significant value compared to the other. A **by-product** is an incidental product from a process which has an insignificant value compared to the main product.

- There are a number of methods to account for by-products and the choice of method will be influenced by the **circumstances of production** and **ease of calculation**.

- A joint product should be processed further **only** if sales value minus further processing costs is greater than sales value at the split-off point.

Quick Quiz

1   Define process costing.

2   Process costing is centred around four key steps.

Step 1 ....

Step 2 ....

Step 3 ....

Step 4 ....

3   Abnormal gains result when actual loss is less than normal or expected loss.

   ☐   True

   ☐   False

4   Normal loss (no scrap value) ⎤   ⎡ Same value as good output (positive cost)

   Abnormal loss   ?   No value

   Abnormal gain   ⎦   ⎣ Same value as good output (negative cost)

5   How is revenue from normal scrap treated?

   A   As an addition to sales revenue
   B   As a reduction in costs of processing
   C   As a bonus to employees
   D   All of the above

6   When there is closing WIP at the end of a process, what is the first step in the four-step approach to process costing questions and why must it be done?

7   What is the difference between a joint product and a by-product?

8   What is meant by the term 'split off' point?

9   Name two methods of apportioning common costs to joint products.

Answers to Quick Quiz

1 **Process costing** is a costing method used where it is not possible to identify separate units of production, or jobs, usually because of the continuous nature of the production processes involved.

2 **Step 1** Determine output and losses

   Step 2 Calculate cost per unit of output, losses and WIP

   Step 3 Calculate total cost of output, losses and WIP

   Step 4 Complete accounts

3 ☑ True

4 Normal loss (no scrap value) ⟶ Same value as good output (positive cost)

   Abnormal loss ⟶ No value

   Abnormal gain ⟶ Same value as good output (negative cost)

5 B

6 It is necessary to calculate the equivalent units of production (by drawing up a statement of equivalent units). Equivalent units of production are notional whole units which represent incomplete work and which are used to apportion costs between work in progress and completed output.

7 A **joint product** is regarded as an important saleable item whereas a by-product is not.

8 The **split-off point** (or the point of separation) is the point at which joint products become separately identifiable in a processing operation.

9 Physical measurement and sales value at split-off point.

Now try the questions below from the Exam Question Bank

Number	Level	Marks	Time
12	Examination	N/A	30 mins

Part D
Decision making

13

Cost-volume-profit (CVP) analysis

Chapter topic list

Study guide reference

			Syllabus reference
16	(a)	Calculate contribution per unit and the contribution/sales ratio	6(a)
16	(b)	Explain the concept of breakeven and margin of safety	6(a)
16	(c)	Use contribution per unit and contribution/sales ratio to calculate breakeven point and martin of safety	6(a)
16	(d)	Analyse the effect on breakeven point and margin of safety of changes in selling price and cost	6(a)
16	(e)	Use contribution per unit and contribution/sales ratio to calculate the sales required to achieve a target profit	6(a)
16	(f)	Construct breakeven and profit/volume charts for a single product or business	6(a)

1 CVP analysis and breakeven point

Cost-volume-profit (CVP) analysis is the study of the interrelationships between costs, volume and profit at various levels of activity.

1.1 Introduction

The management of an organisation usually wishes to know the profit likely to be made if the aimed-for production and sales for the year are achieved. Management may also be interested to know the following.

(a) The **breakeven** point which is the activity level at which there is neither profit nor loss.

(b) The **amount** by which actual **sales can fall** below anticipated sales, **without** a **loss** being incurred.

The breakeven point (BEP) can be calculated arithmetically.

Key term

$$\text{Breakeven point} = \frac{\text{Total fixed costs}}{\text{Contribution per unit}} = \frac{\text{Contribution required to break even}}{\text{Contribution per unit}}$$

$$= \text{Number of units of sale required to break even.}$$

1.2 Example: Breakeven point

Expected sales   10,000 units at $8 = $80,000
Variable cost $5 per unit
Fixed costs $21,000

Required

Compute the breakeven point.

Solution

The contribution per unit is $(8–5)	=	$3
Contribution required to break even	=	fixed costs = $21,000
Breakeven point (BEP)	=	21,000 ÷ 3
	=	7,000 units
In revenue, BEP	=	(7,000 × $8) = $56,000

Sales above $56,000 will result in profit of $3 per unit of additional sales and sales below $56,000 will mean a loss of $3 per unit for each unit by which sales fall short of 7,000 units. In other words, profit will improve or worsen by the amount of contribution per unit.

	7,000 units		7,001 units
	$		$
Revenue	56,000		56,008
Less variable costs	35,000		35,005
Contribution	21,000		21,003
Less fixed costs	21,000		21,000
Profit	0	(= breakeven)	3

2 The contribution/sales (C/S) ratio

The **C/S ratio** is a measure of how much contribution is earned from each $ of sales.

The C/S ratio is calculated as follows.

$$\text{C/S ratio} = \frac{\text{Contribution}}{\text{Sales}} \times 100\%$$

2.1 Example: C/S ratio

The following information relates to Product G which is manufactured by Darling.

Expected sales revenue	10,000 units @ $8 = $80,000
Variable cost	$5 per unit
Fixed costs	$21,000

Required

Calculate the C/S ratio for Product G.

Solution

Contribution	= Selling price – variable costs
	= $8 – $5
	= $3

$$\text{C/S ratio} = \frac{\text{Contribution}}{\text{Sales}} \times 100\%$$

$$= \frac{\$3}{\$8} \times 100\%$$

$$= 37.5\%$$

A C/S ratio of 37.5% means that for every $1 of sales, a contribution of 37.5c is earned.

2.2 An alternative method to calculate breakeven

An alternative way of calculating the breakeven point to give an answer in terms of sales revenue is as follows.

$$\frac{\text{Required contribution}}{\text{C/S ratio}} = \frac{\text{Fixed costs}}{\text{C/S ratio}} = \textbf{Sales revenue at breakeven point}$$

In the example above, the C/S ratio is $\dfrac{\$3}{\$8} = 37.5\%$

Breakeven is where sales revenue equals $\dfrac{\$21,000}{37.5\%} = \$56,000$

At a price of $8 per unit, this represents 7,000 units of sales.

Thus, in order to earn a total contribution of $21,000 and if contribution increases by 37.5c per $1 of sales, sales must be:

$$\frac{\$1}{37.5c} \times \$21,000 = \$56,000$$

Question   C/S ratio

The C/S ratio of product W is 20%. IB Co, the manufacturer of product W, wishes to make a contribution of $50,000 towards fixed costs. How many units of product W must be sold if the selling price is $10 per unit?

Answer

$$\frac{\text{Required contribution}}{\text{C/S ratio}} = \frac{\$50,000}{20\%} = \$250,000$$

∴ Number of units = $250,000 ÷ $10 = 25,000.

3 The margin of safety

The **margin of safety** is the difference in units between the **expected sales volume** and the **breakeven sales volume** and it is sometimes expressed as a percentage of the expected sales volume.

The margin of safety may also be expressed as the difference between the expected/actual sales revenue and breakeven sales revenue, expressed as a percentage of the expected/actual sales revenue.

3.1 Example: margin of safety

Mal de Mer Co makes and sells a product which has a variable cost of $30 and which sells for $40. Budgeted fixed costs are $70,000 and expected sales are 8,000 units.

Required

Calculate the breakeven point and the margin of safety.

Solution

(a)   Breakeven point   = $\dfrac{\text{Total fixed costs}}{\text{Contribution per unit}} = \dfrac{\$70,000}{\$(40-30)}$

                                   =   7,000 units

(b)   Margin of safety   =   8,000 – 7,000 units = 1,000 units

     which may be expressed as $\dfrac{1,000 \text{ units}}{8,000 \text{ units}} \times 100\% \times 100\% = 12\tfrac{1}{2}\%$ of budget

(c)   The margin of safety indicates to management that actual sales can fall short of budget by 1,000 units or 12½% before the breakeven point is reached and no profit at all is made.

4 Breakeven arithmetic and target profits

FORWARD

> At the **breakeven point**, sales revenue equals total costs and there is no profit. At the breakeven point, total contribution = fixed costs.

4.1 Introduction

At **the breakeven point**, S = V + F

     V   = Total variable costs

     F   = Total fixed costs

Subtracting V from each side of the equation, we get:

     S – V = F, that is, **total contribution = fixed costs**

4.2 Example: Breakeven arithmetic

Butterfingers Co makes a product which has a variable cost of $7 per unit.

Required

If fixed costs are $63,000 per annum, calculate the selling price per unit if the company wishes to break even with a sales volume of 12,000 units.

Solution

Contribution required to break even (= Fixed costs)	=	$63,000	
Volume of sales	=	12,000 units	
			$
Required contribution per unit (S – V)	=	$63,000 ÷ 12,000 =	5.25
Variable cost per unit (V)	=		7.00
Required sales price per unit (S)	=		12.25

4.3 Target profits

A similar formula may be applied where a company wishes to achieve a certain profit during a period. To achieve this profit, sales must cover all costs and leave the required profit.

Key term

> The **target profit** is achieved when: S = V + F + P,
>
>   where   P = required profit
>
> Subtracting V from each side of the equation, we get:
>
>   S – V = F + P, so
>
>   Total contribution required   = F + P

4.4 Example: Target profits

Riding Breeches Co makes and sells a single product, for which variable costs are as follows.

	$
Direct materials	10
Direct labour	8
Variable production overhead	6
	24

The sales price is $30 per unit, and fixed costs per annum are $68,000. The company wishes to make a profit of $16,000 per annum.

Required

Determine the sales required to achieve this profit.

Solution

Required contribution = fixed costs + profit = $68,000 + $16,000 = $84,000

Required sales can be calculated in one of two ways.

(a) $\dfrac{\text{Required contribution}}{\text{Contribution per unit}}$ = $\dfrac{\$84,000}{\$(30-24)}$ = 14,000 units, or $420,000 in revenue

(b) $\dfrac{\text{Required contribution}}{\text{C/S ratio}}$ = $\dfrac{\$84,000}{20\%\,^*}$ = $420,000 of revenue, or 14,000 units.

* C/S ratio = $\dfrac{\$30-\$24}{\$30}=\dfrac{\$6}{\$30}$ = 0.2 = 20%.

Question

Target profit

Seven League Boots Co wishes to sell 14,000 units of its product, which has a variable cost of $15 to make and sell. Fixed costs are $47,000 and the required profit is $23,000.

Required

Calculate the sales price per unit.

Answer

Required contribution = fixed costs plus profit
= $47,000 + $23,000
= $70,000
Required sales   14,000 units

	$
Required contribution per unit sold	5
Variable cost per unit	15
Required sales price per unit	20

4.5 Decisions to change sales price or costs

You may come across a problem in which you will be expected to offer advice as to the effect of altering the selling price, variable cost per unit or fixed cost. Such problems are slight variations on basic breakeven arithmetic.

4.5.1 Example: Change in selling price

Stomer Cakes Co bake and sell a single type of cake. The variable cost of production is 15c and the current sales price is 25c. Fixed costs are $2,600 per month, and the annual profit for the company at current sales volume is $36,000. The volume of sales demand is constant throughout the year.

The sales manager, Ian Digestion, wishes to raise the sales price to 29c per cake, but considers that a price rise will result in some loss of sales.

Required

Ascertain the minimum volume of sales required each month to raise the price to 29c.

Solution

The minimum volume of demand which would justify a price of 29p is one which would leave total profit at least the same as before, ie $3,000 per month. Required profit should be converted into required contribution, as follows.

	$
Monthly fixed costs	2,600
Monthly profit, minimum required	3,000
Current monthly contribution	5,600
Contribution per unit (25p – 15c)	10c
Current monthly sales	56,000 cakes

The minimum volume of sales required after the price rise will be an amount which earns a contribution of $5,600 per month, no worse than at the moment. The contribution per cake at a sales price of 29c would be 14c.

$$\text{Required sales} = \frac{\text{required contribution}}{\text{contribution per unit}} = \frac{\$5,600}{14c} = 40,000 \text{ cakes per month.}$$

4.5.2 Example: Change in production costs

Close Brickett Co makes a product which has a variable production cost of $8 and a variable sales cost of $2 per unit. Fixed costs are $40,000 per annum, the sales price per unit is $18, and the current volume of output and sales is 6,000 units.

The company is considering whether to have an improved machine for production. Annual hire costs would be $10,000 and it is expected that the variable cost of production would fall to $6 per unit.

Required

(a)   Determine the number of units that must be produced and sold to achieve the same profit as is currently earned, if the machine is hired.

(b)   Calculate the annual profit with the machine if output and sales remain at 6,000 units per annum.

Solution

The current unit contribution is $(18 − (8 + 2)) = $8

(a)

	$
Current contribution (6,000 × $8)	48,000
Less current fixed costs	40,000
Current profit	8,000

With the new machine fixed costs will go up by $10,000 to $50,000 per annum. The variable cost per unit will fall to $(6 + 2) = $8, and the contribution per unit will be $10.

	$
Required profit (as currently earned)	8,000
Fixed costs	50,000
Required contribution	58,000
Contribution per unit	$10
Sales required to earn $8,000 profit	5,800 units

(b)   **If sales are 6,000 units**

	$	$
Sales (6,000 × $18)		108,000
Variable costs: production (6,000 × $6)	36,000	
sales (6,000 × $2)	12,000	
		48,000
Contribution (6,000 × $10)		60,000
Less fixed costs		50,000
Profit		10,000

Alternative calculation	$
Profit at 5,800 units of sale (see (a))	8,000
Contribution from sale of extra 200 units (× $10)	2,000
Profit at 6,000 units of sale	10,000

4.6 Sales price and sales volume

It may be clear by now that, given no change in fixed costs, **total profit is maximised when the total contribution is at its maximum**. Total contribution in turn depends on the unit contribution and on the sales volume.

An increase in the sales price will increase unit contribution, but sales volume is likely to fall because fewer customers will be prepared to pay the higher price. A decrease in sales price will reduce the unit contribution, but sales volume may increase because the goods on offer are now cheaper. The **optimum combination** of sales price and sales volume is arguably the one which **maximises total contribution**.

4.6.1 Example: Profit maximisation

C Co has developed a new product which is about to be launched on to the market. The variable cost of selling the product is $12 per unit. The marketing department has estimated that at a sales price of $20, annual demand would be 10,000 units.

However, if the sales price is set above $20, sales demand would fall by 500 units for each 50c increase above $20. Similarly, if the price is set below $20, demand would increase by 500 units for each 50c stepped reduction in price below $20.

Required

Determine the price which would maximise C Co's profit in the next year.

Solution

At a price of $20 per unit, the unit contribution would be $(20 − 12) = $8. Each 50c increase (or decrease) in price would raise (or lower) the unit contribution by 50c. The total contribution is calculated at each sales price by multiplying the unit contribution by the expected sales volume.

Unit price	Unit contribution	Sales volume	Total contribution
$	$	Units	$
20.00	8.00	10,000	80,000
(a) **Reduce price**			
19.50	7.50	10,500	78,750
19.00	7.00	11,000	77,000
(b) **Increase price**			
20.50	8.50	9,500	80,750
21.00	9.00	9,000	81,000
21.50	9.50	8,500	80,750
22.00	10.00	8,000	80,000
22.50	10.50	7,500	78,750

The total contribution would be maximised, and therefore profit maximised, at a sales price of $21 per unit, and sales demand of 9,000 units.

Question

Betty Battle Co manufactures a product which has a selling price of $20 and a variable cost of $10 per unit. The company incurs annual fixed costs of $29,000. Annual sales demand is 9,000 units.

New production methods are under consideration, which would cause a $1,000 increase in fixed costs and a reduction in variable cost to $9 per unit. The new production methods would result in a superior product and would enable sales to be increased to 9,750 units per annum at a price of $21 each.

If the change in production methods were to take place, the breakeven output level would be:

A   400 units higher
B   400 units lower
C   100 units higher
D   100 units lower

Answer

	Current	Revised	Difference
	$	$	
Selling price	20	21	
Variable costs	10	9	
Contribution per unit	10	12	
Fixed costs	$29,000	$30,000	
Breakeven point (units)	2,900	2,500	400 lower

$$\text{Breakeven point} = \frac{\text{Total fixed costs}}{\text{Contribution per unit}}$$

$$\text{Current BEP} = \frac{\$29,000}{\$10} = 2,900 \text{ units}$$

Revised BEP $= \dfrac{\$30,000}{\$12} = 2{,}500$ units

The correct answer is therefore B.

5 Breakeven charts and profit/volume charts

- The breakeven point can also be determined graphically using a **breakeven chart** or a **contribution breakeven chart**.
- The **profit/volume (PV) chart** is a variation of the breakeven chart which illustrates the relationship of costs and profits to sales and the margin of safety.

Exam focus point

Remember that you can pick up easy marks in an examination for drawing graphs neatly and accurately. Always use a ruler, label your axes and use an appropriate scale.

5.1 Breakeven charts

The breakeven point can also be determined graphically using a breakeven chart. This is a chart which shows approximate levels of profit or loss at different sales volume levels within a limited range.

A breakeven chart has the following axes.

- A **horizontal** axis showing the **sales/output** (in value or units)
- A **vertical axis** showing $ for **sales revenues** and **costs**

The following lines are drawn on the breakeven chart.

(a) The **sales line**

- Starts at the origin
- Ends at the point signifying expected sales

(b) The **fixed costs line**

- Runs parallel to the horizontal axis
- Meets the vertical axis at a point which represents total fixed costs

(c) The **total costs line**

- Starts where the fixed costs line meets the vertical axis

- Ends at the point which represents anticipated sales on the horizontal axis and total costs of anticipated sales on the vertical axis

The **breakeven point** is the **intersection** of the **sales line** and the **total costs line**.

The distance between the **breakeven point** and the **expected (or budgeted) sales**, in units, indicates the **margin of safety**.

5.1.1 Example: A breakeven chart

The budgeted annual output of a factory is 120,000 units. The fixed overheads amount to $40,000 and the variable costs are 50c per unit. The sales price is $1 per unit.

Required

Construct a breakeven chart showing the current breakeven point and profit earned up to the present maximum capacity.

Solution

We begin by calculating the profit at the budgeted annual output.

	$
Sales (120,000 units)	120,000
Variable costs	60,000
Contribution	60,000
Fixed costs	40,000
Profit	20,000

Breakeven chart (1) is shown on the following page.

The chart is drawn as follows.

(a)   The **vertical axis** represents **money** (costs and revenue) and the **horizontal axis** represents the **level of activity** (production and sales).

(b)   The fixed costs are represented by a **straight line parallel to the horizontal axis** (in our example, at $40,000).

(c)   The **variable costs** are added 'on top of' fixed costs, to give **total costs**. It is assumed that fixed costs are the same in total and variable costs are the same per unit at all levels of output.

The line of costs is therefore a straight line and only two points need to be plotted and joined up. Perhaps the two most convenient points to plot are total costs at zero output, and total costs at the budgeted output and sales.

- At zero output, costs are equal to the amount of fixed costs only, $40,000, since there are no variable costs

- At the budgeted output of 120,000 units, costs are $100,000.

	$
Fixed costs	40,000
Variable costs 120,000 × 50c	60,000
Total costs	100,000

(d)   The sales line is also drawn by plotting two points and joining them up.

- At zero sales, revenue is nil
- At the budgeted output and sales of 120,000 units, revenue is $120,000

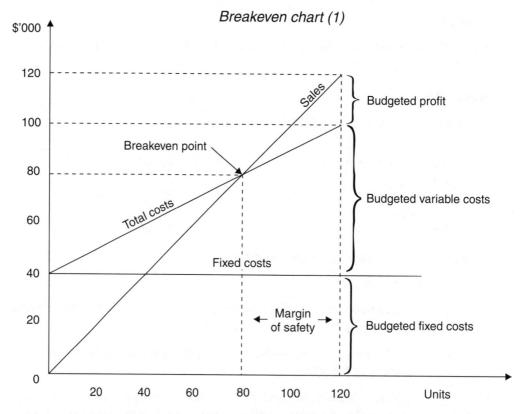

Breakeven chart (1)

The breakeven point is where total costs are matched exactly by total revenue. From the chart, this can be seen to occur at output and sales of 80,000 units, when revenue and costs are both $80,000. This breakeven point can be proved mathematically as:

$$\frac{\text{Required contribution} \ (= \text{fixed costs})}{\text{Contribution per unit}} = \frac{\$40,000}{50\text{c per unit}} = 80,000 \text{ units}$$

The margin of safety can be seen on the chart as the difference between the budgeted level of activity and the breakeven level.

5.2 The value of breakeven charts

Breakeven charts are used as follows.

- To **plan** the production of a company's products
- To **market** a company's products
- To give a **visual display** of breakeven arithmetic

5.2.1 Example: Variations in the use of breakeven charts

Breakeven charts can be used to **show variations** in the possible **sales price**, **variable costs** or **fixed costs**. Suppose that a company sells a product which has a variable cost of $2 per unit. Fixed costs are $15,000. It has been estimated that if the sales price is set at $4.40 per unit, the expected sales volume would be 7,500 units; whereas if the sales price is lower, at $4 per unit, the expected sales volume would be 10,000 units.

Required

Draw a breakeven chart to show the budgeted profit, the breakeven point and the margin of safety at each of the possible sales prices.

Solution

Workings	Sales price $4.40 per unit		Sales price $4 per unit
	$		$
Fixed costs	15,000		15,000
Variable costs (7,500 × $2.00)	15,000	(10,000 × $2.00)	20,000
Total costs	30,000		35,000
Budgeted revenue (7,500 × $4.40)	33,000	(10,000 × $4.00)	40,000

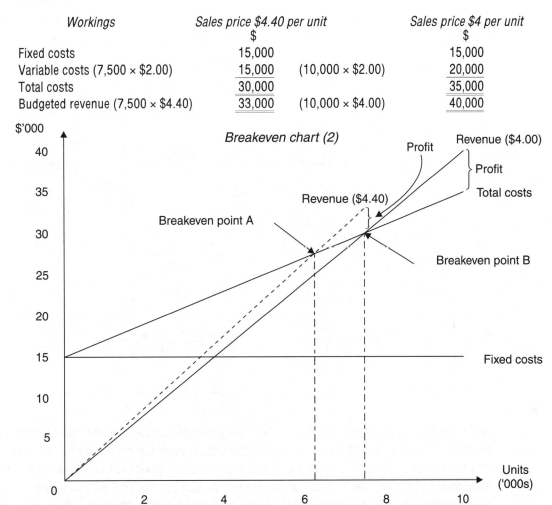

Breakeven chart (2)

(a) **Breakeven point A** is the breakeven point at a sales price of $4.40 per unit, which is 6,250 units or $27,500 in costs and revenues.

$$(check: \frac{Required\ contribution\ to\ breakeven}{Contribution\ per\ unit} \quad \frac{\$15,000}{\$2.40\ per\ unit} = 6,250\ units)$$

The margin of safety (A) is 7,500 units – 6,250 units = 1,250 units or 16.7% of expected sales.

(b) **Breakeven point B** is the breakeven point at a sales price of $4 per unit which is 7,500 units or $30,000 in costs and revenues.

$$(check: \frac{Required\ contribution\ to\ breakeven}{Contribution\ per\ unit} \quad \frac{\$15,000}{\$2\ per\ unit} = 7,500\ units)$$

The margin of safety (B) = 10,000 units – 7,500 units = 2,500 units or 25% of expected sales.

Since a price of $4 per unit gives a higher expected profit and a wider margin of safety, this price will probably be preferred even though the breakeven point is higher than at a sales price of $4.40 per unit.

5.3 Contribution (or contribution breakeven) charts

As an alternative to drawing the fixed cost line first, it is possible to start with that for variable costs. This is known as a **contribution chart**. An example is shown below using the earlier example.

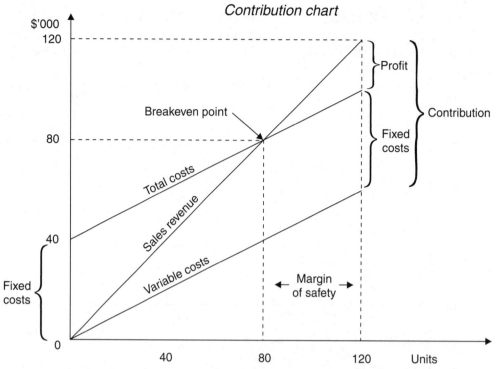

Contribution chart

One of the **advantages** of the contribution chart is that is shows clearly the **contribution** for **different levels of production** (indicated here at 120,000 units, the budgeted level of output) as the 'wedge' shape between the sales revenue line and the variable costs line. At the **breakeven point**, the **contribution equals fixed costs** exactly. At levels of output **above** the **breakeven** point, the **contribution** is **larger**, and not only covers fixed costs, but also leaves a profit. **Below** the **breakeven** point, the **loss** is the amount by which contribution fails to cover fixed costs.

5.4 The profit/volume (P/V) chart

Key term

> The **profit/volume (P/V) chart** is a variation of the breakeven chart which illustrates the relationship of costs and profit to sales, and the margin of safety.

A P/V chart is constructed as follows (look at the chart in the example that follows as you read the explanation).

(a)   'P' is on the y axis and actually comprises not only 'profit' but contribution to profit (in monetary value), extending above and below the x axis with a zero point at the intersection of the two axes, and the negative section below the x axis representing fixed costs. This means that at zero production, the firm is incurring a loss equal to the fixed costs.

(b)   'V' is on the x axis and comprises either volume of sales or value of sales (revenue).

(c)   The profit-volume line is a straight line drawn with its starting point (at zero production) at the intercept on the y axis representing the level of fixed costs, and with a gradient of contribution/unit (or the P/V ratio if sales value is used rather than units). The P/V line will cut the x axis at the breakeven point of sales volume. Any point on the P/V line above the x axis represents the profit to the firm (as measured on the vertical axis) for that particular level of sales.

5.4.1 Example: P/V chart

Let us draw a P/V chart for our example. At sales of 120,000 units, total contribution will be 120,000 × $(1 − 0.5) = $60,000 and total profit will be $20,000.

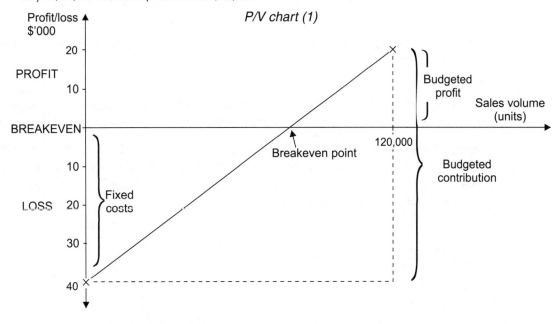

5.5 The advantage of the P/V chart

The P/V chart shows clearly the effect on profit and breakeven point of any changes in selling price, variable cost, fixed cost and/or sales demand. If the budgeted selling price of the product in our example is increased to $1.20, with the result that demand drops to 105,000 units despite additional fixed costs of $10,000 being spent on advertising, we could add a line representing this situation to our P/V chart.

At sales of 105,000 units, contribution will be 105,000 × $(1.20 − 0.50) = $73,500 and total profit will be $23,500 (fixed costs being $50,000).

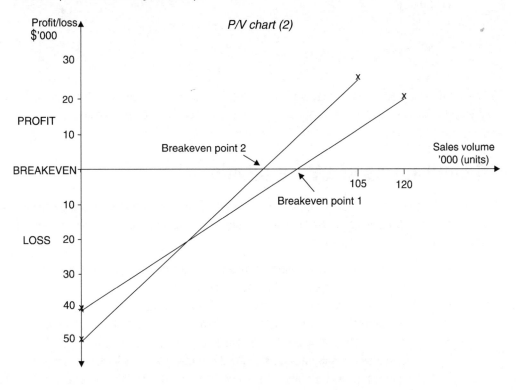

The diagram shows that if the selling price is increased, the breakeven point occurs at a lower level of sales revenue (71,429 units instead of 80,000 units), although this is not a particularly large increase when viewed in the context of the projected sales volume. It is also possible to see that for sales above 50,000 units, the profit achieved will be higher (and the loss achieved lower) if the price is $1.20. For sales volumes below 50,000 units the first option will yield lower losses.

The P/V chart is the clearest way of presenting such information; two conventional breakeven charts on one set of axes would be very confusing.

Changes in the variable cost per unit or in fixed costs at certain activity levels can also be easily incorporated into a P/V chart. The profit or loss at each point where the cost structure changes should be calculated and plotted on the graph so that the profit/volume line becomes a series of straight lines.

For example, suppose that in our example, at sales levels in excess of 120,000 units the variable cost per unit increases to $0.60 (perhaps because of overtime premiums that are incurred when production exceeds a certain level). At sales of 130,000 units, contribution would therefore be 130,000 × $(1 - 0.60) = $52,000 and total profit would be $12,000.

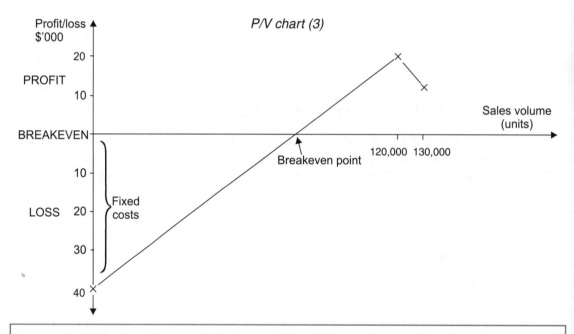

6 Limitations of CVP analysis

Breakeven analysis is a useful technique for managers. Breakeven arithmetic can provide **simple** and **quick** estimates. **Breakeven charts** provide a **graphical representation** of breakeven arithmetic. Breakeven analysis has a number of limitations.

- It **can only apply to a single product** or a single mix of a group of products
- A breakeven chart may be **time-consuming** to prepare
- It **assumes** fixed costs are constant at all levels of output
- It **assumes** that **variable costs** are the **same** per unit at all levels of output
- It **assumes** that **sales prices** are **constant** at all levels of output
- It assumes **production** and **sales** are the **same** (inventory levels are ignored)
- It **ignores** the **uncertainty** in the estimates of fixed costs and variable cost per unit

Chapter Roundup

- **Cost-volume- profit (CVP)/breakeven analysis** is the study of the interrelationships between costs, volume and profits at various levels of activity.

- The **C/S ratio** is a measure of how much contribution is earned from each $1 of sales.

- The **margin of safety** is the difference in units between the **expected sales volume** and the **breakeven sales volume.** It is sometimes expressed as a percentage of the expected sales volume.

- At the **breakeven point**, sales revenue = total costs and there is no profit. At the breakeven point total contribution = fixed costs.

- The breakeven point can also be determined graphically using a **breakeven chart** or a **contribution breakeven chart**.

- The **profit/volume (PV) chart** is a variation of the breakeven chart which illustrates the relationship of costs and profits to sales and the margin of safety.

Quick Quiz

1   What does CVP analysis study?

2   The **breakeven point** is the ....
     or... .

3   Use the following to make up three formulae which can be used to calculate the breakeven point.

Contribution per unit
Contribution per unit
Fixed costs
Fixed costs
Contribution required to breakeven
Contribution required to breakeven
C/S ratio
C/S ratio

(a)   Breakeven point (sales units)   =

        or

(b)   Breakeven point (sales revenue)   =

        or

4   The C/S ratio is a measure of how much profit is earned from each $1 of sales.

☐ True

☐ False

5   The **margin of safety** is the difference in units between the expected sales volume and the breakeven sales volume. How is it sometimes expressed?

6   Profits are maximised at the breakeven point.

☐ True

☐ False

7   At the breakeven point, total contribution = ………………………………… .

8   The total contribution required for a **target profit** = …………………………………………… .

9   Give three uses of breakeven charts.

10   Breakeven charts show approximate levels of profit or loss at different sales volume levels within a limited range. Which of the following are true?

I   The sales line starts at the origin
II   The fixed costs line runs parallel to the vertical axis
III   Breakeven charts have a horizontal axis showing the sales/output (in value or units)
IV   Breakeven charts have a vertical axis showing $ for revenues and costs
V   The breakeven point is the intersection of the sales line and the fixed cost line

A   I and II
B   I and III
C   I, III and IV
D   I, III, IV, and V

11   On a breakeven chart, the distance between the breakeven point and the expected (or budgeted) sales, in units, indicates the ………………………………… .

Answers to Quick Quiz

1   The interrelations between **costs, volume** and **profits** of a product at various activity levels.

2   The **breakeven point** is the number of units of sale required to breakeven or the sales revenue required to breakeven.

3   (a)   Breakeven point (sales units) $= \dfrac{\text{Fixed costs}}{\text{Contribution per unit}}$

$\qquad\qquad$ or $\dfrac{\text{Contribution required to breakeven}}{\text{Contribution per unit}}$

$\qquad$ (b)   Breakeven point (sales revenue) $= \dfrac{\text{Fixed costs}}{\text{C/S ratio}}$

$\qquad\qquad$ or $\dfrac{\text{Contribution required to breakeven}}{\text{C/S ratio}}$

4   False. The C/S ratio is a measure of how much **contribution** is earned from each $1 of sales.

5   As a **percentage** of the budgeted sales volume.

6   False. At the breakeven point there is no profit.

7   At the breakeven point, total contribution = fixed costs

8   Fixed costs + required profit

9   •   To plan the production of a company's products
       •   To market a company's products
       •   To give a visual display of breakeven arithmetic

10   C

11   Margin of safety

Now try the questions below from the Exam Question Bank

Number	Level	Marks	Time
Q13	Examination	–	30 mins

Decision making

14

Chapter topic list

Study guide reference

			Syllabus reference
17	(a)	Explain the importance of the limiting factor concept	6(b)
17	(b)	Identify the limiting factor in given situations	6(b)
17	(c)	Formulate and determine the optimal production solution when there is a single resource constraint	6(b)
17	(d)	Solve make/buy-in problems when there is a single resource constraint	6(b)
17	(e)	Explain the concept of relevant costs	6(b)
17	(f)	Apply the concept of relevant costs in business decisions	6(b)

1 Relevant costs

FAST FORWARD

> **Relevant costs** are future cash flows arising as a direct consequence of a decision.
>
> Relevant costs are **future costs**, **cashflows** and **incremental costs**. Relevant costs are also **differential costs** and **opportunity costs**.

1.1 Relevant costs

Key term

> A **relevant cost** is a future cash flow arising as a direct consequence of a decision.

Decision making should be based on relevant costs.

(a) **Relevant costs are future costs**. A decision is about the future and it cannot alter what has been done already. Costs that have been incurred in the past are totally irrelevant to any decision that is being made 'now'. Such costs are **past costs** or **sunk costs**.

Costs that have been incurred include not only costs that have already been paid, but also costs that have been **committed**. A **committed cost** is a future cash flow that will be incurred anyway, regardless of the decision taken now.

(b) **Relevant costs are cash flows**. Only cash flow information is required. This means that costs or charges which do not reflect **additional cash spending** (such as depreciation and notional costs) should be ignored for the purpose of decision making.

(c) **Relevant costs are incremental costs**. For example, if an employee is expected to have no other work to do during the next week, but will be paid his basic wage (of, say, $100 per week) for attending work and doing nothing, his manager might decide to give him a job which earns the organisation $40. The net gain is $40 and the $100 is irrelevant to the decision because although it is a future cash flow, it will be incurred anyway whether the employee is given work or not.

Other terms are sometimes used to describe relevant costs.

Key term

> **Avoidable costs** are costs which would not be incurred if the activity to which they relate did not exist.

One of the situations in which it is necessary to identify the avoidable costs is in deciding whether or not to **discontinue a product**. The only costs which would be saved are the **avoidable costs** which are usually the variable costs and sometimes some specific costs. Costs which would be incurred whether or not the product is discontinued are known as **unavoidable costs**.

term

> **Differential cost** is the difference in total cost between alternatives.

For example, if decision option A costs $300 and decision option B costs $360, the differential cost is $60.

term

> An **opportunity cost.** The value of the benefit sacrificed when one course of action is chosen, in preference to an alternative.

Suppose for example that there are three options, A, B and C, only one of which can be chosen. The net profit from each would be $80, $100 and $70 respectively.

Since only one option can be selected option B would be chosen because it offers the biggest benefit.

	$
Profit from option B	100
Less opportunity cost (ie the benefit from the most profitable alternative, A)	80
Differential benefit of option B	20

The decision to choose option B would not be taken simply because it offers a profit of $100, but because it offers a differential profit of $20 in excess of the next best alternative.

1.2 Controllable and uncontrollable costs

We came across the term **controllable costs** at the beginning of this Interactive Text. **Controllable costs** are items of expenditure which can be directly influenced by a given manager within a given time span.

As a general rule, **committed fixed costs** such as those costs arising from the possession of plant, equipment and buildings (giving rise to depreciation and rent) are largely **uncontrollable** in the short term because they have been committed by longer-term decisions.

Discretionary fixed costs, for example, advertising and research and development costs can be thought of as being **controllable** because they are incurred as a result of decisions made by management and can be raised or lowered at fairly short notice.

1.3 Sunk costs

term

> A **sunk cost** is a past cost which is not directly relevant in decision making.

The principle underlying decision accounting is that management decisions can only affect the future. In decision making, managers therefore require information about **future costs and revenues** which would be affected by the decision under review. They must not be misled by events, costs and revenues in the past, about which they can do nothing.

Sunk costs, which have been charged already as a cost of sales in a previous accounting period or will be charged in a future accounting period although the expenditure has already been incurred, are irrelevant to decision making.

An example of a sunk cost is development costs which have already been incurred. Suppose that a company has spent $250,000 in developing a new service for customers, but the marketing department's most recent findings are that the service might not gain customer acceptance and could be a commercial failure. The decision whether or not to abandon the development of the new service would have to be taken, but the $250,000 spent so far should be ignored by the decision makers because it is a **sunk cost**.

1.4 Fixed and variable costs

**Exam focus
point**

Unless you are given an indication to the contrary, you should assume the following.

- Variable costs will be relevant costs
- Fixed costs are irrelevant to a decision

This need not be the case, however, and you should analyse variable and fixed cost data carefully. Do not forget that 'fixed' costs may only be fixed in the short term.

1.5 Non-relevant variable costs

There might be occasions when a variable cost is in fact a sunk cost (and therefore a **non-relevant variable cost**). For example, suppose that a company has some units of raw material in inventory. They have been paid for already, and originally cost $2,000. They are now obsolete and are no longer used in regular production, and they have no scrap value. However, they could be used in a special job which the company is trying to decide whether to undertake. The special job is a 'one-off' customer order, and would use up all these materials in inventory.

(a)   In deciding whether the job should be undertaken, the relevant cost of the materials to the special job is nil. Their original cost of $2,000 is a **sunk cost**, and should be ignored in the decision.

(b)   However, if the materials did have a scrap value of, say, $300, then their relevant cost to the job would be the **opportunity cost** of being unable to sell them for scrap, ie $300.

1.6 Attributable fixed costs

There might be occasions when a fixed cost is a relevant cost, and you must be aware of the distinction between **'specific'** or **'directly attributable' fixed costs**, and general fixed overheads.

Directly attributable fixed costs are those costs which, although fixed within a relevant range of activity level are relevant to a decision for either of the following reasons.

(a)   They could increase if certain extra activities were undertaken. For example, it may be necessary to employ an extra supervisor if a particular order is accepted. The extra salary would be an **attributable fixed cost**.

(b)   They would decrease or be eliminated entirely if a decision were taken either to reduce the scale of operations or shut down entirely.

General fixed overheads are those fixed overheads which will be unaffected by decisions to increase or decrease the scale of operations, perhaps because they are an apportioned share of the fixed costs of items which would be completely unaffected by the decisions. General fixed overheads are not relevant in decision making.

1.7 Absorbed overhead

Absorbed overhead is a **notional** accounting cost and hence should be ignored for decision-making purposes. It is **overhead incurred** which may be relevant to a decision.

1.8 The relevant cost of materials

The relevant cost of raw materials is generally their **current replacement cost**, *unless* the materials have already been purchased and would not be replaced once used. In this case the relevant cost of using them is the **higher** of the following.

- Their current resale value
- The value they would obtain if they were put to an alternative use

If the materials have no resale value and no other possible use, then the relevant cost of using them for the opportunity under consideration would be nil.

Question	Relevant cost of materials

O'Reilly Co has been approached by a customer who would like a special job to be done for him, and who is willing to pay $22,000 for it. The job would require the following materials.

Material	Total units required	Units already in inventory	Book value of units in inventory $/unit	Realisable value $/unit	Replacement cost $/unit
A	1,000	0	–	–	6
B	1,000	600	2	2.50	5
C	1,000	700	3	2.50	4
D	200	200	4	6.00	9

Material B is used regularly by O'Reilly Co, and if units of B are required for this job, they would need to be replaced to meet other production demand.

Materials C and D are in inventory as the result of previous over-buying, and they have a restricted use. No other use could be found for material C, but the units of material D could be used in another job as substitute for 300 units of material E, which currently costs $5 per unit (of which the company has no units in inventory at the moment).

Required

Calculate the relevant costs of material for deciding whether or not to accept the contract.

Answer

(a) **Material A** is not yet owned. It would have to be bought in full at the replacement cost of $6 per unit.

(b) **Material B** is used regularly by the company. There are existing inventories (600 units) but if these are used on the contract under review a further 600 units would be bought to replace them. Relevant costs are therefore 1,000 units at the replacement cost of $5 per unit.

(c) 1,000 units of **material C** are needed and 700 are already in inventory. If used for the contract, a further 300 units must be bought at $4 each. The existing inventories of 700 will not be replaced. If they are used for the contract, they could not be sold at $2.50 each. The realisable value of these 700 units is an opportunity cost of sales revenue forgone.

(d) The required units of **material D** are already in inventory and will not be replaced. There is an opportunity cost of using D in the contract because there are alternative opportunities either to sell the existing inventories for $6 per unit ($1,200 in total) or avoid other purchases (of material E), which would cost 300 x $5 = $1,500. Since substitution for E is more beneficial, $1,500 is the opportunity cost.

(e)   **Summary of relevant costs**

	$
Material A (1,000 × $6)	6,000
Material B (1,000 × $5)	5,000
Material C (300 × $4) plus (700 × $2.50)	2,950
Material D	1,500
Total	15,450

1.9 The relevant cost of labour

The relevant cost of labour, in different situations, is best explained by means of an example.

1.9.1 Example: Relevant cost of labour

LW Co is currently deciding whether to undertake a new contract. 15 hours of labour will be required for the contract. LW Co currently produces product L, the standard cost details of which are shown below.

STANDARD COST CARD

PRODUCT L

	$/unit
Direct materials (10kg @ $2)	20
Direct labour (5 hrs @ $6)	30
	50
Selling price	72
Contribution	22

(a)   What is the relevant cost of labour if the labour must be hired from outside the organisation?

(b)   What is the relevant cost of labour if LW Co expects to have 5 hours spare capacity?

(c)   What is the relevant cost of labour if labour is in short supply?

Solution

(a)   Where labour must be hired from outside the organisation, the relevant cost of labour will be the variable costs incurred.

Relevant cost of labour on new contract = 15 hours @ $6 = $90

(b)   It is assumed that the 5 hours spare capacity will be paid anyway, and so if these 5 hours are used on another contract, there is no additional cost to LW plc.

Relevant cost of labour on new contract

	$
Direct labour (10 hours @ $6)	60
Spare capacity (5 hours @ $0)	0
	60

(c)   Contribution earned per unit of Product L produced = $22

If it requires 5 hours of labour to make one unit of product L, the contribution earned per labour hour = $22/5 = $4.40.

Relevant cost of labour on new contract

	$
Direct labour (15 hours @ $6)	90
Contribution lost by not making product L ($4.40 × 15 hours)	66
	154

It is important that you should be able to identify the relevant costs which are appropriate to a decision. In many cases, this is a fairly straightforward problem, but there are cases where great care should be taken.

1.10 The deprival value of an asset

In simple terms, the deprival value of an asset represents the amount of money that a company would have to receive if it were deprived of an asset in order to be no worse off than it already is. The deprival value of an asset is best demonstrated by means of an example.

1.10.1 Example: Deprival value of an asset

A machine cost $14,000 ten years ago. It is expected that the machine will generate future revenues of $10,000. Alternatively, the machine could be scrapped for $8,000. An equivalent machine in the same condition would cost $9,000 to buy now. What is the deprival value of the machine?

Solution

Firstly, let us think about the relevance of the costs given to us in the question.

Cost of machine = $14,000 = past/sunk cost
Future revenues = $10,000 = revenue expected to be generated
Net realisable value = $8,000 = scrap proceeds
Replacement cost = $9,000
When calculating the deprival value of an asset, use the following diagram.

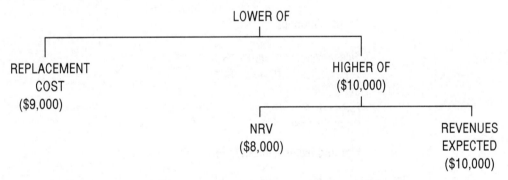

Therefore, the deprival value of the machine is the lower of the replacement cost and $10,000. The deprival value is therefore $9,000.

2 Limiting factors

AST FORWARD

A **limiting factor** is a factor which limits the organisation's activities. In a **limiting factor situation,** contribution will be maximised by earning the biggest possible contribution per unit of limiting factor.

One of the more common decision-making problems is a situation where there are not enough resources to meet the potential sales demand, and so a decision has to be made about what mix of products to produce, using what resources there are as effectively as possible.

> A **limiting factor** is a factor which limits the organisation's activities.

A **limiting factor** could be sales if there is a limit to sales demand but any one of the organisation's resources (labour, materials and so on) may be insufficient to meet the level of production demanded.

2.1 Example: Limiting factors

Suppose Darling Co makes a single product which it sells for $40. The variable costs per unit of the product are as follows.

	$
Direct materials: 6 kg at $2 per kg	12
Direct labour: 2 hours at $6 per hour	12
	24

The fixed costs for the period under consideration are $100,000.

Required

(a) If the availability of direct materials is limited to 60,000 kg, how many units of the product should Darling Co produce and what will be the profit for the period?

(b) If the availability of direct labour is limited to 40,000 hours, how many units of the product should Darling Co produce and what will be the profit for the period?

Solution

(a) **Limiting factor – direct materials**

$$\text{Darling Co can produce} = \frac{60,000 \, \text{kg}}{6 \, \text{kg per unit}}$$

$$= 10,000 \text{ units}$$

Profit statement

	$
Sales revenue (10,000 × $40)	400,000
Variable costs (10,000 × $24)	240,000
Contribution	160,000
Fixed costs	100,000
Profit for period	60,000

(b) **Limiting factor – direct labour**

$$\text{Darling Co can produce} = \frac{40,000 \, \text{hours}}{2 \, \text{hours per unit}}$$

$$= 20,000 \text{ units}$$

Profit statement

	$
Sales revenue (20,000 × $40)	800,000
Variable costs (20,000 × $24)	480,000
Contribution	320,000
Fixed costs	100,000
Profit for period	220,000

2.2 Optimal production solution

It is assumed in limiting factor analysis that management wishes to maximise profit and that **profit will be maximised when contribution is maximised** (given no change in the fixed cost expenditure incurred). In other words, **marginal costing ideas are applied**.

Contribution will be maximised by earning the biggest possible contribution from each unit of limiting factor. For example if grade A labour is the limiting factor, contribution will be maximised by earning the biggest contribution from each hour of grade A labour worked.

The limiting factor decision therefore involves the determination of the contribution earned by each different product from each unit of the limiting factor.

The **optimal production** solution can be determined by following this five-step approach.

Step 1 Identify the limiting factor

Step 2 Calculate contribution per unit for each product

Step 3 Calculate contribution from each product per unit of limiting factor

Step 4 Rank products (make product with highest contribution per unit of limiting factor first)

Step 5 Make products in rank order until scarce resource is used up **(optimal production solution)**

Question
Limiting factor

LF Co makes a single product for which the cost details are as follows.

	$ per unit
Direct material ($3 per kg)	12
Direct labour ($8 per hour)	72
Production overhead	18
Total production cost	102

Demand for next period will be 20,000 units. No inventories are held and only 75,000 kg of material and 190,000 hours of labour will be available. What will be the limiting factor next period?

A Material only
B Labour only
C Material and labour
D There will be no limiting factor next period

Answer

Material required = 20,000 units × ($12/$3) = 80,000 kg

Material is therefore a limiting factor, since only 75,000 kg are available. This eliminates option D.

Labour required = 20,000 units × ($72/$8) = 180,000 hours.

Labour is not a limiting factor, since 190,000 labour hours are available. This eliminates options B and C.

Therefore the correct answer is A.

2.2.1 Example: Optimal production solution

AB Co makes two products, the Ay and the Be. Unit variable costs are as follows.

	Ay $	Be $
Direct materials	1	3
Direct labour ($3 per hour)	6	3
Variable overhead	1	1
	8	7

The sales price per unit is $14 per Ay and $11 per Be. During July 20X2 the available direct labour is limited to 8,000 hours. Sales demand in July is expected to be 3,000 units for Ays and 5,000 units for Bes.

Required

Determine the optimal production solution, assuming that monthly fixed costs are $20,000, and that opening inventories of finished goods and work in progress are nil.

Solution

Step 1   Confirm that the limiting factor is something other than sales demand.

	Ays	Bes	Total
Labour hours per unit	2 hrs	1 hr	
Sales demand	3,000 units	5,000 units	
Labour hours needed	6,000 hrs	5,000 hrs	11,000 hrs
Labour hours available			8,000 hrs
Shortfall			3,000 hrs

Labour is the limiting factor on production.

Step 2   Identify the contribution earned by each product per unit of limiting factor, that is per labour hour worked.

	Ays $	Bes $
Sales price	14	11
Variable cost	8	7
Unit contribution	6	4
Labour hours per unit	2 hrs	1 hr
Contribution per labour hour (= unit of limiting factor)	$3	$4

Although Ays have a higher unit contribution than Bes, two Bes can be made in the time it takes to make one Ay. Because labour is in short supply it is more profitable to make Bes than Ays.

Step 3   Determine the **optimal production solution**. Sufficient Bes will be made to meet the full sales demand, and the remaining labour hours available will then be used to make Ays.

(a)

Product	Demand	Hours required	Hours available	Priority of manufacture
Bes	5,000	5,000	5,000	1st
Ays	3,000	6,000	3,000 (bal)	2nd
		11,000	8,000	

(b)

Product	Units	Hours needed	Contribution per unit $	Total $
Bes	5,000	5,000	4	20,000
Ays	1,500	3,000	6	9,000
		8,000		29,000
Less fixed costs				20,000
Profit				9,000

In conclusion

(a) Unit contribution is **not** the correct way to decide priorities.

(b) Labour hours are the scarce resource, and therefore contribution **per labour hour** is the correct way to decide priorities.

(c) The Be earns $4 contribution per labour hour, and the Ay earns $3 contribution per labour hour. Bes therefore make more profitable use of the scarce resource, and should be manufactured first.

If an examination question asks you to determine the optimal production solution, follow the five-step approach shown below.

Step 1   Identify the limiting factor

Step 2   Calculate contribution per unit for each product

Step 3   Calculate contribution per unit of limiting factor

Step 4   Rank products (make product with highest contribution per unit of limiting factor first)

Step 5   Make products in rank order until scare resource is used up **(optimal production solution)**

A large number of candidates really struggled with this type of question in the December 2004 exam.

---

3 Make/buy-in problems

In a **make/buy-in problem** with no limiting factors, the relevant costs for the decision are the **differential costs** between the two options.

3.1 Introduction

A **make/buy-in problem** involves a decision by an organisation about whether it should make a product/carry out an activity with its own internal resources, or whether it should pay another organisation to make the product/carry out the activity. Examples of make/buy-in problems would be as follows.

(a) Whether a company should manufacture its own components, or buy the components from an outside supplier.

(b) Whether a construction company should do some work with its own employees, or whether it should subcontract the work to another company.

If an organisation has the freedom of choice about whether to make internally or buy externally and has no scarce resources that put a restriction on what it can do itself, the relevant costs for the decision will be the **differential costs** between the two options.

3.1.1 Example: Make/buy-in problem

Buster Co makes four components, W, X, Y and Z, for which costs in the forthcoming year are expected to be as follows.

	W	X	Y	Z
Production (units)	1,000	2,000	4,000	3,000
Unit marginal costs	$	$	$	$
Direct materials	4	5	2	4
Direct labour	8	9	4	6
Variable production overheads	2	3	1	2
	14	17	7	12

Directly attributable fixed costs per annum and committed fixed costs are as follows.

	$
Incurred as a direct consequence of making W	1,000
Incurred as a direct consequence of making X	5,000
Incurred as a direct consequence of making Y	6,000
Incurred as a direct consequence of making Z	8,000
Other fixed costs (committed)	30,000
	50,000

A subcontractor has offered to supply units of W, X, Y and Z for $12, $21, $10 and $14 respectively.

Required

Decide whether Buster Co should make or buy-in the components.

Solution

(a)   **The relevant costs are the differential costs between making and buying**, and they consist of differences in unit variable costs plus differences in directly attributable fixed costs. Subcontracting will result in some fixed cost savings.

	W	X	Y	Z
	$	$	$	$
Unit variable cost of making	14	17	7	12
Unit variable cost of buying	12	21	10	14
	(2)	4	3	2
Annual requirements (units)	1,000	2,000	4,000	3,000
Extra variable cost of buying (per annum)	(2,000)	8,000	12,000	6,000
Fixed costs saved by buying	1,000	5,000	6,000	8,000
Extra total cost of buying	(3,000)	3,000	6,000	(2,000)

(b)   The company would save $3,000 pa by subcontracting component W (where the purchase cost would be less than the marginal cost per unit to make internally) and would save $2,000 pa by subcontracting component Z (because of the saving in fixed costs of $8,000).

(c)   In this example, relevant costs are the variable costs of in-house manufacture, the variable costs of subcontracted units, and the saving in fixed costs.

BPP
LEARNING MEDIA

3.2 Other factors to consider in the make/buy-in problem

(a) If components W and Z are subcontracted, how will the company most profitably use the spare capacity? Would the company's workforce resent the loss of work to an outside subcontractor?

(b) Would the subcontractor be reliable with delivery times, and would he supply components of the same quality as those manufactured internally?

(c) Does the company wish to be flexible and maintain better control over operations by making everything itself?

(d) Are the estimates of fixed cost savings reliable? In the case of Product W, buying is clearly cheaper than making in-house. In the case of product Z, the decision to buy rather than make would only be financially beneficial if the fixed cost savings of $8,000 could really be 'delivered' by management.

Question   Make/buy-in

BB Co makes three components - S, T and W. The following costs have been recorded.

	Component S Unit cost $	Component T Unit cost $	Component W Unit cost $
Variable cost	2.50	8.00	5.00
Fixed cost	2.00	8.30	3.75
Total cost	4.50	16.30	8.75

Another company has offered to supply the components to BB Limited at the following prices.

	Component S	Component T	Component W
Price each	$4	$7	$5.50

Which component(s), if any, should BB Co consider buying in?

A   Buy in all three components
B   Do not buy any
C   Buy in S and W
D   Buy in T only

Answer

BB Co should buy the component if the variable cost of making the component is more than the variable cost of buying the component.

	Component S $	Component T $	Component W $
Variable cost of making	2.50	8.00	5.00
Variable cost of buying	4.00	7.00	5.50
	(1.50)	1.00	(0.50)

The variable cost of making component T is greater than the variable cost of buying it.

∴ BB Co should consider buying in component T only.

The correct answer is D.

3.3 Make/buy-in problems and limiting factors

In a situation where a company must subcontract work to make up a shortfall in its own production capability, its total costs are minimised if those components/products subcontracted are those with the lowest extra variable cost of buying per unit of limiting factor saved by buying.

3.3.1 Example: make/buy-in problems and limiting factors

Green Co manufactures two components, the Alpha and the Beta, using the same machines for each. The budget for the next year calls for the production and assembly of 4,000 of each component. The variable production cost per unit of the final product, the gamma, is as follows.

	Machine hours	Variable cost
		$
1 unit of Alpha	3	20
1 unit of Beta	2	36
Assembly		20
		76

Only 16,000 hours of machine time will be available during the year, and a sub-contractor has quoted the following unit prices for supplying components: Alpha $29; Beta $40. Advise Green Co.

Solution

(a)   There is a shortfall in machine hours available, and some products must be sub-contracted.

Product	Units		Machine hours
Alpha	4,000		12,000
Beta	4,000		8,000
		Required	20,000
		Available	16,000
		Shortfall	4,000

(b)   **The assembly costs are not relevant costs because they are unaffected by the make/buy-in problem.** The units subcontracted should be those which will add least to the costs of Green Co. Since 4,000 hours of work must be sub-contracted, the cheapest policy is to subcontract work which adds the least extra costs (the least extra variable costs) per hour of own-time saved.

(c)

	Alpha	Beta
	$	$
Variable cost of making	20	36
Variable cost of buying	29	40
Extra variable cost of buying	9	4
Machine hours saved by buying	3 hrs	2 hrs
Extra variable cost of buying, per hour saved	$3	$2

It is cheaper to buy Betas than to buy Alphas and so the priority for making the components in-house will be in the reverse order to the preference for buying them from a subcontractor.

(d)

Component	Hrs per unit to make in-house	Hrs required in total	Cumulative hours
Alpha	3 hrs	12,000	12,000
Beta	2 hrs	8,000	20,000
		20,000	
Hours available		16,000	
Shortfall		4,000	

There are enough machine hours to make all 4,000 units of Alpha and 2,000 units of Beta. 4,000 hours production of Beta must be sub-contracted. This will be the cheapest production policy available.

(e)

Component	Machine hours	Number of units	Unit variable cost	Total variable cost
			$	$
Make				
Alpha	12,000	4,000	20	80,000
Beta (balance)	4,000	2,000	36	72,000
	16,000			152,000
Buy	*Hours saved*			
Beta (balance)	4,000	2,000	40	80,000

Total variable costs of components 232,000
Assembly costs (4,000 × $20) 80,000
Total variable costs 312,000

Chapter Roundup

- **Relevant costs** are future cash flows arising as a direct consequence of a decision.

  Relevant costs are **future costs, cashflows** and **incremental costs.** They are also **differential costs** and **opportunity costs.**

- A **limiting factor** is a factor which limits the organisation's activities. In a **limiting factor situation,** contribution will be maximised by earning the biggest possible contribution per unit of limiting factor.

- In a **make/buy-in problem** with no limiting factors, the relevant costs for the decision are the **differential costs** between the two options.

Quick Quiz

1   Relevant costs are:

(a)
(b)
(c)
(d)
(e)

2   Sunk costs are directly relevant in decision making.

☐   True

☐   False

3   The following information relates to machine Z.

Purchase price = $7,000
Expected future revenues = $5,000
Scrap value = $4,000
Replacement cost = $4,500

Complete the following diagram in order to calculate the deprival value of machine Z.

LOWER OF ☐

REPLACEMENT COST ☐

HIGHER OF ☐

NRV ☐

REVENUES ☐

The deprival value of machine Z is ....

4   A limiting factor is a factor which ....

5   When determining the optimal production solution, what five steps are involved?

Step 1 ....

Step 2 ....

Step 3 ....

Step 4 ....

Step 5 ....

6   A sunk cost is:

A   a cost committed to be spent in the current period

B   a cost which is irrelevant for decision making

C   a cost connected with oil exploration in the North Sea

D   a cost unaffected by fluctuations in the level of activity

Answers to Quick Quiz

1   (a)   Future costs
    (b)   Cash flows
    (c)   Incremental costs
    (d)   Differential costs
    (e)   Opportunity costs

2   False

3

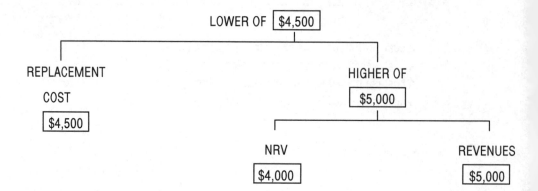

The deprival value of machine Z is **$4,500**.

4   Limits the organisation's activities.

5   **Step 1**   Identify the limiting factor

    Step 2   Calculate contribution per unit for each product

    Step 3   Calculate contribution per unit of limiting factor

    Step 4   Rank products (make product with highest contribution per unit of limiting factor first)

    Step 5   Make products in rank order until scare resource is used up **(optimal production plan)**

6   B

Now try the questions below from the Exam Question Bank

Number	Level	Marks	Time
14	Examination	N/A	30 mins

Capital investment appraisal

15

Chapter topic list

Study guide reference

		Syllabus reference
18/19 (a)	Explain and illustrate the difference between simple and compound interest and between nominal and effective interest rate	6(c)
18/19 (b)	Explain and illustrate compounding and discounting	6(c)
18/19 (c)	Explain the distinction between cash flow and profit and the relevance of cash flow to capital investment appraisal	6(c)
18/19 (d)	Explain and illustrate the net present value (NPV) and internal rate of return (IRR) methods of discounted cash flow	6(c)
18/19 (e)	Calculate present value using annuity and perpetuity formulae	6(c)
18/19 (f)	Calculate payback (discounted and non-discounted)	6(c)
18/19 (g)	Interpret the results of NPV, IRR and payback calculations of investment viability	6(c)

1 Introduction to capital investment appraisal

FAST FORWARD

Long term investments include the purchase of buildings, machinery and equipment. Management will need to have estimates of the initial investment and future costs and revenues of a project in order to make any **long term decisions.**

Long term decisions generally involve looking at the options available when a company (or an individual) puts money into an investment.

If a company invests in a project, it will expect some sort of financial return (or more money) at some point in the future. If the project runs for a number of years then whether or not to invest in the project will involve taking a long term decision.

One of the things companies will need to consider when investing in long term projects is the **time value of money**.

Think about the following question.

'If I have $5 in my pocket **now**, how much will it be worth in four years' time?'

This is a difficult question to answer, but we will be looking at ways in which companies use the concept of the **time value of money** when they are appraising projects and making long term decisions.

2 Interest

FAST FORWARD

Interest is the amount of money which an investment earns over time. **Simple interest** is interest which is earned in equal amounts every year. If interest earned also earns interest itself in later periods, this is known as **compound interest.**

2.1 Simple interest

Key terms

- **Interest** is the amount of money which an investment earns over time.

- **Simple interest** is interest which is earned in equal amounts every year (or month) and which is a given proportion of the original investment (the principal).

If a sum of money is invested for a period of time, then the amount of simple interest which accrues is equal to the number of periods × the interest rate × the amount invested. We can write this as a formula.

The formula for **simple interest** is as follows.

$S = P + nrP$

where	P	=	the original sum invested
	r	=	the interest rate (expressed as a proportion, so 10% = 0.1)
	n	=	the number of periods (normally years)
	S	=	the sum invested after n periods, consisting of the original capital (P) plus interest earned (future value)

2.1.1 Example: Simple interest

Fred invests $1,000 at 10% simple interest per annum.

Required

Calculate how much Fred will have after five years.

Solution

Using the formula $S = P + nrP$

where	P	=	$1,000
	r	=	10%
	n	=	5

$\therefore S = \$1,000 + (5 \times 0.1 \times \$1,000) = \$1,500$

2.2 Compound interest

Interest is normally calculated by means of **compounding**.

If a sum of money is invested at a fixed rate of interest and the interest is added to the original sum of money, then the **interest earned in earlier periods will also earn interest in later periods**.

2.2.1 Example: Compound interest

Suppose that Fred invests $2,000 at 10% interest per annum. After one year, the original principal plus interest will amount to $2,200.

	$
Original investment	2,000
Interest in the first year (10%)	200
Total investment at the end of one year	2,200

(a) **After two years** the total investment will be $2,420.

	$
Investment at end of one year	2,200
Interest in the second year (10%)	220
Total investment at the end of two years	2,420

The second year interest of $220 represents 10% of the original investment, and 10% of the interest earned in the first year.

(b)   Similarly, **after three years**, the total investment will be $2,662.

	$
Investment at the end of two years	2,420
Interest in the third year (10%)	242
Total investment at the end of three years	2,662

Instead of performing the calculations shown above, we could have used the following formula.

The basic formula for **compound interest** is $S = P(1 + r)^n$

where	P	=	the original sum invested
	r	=	the interest rate, expressed as a proportion (so 5% = 0.05)
	n	=	the number of periods (normally years)
	S	=	the sum invested after n periods (future value)

Using the formula for compound interest, $S = P(1 + r)^n$

where	P	=	$2,000
	r	=	10% = 0.1
	n	=	3
	S	=	$2,000 \times 1.10^3$
		=	$2,000 \times 1.331$
		=	$2,662.

The interest earned over three years is $662, which is the same answer that was calculated in the example above.

If today's date is 31 May 20X3, note the following timings of cash flows.

- Time 0 = now (31 May 20X3)
- Time 1 = one year's time (31 May 20X4)
- Time 2 = two year's time (31 May 20X5)

Question
Compound interest

If Fred invests $5,000 now (28 February 20X3) how much will his investment be worth:

(a)   On 28 February 20X6, if the interest rate is 20% per annum?

(b)   On 28 February 20X7, if the interest rate is 15% per annum?

(c)   On 28 February 20X6, if the interest rate is 6% per annum?

Answer

(a)   At 28 February 20X6, n = 3, $5,000 \times 1.20^3$ = $8,640
(b)   At 28 February 20X7, n = 4, $5,000 \times 1.15^4$ = $8,745.03
(c)   At 28 February 20X6, n = 3, $5,000 \times 1.06^3$ = $5,955.08

2.3 Effective interest rates

In the previous examples, interest has been calculated **annually**, but this isn't always the case. Interest may be compounded **daily**, **weekly**, **monthly** or **quarterly**.

The **equivalent annual** rate of interest, when interest is compounded at shorter intervals, is known as an **effective annual rate of interest**.

mula to
rn

Effective Interest Rate $= [(1+r)^{\frac{12}{n}} - 1]$ or $[(1+r)^{\frac{365}{y}} - 1]$

where r is the rate of interest for each time period
         n is the number of months in the time period
         y is the number of days in the time period.

2.3.1 Example: Effective interest rates

Calculate the effective annual rate of interest of:

    (a)   1.5% per month, compound
    (b)   4.5% per quarter, compound
    (c)   9% per half year, compound

Solution

(a) $(1.015)^{12} - 1$ = 0.1956 = 19.56%
(b) $(1.045)^{4} - 1$ = 0.1925 = 19.25%
(c) $(1.09)^{2} - 1$ = 0.1881 = 18.81%

2.4 Nominal interest rates

Most interest rates are expressed as **per annum figures** even when the interest is compounded over periods of less than one year. In such cases, the given interest rate is called a **nominal rate**. We can, however, work out the **effective rate**. It is this effective rate (shortened to one decimal place) which is quoted in advertisements as the **annual percentage rate (APR)**, sometimes called the **compound annual rate (CAR)**.

am focus
int

Students often become seriously confused about the various rates of interest.

- The **NOMINAL RATE** is the interest rate expressed as a per annum figure, eg 12% pa nominal even though interest may be compounded over periods of less than one year.

- Adjusted nominal rate = **EQUIVALENT ANNUAL RATE**

- Equivalent annual rate (the rate per day or per month adjusted to give an annual rate) = **EFFECTIVE ANNUAL RATE**

- Effective annual rate = **ANNUAL PERCENTAGE RATE (APR)** = **COMPOUND ANNUAL RATE (CAR)**

2.5 Example: Nominal and effective rates of interest

A building society may offer investors 10% per annum interest payable half-yearly. If the 10% is a nominal rate of interest, the building society would in fact pay 5% every six months, compounded so that the effective annual rate of interest would be

$[(1.05)^{2} - 1]$ = 0.1025 = 10.25% per annum.

Similarly, if a bank offers depositors a nominal 12% per annum, with interest payable quarterly, the effective rate of interest would be 3% compound every three months, which is

$[(1.03)^4 - 1] = 0.1255 = 12.55\%$ per annum.

Question

Calculate the effective annual rate of interest of

(a)   15% nominal per annum compounded quarterly;
(b)   24% nominal per annum compounded monthly.

Answer

(a)   15% per annum (nominal rate) is 3.75% per quarter. The effective annual rate of interest is
       $[1.0375^4 - 1] = 0.1587 = 15.87\%$

(b)   24% per annum (nominal rate) is 2% per month. The effective annual rate of interest is
       $[1.02^{12} - 1] = 0.2682 = 26.82\%$

3 The principles of discounted cash flow

FAST FORWARD

- The basic principle of **discounting** involves calculating the **present value** of an investment (ie the value of an investment **today** at time 0).

- The term **present value** means the amount of money which must be invested now (for a number of years) in order to earn a future sum (at a given rate of interest).

The basic principle of **discounting** is that if we wish to have $S in n years' time, we need to invest a certain sum **now** (year 0) at an interest rate of r% in order to obtain the required sum of money in the future. In day-to-day terms, we could say that if we wish to have $1,000 in five years' time, how much would we need to invest now at an interest rate of 4%?

3.1 Example: Principles of discounted cash flow

If we wish to have $14,641 in four years' time, how much money would we need to invest now at 10% interest per annum?

Using our compounding formula, $S = P(1 + r)^n$

where	P	=	the original sum invested
	r	=	10% = 0.1
	n	=	4
	S	=	$14,641

$14,641   = $P(1 + 0.1)^4$

$14,641   = $P \times 1.4641$

$\therefore P$ = $\dfrac{\$14,641}{1.4641} = \$10,000$

$10,000 now, with the capacity to earn a return of 10% per annum, is the equivalent in value of $14,641 after four years. We can therefore say that **$10,000 is the present value of $14,641 at year 4, at an interest rate of 10%.**

3.2 Present values

The term **'present value'** simply means the amount of money which must be invested now for n years at an interest rate of r%, to earn a given future sum of money at the time it will be due.

The **discounting formula** is

$$P = S \times \frac{1}{(1+r)^n}$$

where S   is the sum to be received after n time periods
       P   is the present value (PV) of that sum
       r   is the rate of return, expressed as a proportion
       n   is the number of time periods (usually years).

The rate r is sometimes called the **cost of capital**.

Note that this equation is just a rearrangement of the compounding formula.

3.2.1 Example: Present values

(a)   Calculate the present value of $60,000 received at the end of year 6, if interest rates are 15% per annum.

(b)   Calculate the present value of $100,000 received at the end of year 5, if interest rates are 6% per annum.

Solution

The discounting formula, $X = P \times \frac{1}{(1+r)^n}$ is required.

(a)   S   = $60,000
       n   =   6
       r   =   0.15

       PV   = $60,000 \times \frac{1}{1.15^6}$
            = $60,000 \times 0.432$
            = $25,920

(b)   S   = $100,000
       n   =   5
       r   =   0.06

       PV   = $100,000 \times \frac{1}{1.06^5}$
            = $100,000 \times 0.747$
            = $74,700

3.3 Present value tables

Now that you understand the principles of discounting and you are able to calculate present values, you will be happy to hear that you do not need to remember the formula for discounting. This is because the present value tables at the end of this Interactive Text have already calculated all of the discount factors that you will ever need for Paper 4.

Refer to the **present value tables** on page 319.

The use of present value tables is best explained by means of an example.

3.3.1 Example: Present value tables

(a)   Using tables, calculate the present value of $60,000 at year 6, if interest rates are 15% per annum.
(b)   Using tables, calculate the present value of $100,000 at year 5, if interest rates are 6% per annum.

Solution

(a)   Looking at the present value tables at the back of this Interactive Text, look along the row n = 6 (year 6) and down column r = 15% (interest rates are 15% per annum). The required discount rate is 0.432.

The present value of $60,000 at year 6, when interest rates are 15% is therefore:

$60,000 × 0.432 = $25,920

(b)   Looking at the present value tables at the back of this Interactive Text, look along the row n = 5 (year 5) and down column r = 6% (interest rates are 6% per annum). The required discount rate is 0.747.

The present value of $100,000 at year 5, when interest rates are 6% is therefore:

$100,000 × 0.747 = $74,700

Do either of these present values look familiar? Well, both of them should be as they are the same present values that we calculated in the previous example using the discounting formula!

Question   **Present values**

Today's date is 30 April 20X3. If Fred wishes to have $16,000 saved by 30 April 20X8, how much should he invest if interest rates are 5%? Use the present value tables at the back of this Interactive Text.

Answer

30 April 20X3 = Now

30 April 20X4 = time period 5

∴ n   = 5

r   = 5%

Present value = $16,000 × discount rate (where n = 5 and r = 5%)

= $16,000 × 0.784

= $12,544

4 Annuities and perpetuities

FORWARD ▶

- An **annuity** is a constant sum of money received or paid each year for a given number of years.
- A **perpetuity** is an annuity which lasts forever

4.1 Annuities

term

An **annuity** is a constant sum of money received or paid each year for a given number of years.

For example, the present value of a three year annuity of $100 which begins in one year's time when interest rates are 5% is calculated as follows.

Time	Cash flow $	Discount factor 5%	Present value $
1	100	0.952	95.20
2	100	0.907	90.70
3	100	0.864	86.40
			272.30

There is a rather long and complicated formula which can be used to calculate the present value of an annuity. Fortunately there are also **annuity tables** which calculate all of the **annuity factors** that you might ever need for Paper 4.

In order to calculate the present value of a constant sum of money, we can multiply the annual cash flow by the sum of the discount factors for the relevant years. These total factors are known as **cumulative present value factors or annuity factors.**

term

Present value of an annuity = Annuity × annuity factor

4.1.1 Example: Annuity tables

What is the annuity factor (cumulative present value factor) of $1 per annum for five years at 11% interest?

Solution

Refer to the annuity tables on page 320 at the back of this Interactive Text.

Read across to the column headed 11% (r = 11%) and down to period 5 (n = 5). The annuity factor = 3.696

Now look back at the present value tables on page 319 and look in the column n = 11%. The cumulative present value rates for n = 1 to 5 = 0.901 + 0.812 + 0.731 + 0.659 + 0.593 = 3.696. Can you see now why these annuity tables are also called cumulative present value tables?

4.1.2 Example: Present value of an annuity

Fred has to make an annual payment of $1,000 to a car hire company on 30 June 20X3 each year until 30 June 20X8.

Required

Calculate the present value of Fred's total payments if today's date is 1 July 20X2. Use a discount rate of 7%.

301

Solution

The first payment will be in one year's time ie time 1.

There will be six annual payments.

Annuity factor (where n = 6, r = 7%) = 4.767

Present value of payments = $1,000 × annuity factor
$$= \$1,000 \times 4.767$$
$$= \$4,767$$

4.2 Perpetuities

Key term

> A **perpetuity** is an annuity which lasts forever.
>
> The **present value of a perpetuity** $= \dfrac{\text{annuity}}{\text{interest rate}^{\,*}}$
>
> *expressed as a proportion eg 20% = 0.2

4.2.1 Example: A perpetuity

Fred is to receive $35,000 per annum in perpetuity starting in one year's time. If the annual rate of interest is 9% what is the present value of this perpetuity?

Solution

$$PV = \frac{\text{annuity}}{\text{interest rate}}$$

$$\therefore PV = \frac{\$35,000}{0.09}$$

$$= \$388,889$$

4.3 Cash flows and profits

To be successful in business, organisations must make **profits**. Profits are needed in order to pay dividends to shareholders and to allow partners to make drawings.

If an organisation makes a loss, the value of the business falls and if there are long-term losses, the business may eventually collapse.

Net profit measures how much the capital of an organisation has increased over a period of time. Profit is calculated by applying the **matching concept**, that is to say by matching the costs incurred with the sales revenue generated during a period.

4.4 The importance of cash

In addition to being **profitable**, an organisation needs to have enough cash in order to pay for the following.

- Goods and services
- Capital investment (plant, machinery and so on)
- Labour costs
- Other expenses (rent, rates, taxation and so on)
- Dividends

Net cash flow measures the difference in the payments leaving an organisation's bank account and the receipts that are paid into the bank account.

4.5 Net profit and net cash flow

Reasons why net profit and net cash flow differ are mainly due to timing differences.

(a) **Cash is obtained from a transaction which is not reported in the income statement**

- Share issue
- Increase bank overdraft

(b) **Purchase of non-current assets**

Suppose an asset is purchased for $20,000 and depreciation is charged at 10% of the original cost.

- Cash payment during the year = $20,000 (and this does not affect the income statement)
- Depreciation charge = 10% × $20,000 = $2,000. This is charged to the income statement and will reduce overall profits

(c) **Sale of non-current assets**

When an asset is sold there is usually a profit or loss on sale. Suppose an asset with a net book value of $15,000 is sold for $11,000, giving rise to a loss on disposal of $4,000.

- Increase in cash flow during the year = $11,000 sale proceeds. There will be no effect on the income statement
- Loss on sale of non-current assets = $4,000. This will be recorded in the firm's income statement and will reduce overall profits

(d) **Matching receipts from receivables and sales invoices raised**

If goods are sold on credit, the cash receipts will differ from the value of the sales.

(e) **Matching payments to payables and cost of sales**

If materials are bought on credit, the cash payments to suppliers will be different from the value of materials purchased. In turn, the value of the materials purchased will need to be matched against sales for the period.

m focus
nt

It is very important that you fully understand the difference between cash and profit. The examiner noted in December 2005 that this was a problem for many candidates.

5 Capital investment appraisal – net present value method

ST FORWARD

- **Discounted cash flow** involves discounting future cash flows from a project in order to decide whether the project will earn a satisfactory rate of return.
- The two main discounted cash flow **methods** are the **net present value** (NPV) method and the **internal rate of return** (IRR) method.

Discounted cash flow methods can be used to appraise capital investment projects.

Discounted cash flow (DCF) involves the application of discounting arithmetic to the estimated future cash flows (receipts and expenditures) from a capital investment project in order to decide whether the project is expected to earn a satisfactory rate of return.

The two main discounted cash flow methods are as follows.

- The net present value (NPV) method
- The internal rate of return (IRR) method

5.1 The net present value (NPV) method

The **net present value (NPV) method** calculates the present values of all items of income and expenditure related to an investment at a given rate of return, and then calculates a net total. If it is positive, the investment is considered to be acceptable. If it is negative, the investment is considered to be unacceptable.

5.1.1 Example: The net present value of a project

Dog Co is considering whether to spend $5,000 on an item of equipment which will last for two years. The excess of income over cash expenditure from the equipment would be $3,000 in the first year and $4,000 in the second year.

Required

Calculate the net present value of the investment in the equipment at a discount rate of 15%.

Solution

In this example, an outlay of $5,000 now promises a return of $3,000 **during** the first year and $4,000 **during** the second year. It is a convention in DCF, however, that cash flows spread over a year are assumed to occur **at the end of the year**, so that the cash flows of the project are as follows.

	$
Year 0 (now)	(5,000)
Year 1 (at the end of the year)	3,000
Year 2 (at the end of the year)	4,000

A net present value statement is drawn up as follows.

Year	Cash flow $	Discount factor 15%	Present value $
0	(5,000)	1.000	(5,000)
1	3,000	0.870	2,610
2	4,000	0.756	3,024
	Net present value		+ 634

The project has a positive net present value, so it is acceptable.

5.2 The timing of cash flows

Note that annuity tables and the formulae both assume that the first payment or receipt is a year from now. **Always check examination and assessment questions for when the first payment falls**.

For example, if there are five equal annual payments starting now, and the interest rate is 8%, we should use a factor of 1 (for today's payment) + 3.312 (for the other four payments) = 4.312.

5.3 Cash v profit

Remember that it is **cash flow figures** that must be included in your calculations. If depreciation has been deducted from a profit figure, it must be **added back** to give the net cash inflow.

Question	NPV (1)

A company is wondering whether to spend $18,000 on an item of equipment, in order to obtain cash profits as follows.

Year	$
1	6,000
2	8,000
3	5,000
4	1,000

The company requires a return of 10% per annum.

Required

Use the net present value method to assess whether the project to invest in the equipment is viable.

Answer

	Cash flow	Discount factor	Present value
	$	10%	$
0	(18,000)	*1.000	(18,000)
1	6,000	0.909	5,454
2	8,000	0.826	6,608
3	5,000	0.751	3,755
4	1,000	0.683	683
		Net present value	(1,500)

*The initial cost occurs at time 0, now, and therefore the discount factor is 1.00 as $18,000 is the present value of the expenditure now.

The NPV is negative and the project is therefore not viable (since the present value of the costs is greater than the present value of the benefits).

Question	NPV (2)

Daisy Co is considering whether to make an investment costing $28,000 which would earn $8,000 cash per annum (starting in one year's time) for five years.

Required

What is the net present value of the investment at a cost of capital of 11%.

Answer

Year	Cash flow $	Discount factor 11%	Present value $
0	(28,000)	1.000	(28,000)
1	8,000	0.901	7,208
2	8,000	0.812	6,496
3	8,000	0.731	5,848
4	8,000	0.659	5,272
5	8,000	0.593	4,744
		NPV	1,568

Alternatively, you could treat the cash inflows of $8,000 for five years as an annuity.

Year	Cash flow $	Discount factor 11%	Present value $
0	(28,000)	1.000	(28,000)
1-5	8,000	3.696	29,568
			1,568

Question

NPV (3)

Mostly Co is considering a project which would cost $50,000 now and yield $9,000 per annum every year in perpetuity, starting a year from now. The cost of capital is 15%.

Required

Calculate the net present value of the project.

Answer

Year	Cash flow $	Discount factor 15%	Present value $
0	(50,000)	1.0	(50,000)
1 - ∞	9,000	1/0.15	60,000
		NPV	10,000

The net present value of the project is $10,000.

6 Capital investment appraisal – internal rate of return (IRR) method

FAST FORWARD

> The **IRR method** determines the rate of interest (internal rate of return) at which the NPV = 0. The internal rate of return is therefore the rate of return on an investment.

The **internal rate of return (IRR) method** of evaluating investments is an alternative to the NPV method. The NPV method of discounted cash flow determines whether an investment earns a **positive or a negative NPV when discounted at a given rate of interest**. If the NPV is zero (that is, the present values of costs and benefits are equal) the return from the project would be exactly the rate used for discounting.

The **IRR method of discounted cash flow** is a method which determines the rate of interest (the internal rate of return) at which the NPV is 0. The internal rate of return is therefore the rate of return on an investment.

The IRR method will indicate that a project is viable **if the IRR exceeds the minimum acceptable rate of return**. Thus if the company expects a minimum return of, say, 15%, a project would be viable if its IRR is more than 15%.

6.1 Example: The IRR method over one year

If $500 is invested today and generates $600 in one year's time, the internal rate of return (r) can be calculated as follows.

$$PV \text{ of cost} = PV \text{ of benefits}$$
$$500 = \frac{600}{(1+r)}$$
$$500(1+r) = 600$$
$$1+r = \frac{600}{500} = 1.2$$
$$r = 0.2 = 20\%$$

The arithmetic for calculating the IRR is more complicated for investments and cash flows extending over a period of time longer than one year. An approximate IRR can be calculated using either a **graphical method** or by a technique known as the **interpolation** method.

6.2 Graphical approach

A useful way to **estimate** the IRR of a project is to **find the project's NPV at a number of discount rates** and **sketch a graph of NPV against discount rate**. You can then use the sketch to estimate the **discount rate at which the NPV is equal to zero** (the point where the curve cuts the axis).

6.2.1 Example: graphical approach

A project might have the following NPVs at the following discount rates.

Discount rate %	NPV $
5	5,300
10	400
15	(1,700)
20	(2,900)

This could be sketched on a graph as follows.

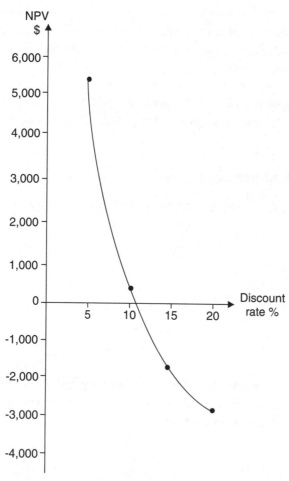

Reading from the graph, the IRR can be **estimated as 11%.**

6.3 The interpolation method

Using the interpolation method, the IRR is calculated by first of all finding the NPV at each of two interest rates. Ideally, one interest rate should give a small positive NPV and the other a small negative NPV. The IRR would then be somewhere between these two interest rates: above the rate where the NPV is positive, but below the rate where the NPV is negative.

Key term

The IRR, where the NPV is zero, can be calculated as follows.

$$\textbf{IRR} = a\% + \left[\frac{NPV_A}{NPV_A - NPV_B} \times (b - a) \right]\%$$

where a is one interest rate
  b is the other interest rate
  NPV_A is the NPV at rate a
  NPV_B is the NPV at rate b

Using the information from the graphical approach example above.

a = 10%
b = 15%
NPV_A = $400
NPV_B = $(1,700)

$$IRR = 10\% + \frac{400}{(400 + 1,700)} \times (15 - 10) \%$$
$$= 10\% + 0.95\%$$
$$= 10.95\%$$

Question

The net present value of an investment at 15% is $50,000 and at 20% is - $10,000. The internal rate of return of this investment (to the nearest whole number) is:

A   16%
B   17%
C   18%
D   19%

Answer

$$\text{IRR} = a\% + \left[\frac{\text{NPV}_A}{\text{NPV}_A - \text{NPV}_B} \times (b-a) \right]\%$$

Where a   =   one interest rate = 15%
      b   =   other interest rate = 20%
      NPV_A =   NPV at rate a = $50,000
      NPV_B =   NPV at rate b = $10,000

$$\text{IRR} = 15\% + \left[\frac{\$50,000}{\$50,000 - (-10,000)} \times (20-15) \right]\%$$

$$= 15\% + 4.17\%$$
$$= 19.17\%$$
$$= 19\%$$

The correct answer is therefore D.

7 Capital investment appraisal – payback method

ST FORWARD The **payback period** is the time that is required for the cash inflows from a capital investment project to equal the cash outflows.

7.1 What is the payback period?

The **payback period** is the time that is required for the total of the cash inflows of a capital investment project to equal the total of the cash outflows.

Before the payback period can be calculated, management must have details of the following.

- The initial cash outflow for the project under consideration
- Estimates of any future cash inflows or savings

7.2 Example: Payback method

Ruby Co is considering a new project which will require an initial investment $60,000. The estimated profits before depreciation are as follows.

Year	Estimated profits before depreciation
	$
1	20,000
2	30,000
3	40,000
4	50,000
5	60,000

The payback period is calculated by considering the cumulative estimated profits before depreciation.

Year	Estimated profits before depreciation	Cumulative estimated profits before depreciation
	$	$
1	20,000	20,000
2	30,000	50,000
3	40,000	90,000
4	50,000	140,000
5	60,000	200,000

Initially, it appears that the initial investment of $60,000 is paid back in year 3. If the cash flows accrue evenly throughout the year, we can calculate the payback period as follows.

At the end of year 2, $50,000 of the cash invested has been 'paid back'.

At the end of year 3, $90,000 of the cash invested has been 'paid back'.

The point at which the $60,000 investment has been 'paid back' is actually:

2 years + ($10,000/$40,000 × 12 months) = 2 years and 3 months

If, on the other hand, the cash flows are received at the end of the year then the payback period would be 3 years.

7.3 Using the payback period to appraise capital investment projects

There are two ways in which the payback period can be used to appraise projects.

(a)   If two or more projects are under consideration, the usual decision is to accept the project with the **shortest payback period.**

(b)   If the management of a company have a **payback period limit**, then only projects with payback periods which are less than this limit would be considered for investment.

7.4 Example: Project appraisal – payback method

Suppose Ruby Co has a payback period limit of two years, and is considering investing in one of the following projects, both of which require an initial investment of $400,000. Cashflows accrue evenly throughout the year.

	Project A			Project B	
Year		Cash inflow	Year		Cash inflow
		$			$
1		100,000	1		200,000
2		200,000	2		180,000
3		100,000	3		120,000
4		150,000	4		100,000
5		150,000	5		100,000

Required

Which project is acceptable from the point of view of the payback period?

Solution

Firstly, we need to calculate the payback periods for Projects A and B.

Project A

Year	Cash inflow	Cumulative cash inflow
	$	$
1	100,000	100,000
2	200,000	300,000
3	100,000	400,000
4	150,000	550,000
5	150,000	700,000

Project A has a payback period of 3 years.

Project B

Year	Cash inflow	Cumulative cash inflow
	$	$
1	200,000	200,000
2	180,000	380,000
3	120,000	500,000
4	100,000	600,000
5	100,000	700,000

Project B has a payback period of between 2 and 3 years.

Payback period = 2 years + ($20,000/$120,000 × 12 months)
= 2 years + 2 months

Since Ruby Co has a payback period limit of two years, neither project should be invested in (as both payback periods are greater than two years). If, however, Ruby Co did not have a payback limit, it should invest in Project B because it has the shorter payback period of the two projects.

![Pencil icon] **Question** Payback

A business is considering investing in one of the following projects on 1 April 20X3. The initial investment and estimated cash inflows are as follows.

	Project X	Project Y
	$	$
Initial investment on 1 April 20X3	250,000	300,000
Cash inflow on 31 March 20X4	50,000	50,000
Cash inflow on 31 March 20X5	150,000	180,000
Cash inflow on 31 March 20X6	150,000	280,000
Cash inflow on 31 March 20X7	70,000	25,000
Cash inflow on 31 March 20X8	130,000	30,000

The business has a payback period limit of three years and will not invest in projects which have a payback period greater than this.

Cash inflows are spread evenly throughout the year

Required

From the point of view of the payback period, identify which project the business should invest in and explain your answer.

Answer

Payback period – Project X

Date	Cash inflows	Cumulative cash inflows
	$	$
31 March 20X4	50,000	50,000
31 March 20X5	150,000	200,000
31 March 20X6	150,000	350,000
31 March 20X7	70,000	420,000
31 March 20X8	130,000	550,000

The payback period is between years 2 and 3.

Payback period = 2 years + ($50,000/$150,000 × 12 months)

= 2 years + 4 months

The investment in Project X is a possibility because the payback period is less than three years.

Payback period – Project Y

Date	Cash inflows	Cumulative cash inflows
	$	$
31 March 20X4	50,000	50,000
31 March 20X5	180,000	230,000
31 March 20X6	280,000	510,000
31 March 20X7	25,000	535,000
31 March 20X8	30,000	565,000

The payback period for Project Y is also between 2 and 3 years,

Payback period = 2 years + ($70,000/$280,000 × 12 months)

= 2 years + 3 months

The investment in Project Y is also a possibility because the payback period is less than three years.

The business should invest in Project Y because it has the shortest payback period (2 years and 3 months).

Payback is often used as an initial step in appraising a project. However, a project should not be evaluated on the basis of payback alone. If a project passes the 'payback test' ie if it has a payback period that is less than the payback period limit of the company then it should be evaluated further with a more sophisticated project appraisal technique (such as the NPV or IRR methods studied earlier in this chapter).

7.5 Discounted payback

The payback method of project appraisal was described earlier in this section. Payback can be combined with DCF, and a discounted payback period calculated.

> The **discounted payback period** is the time it will take before a project's cumulative NPV turns from being negative to being positive.

For example if we have a cost of capital of 10% and a project with the cash flows shown below, we can calculate a discounted payback period.

Year	Cash flow	Discount factor	Present value	Cumulative NPV
	$	10%	$	$
0	(100,000)	1.000	(100,000)	(100,000)
1	30,000	0.909	27,270	(72,730)
2	50,000	0.826	41,300	(31,430)
3	40,000	0.751	30,040	(1,390)
4	30,000	0.683	20,490	19,100
5	20,000	0.621	12,420	31,520
		NPV =	31,520	

The discounted payback period is early in year 4.

A company can set a target discounted payback period, and choose not to undertake any projects with a discounted payback period in excess of a certain number of years, say five years.

Chapter Roundup

- **Long term investments** include the purchase of buildings, machinery and equipment. Management will need to have estimates of the initial investment and future costs and revenues of a project in order to make any **long term decisions.**

- **Interest** is the amount of money which an investment earns over time. **Simple interest** is interest which is earned in equal amounts every year. If interest earned also earns interest itself in later periods, this is known as **compound interest.**

- The basic principle of **discounting** involves calculating the **present value** of an investment (ie the value of an investment **today** at time 0).

- The term **present value** means the amount of money which must be invested now (for a number of years) in order to earn a future sum (at a given rate of interest).

- An **annuity** is a constant sum of money received or paid each year for a given number of years.

- **A perpetuity** is an annuity which lasts forever.

- **Discounted cash flow** involves discounting future cash flows from a project in order to decide whether the project will earn a satisfactory rate of return.

- The two main discounted cash flow methods are the **net present value (NPV) method** and the **internal rate of return (IRR) method**.

- The **IRR method** determines the rate of interest (internal rate of return) at which the NPV = 0. The internal rate of return is therefore the rate of return on an investment.

- The **payback period** is the time that is required for the cash inflows from a capital investment project to equal the cash outflows.

Quick Quiz

1   What does the term present value mean?

2   The discounting formula is $P = S \times \dfrac{1}{(1+r)^n}$

        Where

        S   =
        P   =
        r   =
        n   =

        (a)   the rate of return (as a proportion)
        (b)   the sum to be received after n time periods
        (c)   the PV of that sum
        (d)   the number of time periods

3   An annuity is a sum of money received every year.

        ☐   True
        ☐   False

4   What is a perpetuity?

5   What is the formula for the present value of a perpetuity?

6   What are the two usual methods of capital expenditure appraisal using discounted cash flow methods?

7   What is the payback period?

Answers to Quick Quiz

1   The amount of money which must be invested now for n years at an interest rate of r% to give a future sum of money at the time it will be due.

2
S   =   (b)
P   =   (c)
r   =   (a)
n   =   (d)

3   ☑   False

It is a **constant** sum of money **received** or **paid** each year for a **given number** of years.

4   An annuity which lasts forever.

5    $PV = \dfrac{\text{annuity}}{\text{interest rate}}$

6   The net present value (NPV) method

The internal rate of return (IRR) method

7   The payback period is the time that is required for the cash inflows of a capital investment project to equal the cash outflows.

Now try the questions below from the Exam Question Bank

Number	Level	Marks	Time
Q15	Examination	N/A	20 mins

Mathematical tables

PRESENT VALUE TABLE

Present value of 1 ie $(1+r)^{-n}$

where   r = discount rate

         n = number of periods until payment

Periods (n)	\ Discount rates (r)									
	1%	2%	3%	4%	5%	6%	7%	8%	9%	10%
1	0.990	0.980	0.971	0.962	0.952	0.943	0.935	0.926	0.917	0.909
2	0.980	0.961	0.943	0.925	0.907	0.890	0.873	0.857	0.842	0.826
3	0.971	0.942	0.915	0.889	0.864	0.840	0.816	0.794	0.772	0.751
4	0.961	0.924	0.888	0.855	0.823	0.792	0.763	0.735	0.708	0.683
5	0.951	0.906	0.863	0.822	0.784	0.747	0.713	0.681	0.650	0.621
6	0.942	0.888	0.837	0.790	0.746	0.705	0.666	0.630	0.596	0.564
7	0.933	0.871	0.813	0.760	0.711	0.665	0.623	0.583	0.547	0.513
8	0.923	0.853	0.789	0.731	0.677	0.627	0.582	0.540	0.502	0.467
9	0.914	0.837	0.766	0.703	0.645	0.592	0.544	0.500	0.460	0.424
10	0.905	0.820	0.744	0.676	0.614	0.558	0.508	0.463	0.422	0.386
11	0.896	0.804	0.722	0.650	0.585	0.527	0.475	0.429	0.388	0.350
12	0.887	0.788	0.701	0.625	0.557	0.497	0.444	0.397	0.356	0.319
13	0.879	0.773	0.681	0.601	0.530	0.469	0.415	0.368	0.326	0.290
14	0.870	0.758	0.661	0.577	0.505	0.442	0.388	0.340	0.299	0.263
15	0.861	0.743	0.642	0.555	0.481	0.417	0.362	0.315	0.275	0.239

Periods (n)	11%	12%	13%	14%	15%	16%	17%	18%	19%	20%
1	0.901	0.893	0.885	0.877	0.870	0.862	0.855	0.847	0.840	0.833
2	0.812	0.797	0.783	0.769	0.756	0.743	0.731	0.718	0.706	0.694
3	0.731	0.712	0.693	0.675	0.658	0.641	0.624	0.609	0.593	0.579
4	0.659	0.636	0.613	0.592	0.572	0.552	0.534	0.516	0.499	0.482
5	0.593	0.567	0.543	0.519	0.497	0.476	0.456	0.437	0.419	0.402
6	0.535	0.507	0.480	0.456	0.432	0.410	0.390	0.370	0.352	0.335
7	0.482	0.452	0.425	0.400	0.376	0.354	0.333	0.314	0.296	0.279
8	0.434	0.404	0.376	0.351	0.327	0.305	0.285	0.266	0.249	0.233
9	0.391	0.361	0.333	0.308	0.284	0.263	0.243	0.225	0.209	0.194
10	0.352	0.322	0.295	0.270	0.247	0.227	0.208	0.191	0.176	0.162
11	0.317	0.287	0.261	0.237	0.215	0.195	0.178	0.162	0.148	0.135
12	0.286	0.257	0.231	0.208	0.187	0.168	0.152	0.137	0.124	0.112
13	0.258	0.229	0.204	0.182	0.163	0.145	0.130	0.116	0.104	0.093
14	0.232	0.205	0.181	0.160	0.141	0.125	0.111	0.099	0.088	0.078
15	0.209	0.183	0.160	0.140	0.123	0.108	0.095	0.084	0.074	0.065

ANNUITY TABLE

Present value of annuity of 1, ie $\dfrac{1-(1+r)^{-n}}{r}$

where   r = discount rate

n = number of periods.

Periods	Discount rates (r)									
(n)	1%	2%	3%	4%	5%	6%	7%	8%	9%	10%
1	0.990	0.980	0.971	0.962	0.952	0.943	0.935	0.926	0.917	0.909
2	1.970	1.942	1.913	1.886	1.859	1.833	1.808	1.783	1.759	1.736
3	2.941	2.884	2.829	2.775	2.723	2.673	2.624	2.577	2.531	2.487
4	3.902	3.808	3.717	3.630	3.546	3.465	3.387	3.312	3.240	3.170
5	4.853	4.713	4.580	4.452	4.329	4.212	4.100	3.993	3.890	3.791
6	5.795	5.601	5.417	5.242	5.076	4.917	4.767	4.623	4.486	4.355
7	6.728	6.472	6.230	6.002	5.786	5.582	5.389	5.206	5.033	4.868
8	7.652	7.325	7.020	6.733	6.463	6.210	5.971	5.747	5.535	5.335
9	8.566	8.162	7.786	7.435	7.108	6.802	6.515	6.247	5.995	5.759
10	9.471	8.983	8.530	8.111	7.722	7.360	7.024	6.710	6.418	6.145
11	10.368	9.787	9.253	8.760	8.306	7.887	7.499	7.139	6.805	6.495
12	11.255	10.575	9.954	9.385	8.863	8.384	7.943	7.536	7.161	6.814
13	12.134	11.348	10.635	9.986	9.394	8.853	8.358	7.904	7.487	7.103
14	13.004	12.106	11.296	10.563	9.899	9.295	8.745	8.244	7.786	7.367
15	13.865	12.849	11.938	11.118	10.380	9.712	9.108	8.559	8.061	7.606

Periods										
(n)	11%	12%	13%	14%	15%	16%	17%	18%	19%	20%
1	0.901	0.893	0.885	0.877	0.870	0.862	0.855	0.847	0.840	0.833
2	1.713	1.690	1.668	1.647	1.626	1.605	1.585	1.566	1.547	1.528
3	2.444	2.402	2.361	2.322	2.283	2.246	2.210	2.174	2.140	2.106
4	3.102	3.037	2.974	2.914	2.855	2.798	2.743	2.690	2.639	2.589
5	3.696	3.605	3.517	3.433	3.352	3.274	3.199	3.127	3.058	2.991
6	4.231	4.111	3.998	3.889	3.784	3.685	3.589	3.498	3.410	3.326
7	4.712	4.564	4.423	4.288	4.160	4.039	3.922	3.812	3.706	3.605
8	5.146	4.968	4.799	4.639	4.487	4.344	4.207	4.078	3.954	3.837
9	5.537	5.328	5.132	4.946	4.772	4.607	4.451	4.303	4.163	4.031
10	5.889	5.650	5.426	5.216	5.019	4.833	4.659	4.494	4.339	4.192
11	6.207	5.938	5.687	5.453	5.234	5.029	4.836	4.656	4.486	4.327
12	6.492	6.194	5.918	5.660	5.421	5.197	4.988	4.793	4.611	4.439
13	6.750	6.424	6.122	5.842	5.583	5.342	5.118	4.910	4.715	4.533
14	6.982	6.628	6.302	6.002	5.724	5.468	5.229	5.008	4.802	4.611
15	7.191	6.811	6.462	6.142	5.847	5.575	5.324	5.092	4.876	4.675

BPP
LEARNING MEDIA

Question Bank

1 Management information

(a)   Which of the following statements is/are true?

     I   Information is the raw material for data processing

     II   External sources of information include an organisation's financial accounting records

     III   The main objective of a non-profit making organisation is usually to provide goods and services

     A   I and III only
     B   I, II and III
     C   II and III only
     D   III only

(b)   Which of the following statements is not true?

     A   Management accounts detail the performance of an organisation over a defined period and the state of affairs at the end of that period

     B   There is no legal requirement to prepare management accounts

     C   The format of management accounts is entirely at management discretion

     D   Management accounts are both an historical record and a future planning tool

(c)   Which of the following statements is not correct?

     A   Financial accounting information can be used for internal reporting purposes.

     B   Routine information can be used to make decisions regarding both the long term and the short term

     C   Management accounting provides information relevant to decision making, planning, control and evaluation of performances

     D   Cost accounting can be used to provide inventory valuations for internal reporting only

2 The role of information technology

(a)   Which of the following is an output device?

     A   Screen
     B   Keyboard
     C   CPU
     D   Disk

(b)   A method of input which involves a machine that is able to read characters by using lasers to detect the shape of those characters is known as

     A   MICR
     B   OCR
     C   OMR
     D   CPU

3 Cost classification

WH Co is a member of a trade association which operates an inter-company comparison scheme. The scheme is designed to help its member companies to monitor their own performance against that of other companies in the same industry.

At the end of each year, the member companies submit detailed annual accounts to the scheme organisers. The results are processed and a number of performance ratios are published and circulated to members. The ratios indicate the average results for all member companies.

Your manager has given you the following extract, which shows the average profitability and asset turnover ratios for the latest year. For comparison purposes, WH Co's accounts analyst has added the ratios for your company.

	Results for year 4	
	Trade association	
	average	*WH Limited*
Return on capital employed	20.5%	18.4%
Net profit margin	5.4%	6.8%
Asset turnover	3.8 times	2.7 times
Gross profit margin	14.2%	12.9%

Required

As one of the accounting technicians for WH Co, your manager has asked you to prepare a report for the Senior Management Committee. The report should cover an explanation of what each ratio is designed to show.

4 Cost behaviour

A company manufactures and retails clothing.

(a)   You are required to group the costs which are listed below and numbered 1 to 20 into the following classifications (each cost is intended to belong to only one classification).

(i)   Direct materials
(ii)   Direct labour
(iii)   Direct expenses
(iv)   Indirect production overhead
(v)   Research and development costs
(vi)   Selling and distribution costs
(vii)   Administration costs
(viii) Finance costs

1   Lubricant for sewing machines
2   Floppy disks for general office computer
3   Maintenance contract for general office photocopying machine
4   Telephone rental plus metered calls
5   Interest on bank overdraft
6   Performing Rights Society charge for music broadcast throughout the factory
7   Market research undertaken prior to a new product launch
8   Wages of security guards for factory
9   Carriage on purchases of basic raw material
10   Royalty payable on number of units of product XY produced
11   Road fund licences for delivery vehicles
12   Parcels sent to customers

13   Cost of advertising products on television
14   Audit fees
15   Chief accountant's salary
16   Wages of operatives in the cutting department
17   Cost of painting advertising slogans on delivery vans
18   Wages of storekeepers in materials store
19   Wages of fork lift truck drivers who handle raw materials
20   Developing a new product in the laboratory

(b)   Explain why it is necessary to classify costs by their behaviour.

(c)   Explain and show by drawing two separate diagrams what is meant by the following.

    (i)   A semi-variable cost
    (ii)   A stepped fixed cost

    Give one example of each.

5 Materials

The following transactions took place during May 20X3. You are required to calculate the value of all issues and of closing inventory using each of the following methods of valuation.

(a)   FIFO
(b)   LIFO
(c)   Cumulative weighted average pricing

TRANSACTIONS DURING MAY 20X3

	Quantity	Unit cost	Total cost
	Units	$	$
Opening balance, 1 May	100	2.00	200
Receipts, 3 May	400	2.10	840
Issues, 4 May	200		
Receipts, 9 May	300	2.12	636
Issues, 11 May	400		
Receipts, 18 May	100	2.40	240
Issues, 20 May	100		
Closing balance, 31 May	200		
			1,916

6 Labour

A team of five employees is rewarded by means of a group incentive scheme. The team receives a basic hourly rate for output up to and including 200 units per day.
The basic rate of pay for members of the team is:

	Number of employees	Hourly rate
		$
Team leader	1	14
Operatives	3	10
Junior operative	1	6

For outputs exceeding 200 units per day the hourly rate for all members of the team is increased, for all hours worked that day. The increases in hourly rates, above the basic hourly rate, are as follows.

Output per day	Increase in hourly rate
Units	%
201 to 250	10
251 to 280	12
281 to 300	15

Due to a limitation on machine capacity it is not possible to exceed an output of 300 units per day.

Required

Prepare a graph to show the hourly group remuneration cost for the range of output from zero to 300 units per day.

7 Expenses

Listed below are fifteen entries in the cash book of Beancounters, a small firm of accountants. You are required to code up the invoices according to the sort of expense you think has been incurred.

Nominal codes	*Nominal account*
0010	Advertising
0020	Bank charges
0030	Books and publications
0040	Cleaning
0050	Computer supplies
0060	Heat and light
0070	Motor expenses
0080	Motor vehicles
0090	Office equipment
0100	Printing, postage and stationery
0110	Rates
0120	Rent
0130	Repairs and maintenance
0140	Staff training
0150	Staff welfare
0160	Subscriptions
0170	Telephone
0180	Temporary staff
0190	Travel

	$	Code
Strange (Properties) Co	4,000.00	
Yorkshire Electricity Co	1,598.27	
Dudley Stationery Co	275.24	
Dora David (cleaner)	125.00	
BPP Professional Education	358.00	
ACCA	1,580.00	
British Telecom	1,431.89	
Kall Kwik (Stationers)	312.50	
Interest to 31.3.X3	2,649.33	
L & W Office Equipment	24.66	
Avis	153.72	
Federal Express	32.00	
Starriers Garage Co	79.80	

8 Overheads and absorption costing

Uttoxeter Co has a budgeted production overhead of $50,000 and a budgeted activity of 25,000 direct labour hours and therefore a recovery rate of $2 per direct labour hour ($50,000 ÷ 25,000 direct labour hours). Calculate the under-/over-absorbed overhead, and explain the reasons for the under/over absorption, in the following circumstances.

(a) Actual overheads cost $47,000 and 25,000 direct labour hours are worked.
(b) Actual overheads cost $50,000 and 21,500 direct labour hours are worked.
(c) Actual overheads cost $47,000 and 21,500 direct labour hours are worked.

9 Marginal costing and absorption costing

A company manufactures a single product with a selling price of $28 per unit. Variable production costs per unit of product are:

Direct material	$6.10
Direct labour	$5.20
Variable overhead	$1.60

Fixed production overheads are $30,000 per month. Administration overheads are semi-variable in nature: variable costs are 5% of sales and fixed costs are $13,000 per month.

Production and sales quantities over a two month period are:

	Production	Sales
Month 1	4,000 units	3,500 units
Month 2	3,600 units	3,800 units

There is no finished inventory at the beginning of Month 1.

The company has prepared the following profit statement for each of the two months using the absorption costing method.

Profit statement

	Month 1		Month 2	
	$	$	$	$
Sales		98,000		106,400
Production cost of sales:				
Opening inventory	–		10,200	
Cost of production	81,600		76,440	
Closing inventory *	(10,200)		(6,370)	
		71,400		80,270
Gross profit		26,600		26,130
Administration overhead		17,900		18,320
Net profit		8,700		7,810

* Inventory valuation: End Month 1 $81,600 × (500 ÷ 4,000 units)
              End Month 2 $76,440 × (300 ÷ 3,600 units)

Required

(a) Prepare a profit statement for each of the two months using the marginal costing method.

(b) Provide a reconciliation of the absorption costing and marginal costing profits for Month 2, supported by a full explanation of the difference.

10 Cost bookkeeping

In the absence of the accountant, you have been asked to prepare a month's cost accounts for Saucy Sauces Co, a company which operates an interlocking cost accounting system which is not integrated with the financial accounts. The cost clerk has provided you with the following information.

(a) Balances at beginning of month

	$
Stores ledger control account	72,800
Work in progress control account	46,000
Finished goods control account	31,400
Cost ledger control account	150,200

(b) Information relating to events during the month

	$
Materials purchased	57,400
Materials issued to:	
Production	42,600
Service departments	8,400
Gross factory wages paid	117,800

Of these gross wages, $39,000 were indirect wages.

	$
Production overheads incurred (excluding the items shown above)	3,940
Raw materials inventories written off, damaged	2,400
Selling overheads incurred and charged to cost of sales	21,000
Sales	176,000
Material and labour cost of goods sold	105,600

(c) Balances at end of the month

	$
Inventories of work in progress	61,280

(d) The company operates a marginal costing system.

Required

Prepare the following for the month.

(a) Cost ledger control account
(b) Stores ledger control account
(c) Factory wages control account
(d) Production overhead control account
(e) Work in progress (WIP) control account
(f) Finished goods control account
(g) Selling overhead control account
(h) Sales account
(i) Cost of sales account
(j) Costing income statement
(k) Trial balance at month end

11 Job, batch and service costing

A company manufactures carpet for the hotel industry. No finished inventories are carried as the company only manufactures specifically to customer order. At the end of Month 6, one incomplete job (Job X124) remained in progress. Production costs incurred on the job to the end of Month 6 were:

Direct material	$7,220
Direct labour	$6,076
Production overhead	$10,416

During Month 7, the company accepted two further jobs (Job X125 and Job X126) and incurred prime costs as follows.

	Job X124	Job X125	Job X126
Direct material issued from stores	$6,978	$18,994	$12,221
Direct material returned to stores	Nil	($700)	($2,170)
Direct material transfers	Nil	$860	($860)
Direct labour hours	780	2,364	1,510

Direct labour is paid at a rate of $7.00 per hour. Production overheads are absorbed at a rate of $12.00 per direct labour hour.

During Month 7, Jobs X124 and X125 were completed. On completion of a job, 20% of the total production cost is added in order to recover distribution, selling and administration costs. The amounts involved to customers during Month 7 for the completed jobs were:

Job X124	$60,000
Job X125	$79,000

Required

(a) For each of the jobs calculate the following total costs:

    (i)   Direct material.

    (ii)   Direct labour.

    (iii) Production overhead.

(b) Calculate the total cost and profit/(loss) of each of Job X124 and X125.

12 Process costing

Chemicals X, Y and Z are produced from a single joint process. The information below relates to the period just ended.

Input to process:	Direct materials	3,200 litres, cost $24,000
	Direct labour	$48,000

Factory overheads are absorbed at 120% of prime cost

Output from process:	Chemical X	1,440 litres
	Chemical Y	864 litres
	Chemical Z	576 litres
	Scrap	10% of input, credited to the process account at sales value as it occurs
Selling prices:	Chemical X	$100 per litre
	Chemical Y	$80 per litre
	Chemical Z	$60 per litre
	Scrap	$16 per litre

Required

Calculate for the period just ended:

(a)   The joint process costs to be apportioned to the joint products.

(b)   The total sales value of the output of the three products.

(c)   The share of the joint process costs charged to Chemical X, using the volume of output method of apportionment.

(d)   The share of the joint process costs charged to Chemical Y, using the sales value method of apportionment.

13 Cost-volume-profit (CVP) analysis

A building company constructs a standard unit which sells for $30,000. The company's costs can be readily identifiable between fixed and variable costs.

Budgeted data for the coming six months includes the following.

	Sales Units	Profit $
January	18	70,000
February	20	100,000
March	30	250,000
April	22	130,000
May	24	160,000
June	16	40,000

You are told that the fixed costs for the six months have been spread evenly over the period under review to arrive at the monthly profit projections.

Required

(a)   Calculate the total fixed costs for the period using the high-low method.

(b)   Calculate the breakeven point in terms of both units and sales revenue.

(c)   Prepare a breakeven chart for the six months under review. Make sure that your graph shows the following.

- Total sales
- Costs (fixed, variable and total)
- Output
- Breakeven point
- Margin of safety
- Total budgeted sales

14 Decision making

ABC Co makes three products, all of which use the same machine which is available for 50,000 hours per period.

The standard costs of the products per unit are as follows.

	Product A $	Product B $	Product C $
Direct materials	70	40	80
Direct labour:			
Machinists ($8 per hour)	48	32	56
Assemblers ($6 per hour)	36	40	42
Total variable cost	154	112	178
Selling price per unit	$200	$158	$224
Maximum demand (units)	3,000	2,500	5,000

Fixed costs are $300,000 per period.

ABC Co could buy in similar quality products at the following unit prices.

A $175
B $140
C $200

Required

(a) Calculate the deficiency in machine hours for the next period.
(b) Determine the priority ranking for internal manufacture.
(c) Determine which product(s) and quantities (if any) should be bought externally.

15 Capital investment appraisal

(a) Distinguish between net profit and net cash flow and explain the rationale for discounting cash flows in the appraisal of capital investment project viability.

(b) A company is considering an investment in new equipment. The company has a cost of capital of 12% per annum.

Required

Calculate:

(i) The net present value (NPV).
(ii) The internal rate of return (IRR).
(iii) The discounted payback period.

of the investment project, using the following information as appropriate.

Year	Cash flow $'000	Discount factor 12%	Discount factor 20%
0	(460)	1.000	1.000
1	50	0.893	0.833
2	140	0.797	0.694
3	180	0.712	0.579
4	250	0.636	0.482
5	160	0.567	0.402
6	(40)	0.507	0.335

Answer Bank

1 Management information

(a)   D   **Data** is the raw material for data processing. **Information** is data that has been processed in such a way as to be meaningful to the person who receives it. Statement I is therefore incorrect.

An organisation's financial accounting records are an example of an **internal** source of information. Statement II is therefore incorrect.

The main objective of a non-profit making organisation is usually to provide goods and services. Statement III is therefore correct.

(b)   A   **Financial accounts** (not management accounts) detail the performance of an organisation over a defined period and the state of affairs at the end of that period. **Management accounts** are used to aid management record, plan and control the organisation's activities and to help the decision-making process.

(c)   D   Cost accounting can be used to provide inventory valuations for external reporting also.

2 The role of information technology

(a)   A   A **screen** is an output device.

A **keyboard** is an input device.

The **CPU** performs the processing function.

A **disk** is a storage device.

(b)   B   **MICR** is the recognition of characters by a machine that reads special formatted characters printed in magnetic ink.

OMR involves marking a pre-printed source document which is then read by a device which translates the marks on the document into machine code.

CPU is the central processing unit.

Option B is therefore correct.

3 Cost classification

WH Co
REPORT

To: Senior Management Committee   Date: 12 December 20X4
From: Accounting Technician
Subject: Profitability and asset turnover ratios

We have received the Trade Association results for year 4 and this report looks in detail at the profitability and asset turnover ratios.

What each ratio is designed to show

(a)   Return on capital employed (ROCE)/Return on investment (ROI)

This ratio shows the percentage rate of profit which has been earned on the capital invested in the business, that is the return on the resources controlled by management. The expected return varies depending on the type of business and it is usually calculated as follows.

$$\text{Return on capital employed} = \frac{\text{Profit before interest and tax}}{\text{Capital employed}} \times 100\%$$

Other profit figures can be used, as well as various definitions of capital employed.

(b) Net profit margin

This ratio shows the net profit as a percentage of turnover. The net profit is calculated before interest and tax and it is the profit over which operational mangers can exercise day to day control.

$$\text{Net profit margin} = \frac{\text{Net profit}}{\text{Turnover}} \times 100\%$$

(c) Asset turnover

This ratio shows how effectively the assets of a business are being used to generate sales.

$$\text{Asset turnover} = \frac{\text{Sales revenue}}{\text{Capital employed}}$$

If the same figure for capital employed is used as in ROCE, then ratios (i) to (iii) can be related together as follows.

(i) ROCE = (ii) net profit margin × (iii) asset turnover

(d) Gross profit margin

This ratio measures the profitability of sales.

$$\text{Gross margin} = \frac{\text{Gross profit}}{\text{Turnover}} \times 100\%$$

The gross profit is calculated as sales revenue less the cost of goods sold, and this ratio therefore focuses on the company's manufacturing and trading activities.

4 Cost behaviour

(a)
(i)	Direct materials	9
(ii)	Direct labour	16
(iii)	Direct expenses	10
(iv)	Indirect production overhead	1, 6, 8, 18, 19
(v)	Research and development costs	20
(vi)	Selling and distribution costs	7, 11, 12, 13, 17
(vii)	Administration costs	2, 3, 4, 14, 15
(viii)	Finance costs	5

(b) The classification of costs according to their behaviour serves a number of purposes.

(i) In planning it is necessary to know how costs will vary at various possible levels of activity so that a level of activity appropriate to the overall resources of the business may be chosen.

(ii) To maintain control of the business it is necessary to compare actual and expected results. Managers must therefore know what expected costs are likely to be at various levels of activity.

(iii) Cost classification also aids control by emphasising which costs are fixed within a given time span, and which costs may be varied by management action.

(iv) Where marginal costing is used for decision making, the distinction between fixed and variable costs is fundamental. Management decisions will be based on the contribution achieved by various levels of activity, and fixed costs are not taken into account when calculating contribution.

(c)   (i)

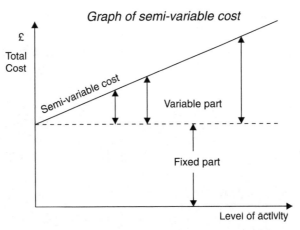

Graph of semi-variable cost

A semi-variable cost is a cost which contains both fixed and variable elements. The fixed cost is a constant amount of expenditure which is incurred regardless of the level of activity.

An example is a telephone bill. The rental charge is a fixed amount which is incurred regardless of the level of usage of the telephone. A variable cost is then incurred for each unit used.

(ii)

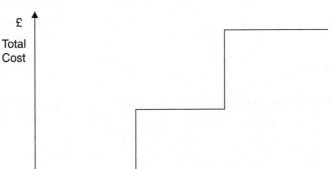

Graph of stepped fixed cost

A stepped fixed cost is a cost which is fixed within a range of levels of activity. It remains constant until a certain level of activity and then the expenditure increases to a higher level, remaining constant until the next step is reached.

An example of a stepped fixed cost is supervisory salaries. One supervisor may be needed until production reaches a certain level and then two supervisors are required, and so on.

5 Materials

(a)   FIFO

Date of issue	Quantity issued	Value		Cost of issues
	Units	$	$	$
4 May	200	100 at $2.00	200	
		100 at $2.10	<u>210</u>	
				410
11 May	400	300 at $2.10	630	
		100 at $2.12	<u>212</u>	
				842
20 May	100	100 at $2.12		<u>212</u>
				1,464
Closing inventory value	200	100 at $2.12	212	
		100 at $2.40	<u>240</u>	
				<u>452</u>
				1,916

The cost of materials issued plus the value of closing inventory equals the cost of purchases plus the value of opening inventory ($1,916).

(b)   LIFO

Date of issue	Quantity issued	Value		Cost of issues
	Units		$	$
4 May	200	200 at $2.10		420
11 May	400	300 at $2.12	636	
		100 at $2.10	<u>210</u>	
				846
20 May	100	100 at $2.40		<u>240</u>
				1,506
Closing inventory value	200	100 at $2.10	210	
		100 at $2.00	<u>200</u>	
				<u>410</u>
				1,916

The cost of materials issued plus the value of closing inventory equals the cost of purchases plus the value of opening inventory ($1,916).

(c) Cumulative weighted average

Date	Received	Issued	Balance	Total Inventory value	Unit cost	Price of issue
	Units	Units	Units	$	$	$
Opening inventory			100	200	2.00	
3 May	400			840	2.10	
			500*	1,040	2.08	
4 May		200		(416)	2.08	416
			300	624	2.08	
9 May	300			636	2.12	
			600*	1,260	2.10	
11 May		400		(840)	2.10	840
			200	420	2.10	
18 May	100			240	2.40	
			300*	660	2.20	
20 May		100		(220)	2.20	220
Cost of issues						1,476
Closing inventory			200	440	2.20	440
						1,916

* A new unit inventory value is calculated whenever a new receipt of materials occurs.

The cost of materials issued plus the value of closing inventory equals the cost of purchases plus the value of opening inventory ($1,916).

6 Labour

Basic hourly rate = (1 × $14) + ($3 × $10) + (1 × $6) = $50.

Output per day Units	Increase %	Hourly group remuneration $
201 to 250	10	55.00
251 to 280	12	56.00
281 to 300	15	57.50

Graph of group hourly remuneration cost for output ranging from zero to 300 units per day

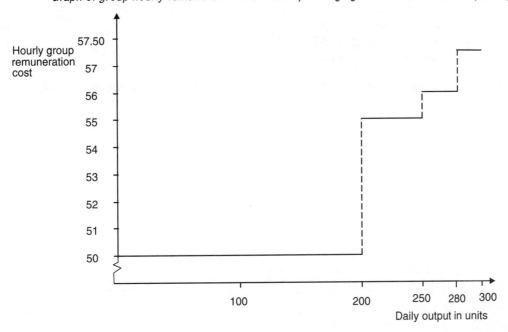

7 Expenses

	$	Code
Strange (Properties) Co	4,000.00	0120
Yorkshire Electricity Co	1,598.27	0060
Dudley Stationery Co	275.24	0100
Dora David (Cleaner)	125.00	0040
BPP Professional Education	358.00	0140
ACCA	1,580.00	0160
British Telecom	1,431.89	0170
Kall Kwik (Stationers)	312.50	0100
Interest to 31.3.X3	2,649.33	0020
L & W Office Equipment	24.66	0090
Avis	153.72	0190
Federal Express	32.00	0100
Starriers Garage Co	79.80	0070

8 Overheads and absorption costing

(a)

	$
Actual overhead	47,000
Absorbed overhead (25,000 × $2)	50,000
Over-absorbed overhead	3,000

Here there is over absorption because although the actual and estimated direct labour hours are the same, actual overheads cost *less* than expected and so too much overhead has been charged against profit.

(b)

	$
Actual overhead	50,000
Absorbed overhead (21,500 × $2)	43,000
Under-absorbed overhead	7,000

Here there is under absorption because although estimated and actual overhead costs were the same, fewer direct labour hours were worked than expected and hence insufficient overheads have been charged against profit.

(c)

	$
Actual overhead	47,000
Absorbed overhead (21,500 × $2)	43,000
Under-absorbed overhead	4,000

The reason for the net under absorption is a combination of the reasons in (a) and (b).

9 Marginal costing and absorption costing

(a)   PROFIT STATEMENT – MARGINAL COSTING

	Month 1		Month 2	
	$	$	$	$
Sales		98,000		106,400
Variable cost of sales:				
Opening inventory	–		7,150	
Cost of production (W1)	57,200		51,480	
Closing inventory (W2)	(7,150)		(4,290)	
		50,050		54,340
Contribution		47,950		52,060
Less fixed production overheads		(30,000)		(30,000)
Less fixed administration overheads		(13,000)		(13,000)
Profit		4,950		9,060

Workings

(1)   *Cost of production*

	$ per unit
Direct material	6.10
Direct labour	5.20
Variable overhead	1.60
Variable administration overhead	1.40
Total variable costs	14.30

Variable cost of sales – Month 1	= 4,000 × $14.30
	= $57,200
Variable cost of sales – Month 2	= 3,600 × $14.30
	= $51,480

(2)   Closing inventory

Opening inventory + production – sales = closing inventory
0 + 4,000 – 3,500 = 500
Month 1 closing inventory = 500 units @ $14.30
                = $7,150
∴ Month 2 closing inventory = 500 + 3,600 – 3,800 = 300
                = 300 units @ $14.30
                = $4,290

(b)

		Month 2
		$
Marginal costing profit		9,060
Adjust for fixed overhead inventory:		
Fixed overhead in opening inventory	$\left(\dfrac{500}{4,000} \times \$30,000\right)$	(3,750)
Fixed overhead in closing inventory	$\left(\dfrac{300}{3,600} \times \$30,000\right)$	2,500
Absorption costing profit		7,810

10 Cost bookkeeping

(a)   COST LEDGER CONTROL ACCOUNT (CLC)

	$		$
Sales account	176,000	Opening balance b/f	150,200
Profit and loss account	4,340	Stores ledger control	57,400
Closing balance c/f	170,000	Factory wages control	117,800
		Production overhead control	3,940
		Selling overheads control	21,000
	350,340		350,340
		Opening balance b/f	170,000

(b)   STORES LEDGER CONTROL ACCOUNT

	$		$
Opening balance b/f	72,800	WIP control	42,600
Purchases - CLC	57,400	Production overhead control	8,400
		Income statement	
		(inventory written off)	2,400
		Closing balance c/f	76,800
	130,200		130,200
Balance b/f	76,800		

(c)   FACTORY WAGES CONTROL ACCOUNT

	$		$
Gross wages – CLC	117,800	WIP control (bal figure)	78,800
		Production overhead control	39,000
	117,800		117,800

(d)   PRODUCTION OVERHEAD CONTROL ACCOUNT

	$		$
Stores ledger control	8,400	Income statement	
Factory wages control	39,000	(balancing figure)	51,340
Other costs - CLC	3,940		
	51,340		51,340

(e)   WORK IN PROGRESS (WIP) CONTROL ACCOUNT

	$		$
Opening balance b/f	46,000	Finished goods control	
Stores ledger control	42,600	(balancing figure)	106,120
Factory wages control	78,800	Closing balance	61,280
	167,400		167,400
Balance b/f	61,280		

(f)   FINISHED GOODS CONTROL ACCOUNT

	$		$
Opening balance b/f	31,400	Cost of sales	105,600
WIP control	106,120	Closing balance c/f	31,920
	137,520		137,520
Balance b/f	31,920		

(g)   SELLING OVERHEAD CONTROL ACCOUNT

	$		$
CLC	21,000	Cost of sales a/c	21,000

(h)

SALES ACCOUNT

	$		$
Income statement	176,000	CLC – sales	176,000

(i)

COST OF SALES ACCOUNT

	$		$
Finished goods control	105,600	Income statement	126,600
Selling overheads control	21,000		
	126,600		126,600

(j)

COSTING PROFIT AND LOSS ACCOUNT

	$		$
Cost of sales a/c	126,600	Sales a/c	176,000
Production overhead	51,340	Loss (balance) CLC	4,340
Stores ledger control	2,400		
(inventory written off)			
	180,340		180,340

(k)

TRIAL BALANCE AT MONTH END

	$	$
Cost ledger control account		170,000
Stores ledger control account	76,800	
Work in progress control account	61,280	
Finished goods control account	31,920	
	170,000	170,000

11 Job, batch and service costing

(a)

		Job X124 $	Job X125 $	Job X126 $
Direct material				
Month 6		7,220	–	–
Month 7 – issues		6,978	18,994	12,221
Month 7 – returns		–	(700)	(2,170)
Month 7 – transfers		–	860	(860)
(i)	Total direct material	14,198	19,154	9,191
Direct labour				
Month 6		6,076	–	–
Month 7 (@ $7 per hour)		5,460 (780 hrs)	16,548 (2,364 hrs)	10,570 (1,510 hrs)
(ii)	Total direct labour	11,536	16,548	10,570
Production overhead				
Month 6		10,416		
Month 7 (@ $12 per dir. labour hour)		9,360 (780 hrs)	28,368 (2,364 hrs)	18,120 (1,510 hrs)
(iii)	Total production overhead	19,776	28,368	18,120
Invoiced to customers		60,000	79,000	
Total production cost ((i)+(ii)+(iii))		(45,510)	(64,070)	
20% total production cost		(9,102)	(12,814)	
Total cost		54,612	76,884	
Profit on job		5,388	2,116	

12 Process costing

(a) Joint process costs

		$
Direct materials		24,000
Direct labour		48,000
		72,000
Factory overhead (120% × $72,000)		86,400
		158,400
Scrap proceeds *		(5,120)
Joint process costs		153,280

* Scrap   = 10% × 3,200 litres
  = 320 litres @ $16 per litre
  = $5,120

(b) Total sales value

	Chemical X	Chemical Y	Chemical Z
Output	1,440 litres	864 litres	576 litres
Selling price	× $100	× $80	× $60
Sales value of output	$144,000	$69,120	$34,560

Total sales value   = $(144,000 + 69,120 + 34,560)
  = $247,680

(c) Total output   = (1,440 + 864 + 576) litres

  = 2,880 litres

Total joint process costs = $153,280

∴ Share of joint process costs charged to chemical X

$$= \frac{1,440}{2,880} \times \$153,280 = \$76,640$$

(d) Total sales value = $247,680

Total joint process costs = $153,280

∴ Share of joint process costs charged to chemical Y

$$= \frac{69,120}{247,680} \times \$153,280$$

= $42,776 (to the nearest $)

13 Cost-volume-profit (CVP) analysis

(a)

	Units	Profit $'000
High - March	30	250
Low - June	16	40
	14	210

Variable cost per unit ($210,000/14)	$15,000

	$'000
Taking March as an example	
Sales (30 × $30,000)	900
Profit	250
Total costs	650
Variable costs (30 × $15,000)	450
Fixed costs	200

Fixed costs for the six months = 6 × $200,000 = $1,200,000.

(b)

Per unit	$'000
Selling price	30
Variable cost	15
Contribution	15

Breakeven point is where total contribution = fixed costs. Breakeven point is therefore where $15,000N − $1,200,000, where N is the breakeven quantity of units.

N = $(1,200,000/15,000) = 80 units

Breakeven sales revenue = 80 × $30,000 = $2,400,000

Breakeven chart

Note that at 80 units, the variable cost is 80 × $15,000 = $1,200,000.

14 Decision making

(a)

	Product A	Product B	Product C	Total
Machine hours required per unit	6	4	7	
Maximum demand (units)	3,000	2,500	5,000	
Total machine hours required	18,000	10,000	35,000	63,000
Machine hours available				50,000
Deficiency in machine hours for next period				13,000

(b)

	Product A $ per unit	Product B $ per unit	Product C $ per unit
External purchase price	175	140	200
Variable cost of internal manufacture	154	112	178
Saving through internal manufacture	21	28	22
Machine hours per unit	6	4	7
Saving per machine hour	$3.50	$7.00	$3.14
Priority ranking for internal manufacture	2	1	3

(c) Since all products can be sold for more than their bought-in cost, unsatisfied demand should be met through external purchases. Purchases should be made in the reverse order of the above ranking shown in (b), until the deficiency in machine hours (13,000) has been covered.

Some units of Product C should therefore be purchased from the external supplier.

Number of units of C to be purchased = $\frac{13000\ hours}{7}$ (from (a))

= 1,858 units

15 Capital investment appraisal

(a) Net profit measures how much the capital of an organisation has increased over a period of time. Profit is calculated by applying the matching concept, that is to say by matching the costs incurred with the sales revenue generated during a period.

Net cash flow measures the difference in the payments leaving a business's bank account and the receipts that are paid into the bank account.

Reasons why net profit and net cashflow will differ are mainly due to timing differences and include the following:

- Receipts from debtors and sales invoices raised
- Payments to creditors and matching costs against sales
- Purchase of inventory and matching costs against sales
- Investment in capital assets and writing off the asset (via a depreciation charge) in the income statement.

Discounting cashflows in the appraisal of capital investment project viability means that the time value of money is reflected. Therefore, cashflows which are received earliest have a greater earning capacity.

(b)

Year	Cash flow $'000	Discount factor 12%	Discount factor 20%	Present value 12%	Present value 20%
0	(460)	1.000	1.000	(460.0)	(460.0)
1	50	0.893	0.833	44.7	41.7
2	140	0.797	0.694	111.6	97.2
3	180	0.712	0.579	128.2	104.2
4	250	0.636	0.482	159.0	120.5
5	160	0.567	0.402	90.7	64.3
6	(40)	0.507	0.335	(20.3)	(13.4)
		Net present value		53.9	(45.5)

(i) The net present value at 12% cost of capital is $53,900.

(ii) The IRR can be calculated using the following formula.

$$IRR = a\% + \left[\frac{NPV_A}{NPV_A - NPV_B} \times (b-a) \right] \%$$

Where a = one interest rate (12%)

  b = the other interest rate (20%)

NPV_A = NPV at rate a ($53,900)

NPV_B = NPV at rate b(−$45,500)

$$\therefore \quad IRR = 12\% + \left[\frac{53,900}{53,900 - -(45,500)} \times (20-12) \right] \%$$

$$= 12\% + 4.3\%$$

$$= 16.3\%$$

$$= 16\% \text{ (to the nearest whole per cent)}$$

(iii)

Year	Discounted cashflow at 12%	Cumulative discounted cashflow at 12%
0	(460.0)	(460.0)
1	44.7	(415.3)
2	111.6	(303.7)
3	128.2	(175.5)
4	159.0	(16.5)
5	90.7	74.2
6	(20.3)	53.9

The investment is 'paid back' between years 4 and 5.

$$\frac{16.5 \,(\text{Year 4 cumulative cashflow balance})}{90.7 \,(\text{Year 5 discounted cashflow})} = 0.2$$

Therefore the discounted payback period is 4.2 years or 5 years (if the cashflows are assumed to arise at the end of each year).

Key terms and index

REVIEW FORM & FREE PRIZE DRAW

All original review forms from the entire BPP range, completed with genuine comments, will be entered into one of two draws on 31 January 2008 and 31 July 2008. The names on the first four forms picked out on each occasion will be sent a cheque for £50.

Name: _____   Address: _____

_____

_____

How have you used this Interactive Text?
(Tick one box only)

☐ Home study (book only)

☐ On a course: college _____

☐ With 'correspondence' package

☐ Other _____

Why did you decide to purchase this Interactive Text? *(Tick one box only)*

☐ Have used BPP Texts in the past

☐ Recommendation by friend/colleague

☐ Recommendation by a lecturer at college

☐ Saw advertising

☐ Other _____

Which BPP products have you used?

☑ Text   ☐ Kit   ☐ i-Pass   ☐ i-Learn

During the past six months do you recall seeing/receiving any of the following?
(Tick as many boxes as are relevant)

☐ Our advertisement in *ACCA Student Accountant*

☐ Other advertisement _____

☐ Our brochure with a letter through the post

☐ Our website www.bpp.com

Which (if any) aspects of our advertising do you find useful?
(Tick as many boxes as are relevant)

☐ Prices and publication dates of new editions

☐ Information on Interactive Text content

☐ Facility to order books off-the-page

☐ None of the above

Your ratings, comments and suggestions would be appreciated on the following areas

	Very useful	Useful	Not useful
Introductory section (How to use this Interactive Text)	☐	☐	☐
Key terms	☐	☐	☐
Examples	☐	☐	☐
Activities and answers	☐	☐	☐
Key learning points	☐	☐	☐
Quick quizzes	☐	☐	☐
Exam alerts	☐	☐	☐
Question Bank	☐	☐	☐
Answer Bank	☐	☐	☐
List of key terms and index	☐	☐	☐
Structure and presentation	☐	☐	☐
Icons	☐	☐	☐

	Excellent	Good	Adequate	Poor
Overall opinion of this Interactive Text	☐	☐	☐	☐

Do you intend to continue using BPP products?   ☐ Yes   ☐ No

Please note any further comments and suggestions/errors on the reverse of this page. The BPP author of this edition can be emailed at julietgood@bpp.com

Please return this form to: Mary Maclean, CAT Range Manager, BPP Learning Media Ltd, FREEPOST, London, W12 8BR

REVIEW FORM & FREE PRIZE DRAW (continued)

Please note any further comments and suggestions/errors below

FREE PRIZE DRAW RULES

1 Closing date for 31 January 2008 draw is 31 December 2007. Closing date for 31 July 2008 draw is 30 June 2008.

2 No purchase necessary. Entry forms are available upon request from BPP Learning Media Ltd. No more than one entry per title, per person. Draw restricted to persons aged 16 and over.

3 Winners will be notified by post and receive their cheques not later than 6 weeks after the relevant draw date.

4 The decision of the promoter in all matters is final and binding. No correspondence will be entered into.